D0231632

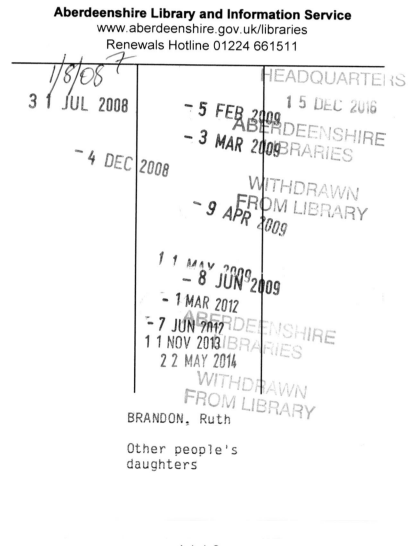

1/8/08

3 1 JUL 2008

HEADQUARTERS

1 5 DEC 2016

- 5 FEB 2009

ABERDEENSHIRE

- 3 MAR 2009 BRARIES

- 4 DEC 2008

WITHDRAWN
FROM LIBRARY
- 9 APR 2009

1 1 MAY 2009
- 8 JUN 2009
- 1 MAR 2012
- 7 JUN 2012 RDEENSHIRE
1 1 NOV 2013 IBRARIES
2 2 MAY 2014

WITHDRAWN
FROM LIBRARY

BRANDON, Ruth

Other people's
daughters

A L I S

2621738

Other People's Daughters

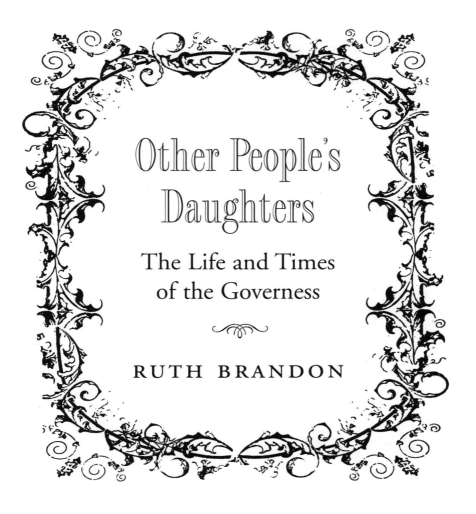

Other People's Daughters

The Life and Times of the Governess

RUTH BRANDON

Weidenfeld & Nicolson

LONDON

First published in Great Britain in 2008
by Weidenfeld & Nicolson

A CIP catalogue record for this book is
available from the British Library.

ISBN-13 9 78029 785 113 4

Typeset by Input Data Services Ltd, Frome

Printed in Great Britain by Butler and Tanner,
Frome and London

Weidenfeld & Nicolson

An imprint of the Orion Publishing Group
Orion House, 5 Upper St Martin's Lane,
London WC2H 9EA

www.orionbooks.co.uk

To Nicky Brooker and Annette Kobak – Girton girls
and in memory of June Benn

Contents

Acknowledgements

I should like to thank the Authors' Foundation for their kind and generous support.

Jennifer Sharp first suggested I might write a book about governesses. Allan and Bindi Doig, Lyndall Gordon, Sheila Hillier, Jan Marsh, Joanna Martin, Thomas Methuen-Campbell, Jinty Nelson, Miranda Seymour and Susan Skedd all offered much appreciated help of various kinds, as did Bruce Barker-Benfield and his staff at the Bodleian Library in Oxford, Kate Perry at Girton College, Cambridge, the staff at London Metropolitan Archives, and Nikki Bosworth at the Pembrokeshire Record Office. Thanks to them all.

I am especially grateful to my editors, Maya Baran, Helen Garnons-Williams and Kelly Falconer; and to my agent, Clare Alexander.

List of Illustrations

Bessie Rayner-Parkes (Madame Belloc).
Girton students. © The Mistress and Fellows, Girton College.
Emily Davies. © The Mistress and Fellows, Girton College.

While every effort has been made to trace copyright holders, if any
have been inadvertently overlooked, the publisher will be happy to
acknowledge them in future editions.

Other People's Daughters

1

'There is nobody in the house with whom I can be on equal terms'[1]

The governess is an ancient institution. Traditionally she was employed by aristocratic families to live in their houses and educate their daughters. But during the nineteenth century, as the newly rich English middle classes did their best to imitate aristocratic lifestyles, governessing became both a normal method of educating middle-class girls and a way of keeping destitute ladies off the streets. If a middle-class woman had neither a husband to support her nor money of her own, this was almost the only way in which society allowed her to earn a living. In the 1851 census, 25,000 women – that is, 2 per cent of all unmarried women between twenty and forty – described themselves as governesses.

This is a large number, but not, on the face of it, a large percentage. However, it must be remembered that most unmarried women, like most of the population, were working class and would have found jobs as servants or in the rapidly expanding factories. And since no middle-class woman worked unless circumstances compelled her to do so, that 2 per cent must mean that almost every respectable lady who was forced to earn her own living became a governess.

All these governesses certainly wrote letters; many doubtless kept journals. But the direct sources – journals and letters – that would tell us about these lives from the inside are oddly lacking. Governesses may be glimpsed in the memoirs of their pupils and employers; they figure as heroines in many novels. And the realities of their lives may be inferred from the copious journalism they inspired, often taking the form of advice columns offering answers to readers' questions. Yet despite the volumes of paper they must have generated, there is comparatively little first-hand testimony from the governesses themselves. They were not only insignificant, they were poor. That was why they were governesses. And the possessions of the poor rarely survive.

My selection of subjects is therefore rather arbitrary. Because people are naturally more interested in preserving papers that relate to the famous, several have celebrity connections: Eliza Bishop's and Everina Wollstonecraft's letters, as well as Claire Clairmont's letters and journals, were kept only because they were related to persons so notorious that any scrap of paper that might throw light on them, however tangentially, was felt worthy of preservation. Others, like Anna Jameson or Mary Wollstonecraft, became famous in their own right. And a few documents surfaced by a lucky chance. Penrice Castle, where Agnes Porter ended her working life, has never been sold out of the family; her journals turned up in a drawer there more than a century and a half after her death. Nelly Weeton's letter-books were found mouldering on a junk-shop shelf. Although Anna Leonowens published her Siamese memoirs, the book fell into obscurity and the true, revealing story of her life would not have emerged had not a quirk of fate made her the notorious heroine of a best-seller, followed by the Hollywood hit musical *The King and I.*

Yet despite this dependence on chance survival, these seven lives, or (in some cases) groups of lives, tell a coherent story: of education as a tool for equality versus ignorance as the perpetuator of inequality. The governess, herself only partially educated, could teach only as much as she herself had learned; and this meant that so long as governessing remained the chief educational system for middle-class girls, women could never aspire to equality with men.

Agnes Porter, my first subject, is essentially an eighteenth-century figure. Her employers, the Earl of Ilchester and his family, were landed aristocrats; Miss Porter absorbed their values and served them loyally, while they, for their part, treated her generously, as befitted the old family retainer she had by the end become. She is a sort of ideal type, a model of what governesses were supposed to be; and in the same way, her employers' lifestyle – expansive, leisured, rooted – embodied everything the nineteenth-century middle classes aimed at from afar.

Mary Wollstonecraft, born in 1759, was only nine years younger than Miss Porter. But Mary and her sisters occupied a very different intellectual world: that of the fierce battles raging around the Enlightenment, and the revolutions in America and France that were based upon its values. This extraordinary woman fought her way out of governessing to become a radical journalist: her *Vindication of the Rights of Woman*, published in 1792, claimed full equality for women, which could only be achieved through a fundamental change in the educational system. But in the blanket of reaction that descended after England declared war on France in 1793, such ideas became almost treasonous; and Mary's two sisters Eliza and Everina, who spent their lives as governesses, found themselves blown from post to post, in a desperate search for families who would employ them. Their lives – powerless and desperate – would set the pattern for lone women for the next century.

Claire Clairmont, born in 1798, was the stepsister of Wollstonecraft's orphaned daughter Mary Shelley (née Godwin). Claire was determined not to become a governess, and managed to avoid it several times before succumbing to the inevitable in 1824. Unlike the brilliant circle around Mary and her husband Shelley, among whom chance had deposited her, there was never any prospect of escape for Claire. She possessed neither the money nor the talent that might have allowed her to live independently. In the twenty years of working life before a legacy rescued her, governessing showed her the world. But it was never her world, and it filled her with bitterness.

Nelly Weeton, a little older than Claire, was born near Wigan, in Lancashire, and lived her life in and around the growing industrial towns of north-west England. She was not a governess for long – only four years, between 1810 and 1814 – and, unusually, took the job voluntarily, for she had enough money to live on, in a small way. But she felt that anything – even governessing – was preferable to the absolute solitude that, for a lone woman too poor to entertain or keep a servant, was its alternative. Yet governessing, too, was lonely, and that loneliness eventually drove her into a disastrous marriage. Nelly's life reflects the narrow choices for a single woman in a man's world.

Anna Leonowens, though of English descent, was not really an Englishwoman; and this detachment from the rigid and stifling rules of class was perhaps what enabled her to survive as successfully as she did. Born and raised in India, and married young, at twenty-eight she found herself a widow with two children to support. In 1862 she took a post in Bangkok teaching the numerous children of the king of Siam. She stayed for five years and made a career out of her adventures. Her story is (among other things) about the governess as ambassador.

With Anna Jameson, the governess's tale takes another turn, into a more modern world. Like Mary Wollstonecraft, Mrs Jameson was one of those rare people able to stand outside their times and look objectively at a situation – women's subjection to men – by which most of her contemporaries were quite simply engulfed. Freed for the fight by an absent husband who supported her financially, she began, in 1846, to question this powerlessness, of which the governess was so intrinsic a part. But although she shocked many and entranced a few, she was able to go only so far; while women's thraldom was unacceptable, she could not in the end bring herself to question men's natural leadership.

It was left to the next generation to contemplate true equality. Barbara Leigh Smith, Bessie Rayner Parkes and Emily Davies, alone of my subjects, were never themselves governesses, yet they led the fight to ensure that women might take up any profession they wanted – not just governessing – and still remain respectable; which, as Mary Wollstonecraft had realized, had to begin with equal education for all. And they recognized, crucially, that in the end the interests of women would be furthered only by women themselves. In this struggle even well-meaning men could not be relied on; for this was a matter in which men's and women's interests were diametrically opposed.

Virtually everyone who wrote about governessing portrayed it as hateful. For Jane Austen, to become a governess was to 'retire from all the pleasures of life, of rational intercourse, equal society, peace and hope, to penance and mortification for ever'. She made this remark in *Emma*, where Jane Fairfax is passing her last weeks of freedom before taking up a 'situation'. Jane compares it to slavery: 'widely different certainly as to the guilt of those who carry it on; but as to the greater misery of the victims, I do not know where it lies'.[2]

Twenty-five years later, things had not improved. According to the

1841 *Ladies' Journal* the governess could be recognized by her 'plain and quiet style of dress; a deep straw bonnet with green or brown veil and on her face a fixed look of despair'.[3] Sir George Stephen, an old anti-slavery campaigner who subsequently took up the governesses' cause, went even further. In his *Guide to Service: The Governess*, published in 1844, a handbook of good practice in a series whose previous books had included clerks, grooms, housemaids and dairy-maids, he wrote:

> We must acknowledge that in . . . describing the office of governess we have had a sickening feeling at heart, such as we have not experienced in tracing any other department of active life. In every other human pursuit there may be found the encouragement of expectation . . . The servant may become master, the labourer may rise into an employer . . . but the governess, and the governess alone, though strictly a member of a liberal profession, has neither hope nor prospect open in this world.[4]

All the advice manuals likewise assumed that governesses must be at best discontented, at worst thoroughly miserable.

Yet this was not, on the face of it, the experience of the women whose lives this book examines. Or at least not most of them: for Eliza Bishop and Everina Wollstonecraft, their lives as governesses were little short of hellish. The Brontë sisters, too (whose lives are not examined at length but whose correspondence and novels are frequently referred to), hated the job. For the rest, however, their actual day-to-day existences seem quite often to have been not just bearable but actively pleasant. Agnes Porter genuinely loved her pupils and enjoyed the hours she spent with them. Mary Wollstonecraft's pupils idolized her and she led a lively social life with her employers. Claire Clairmont's Russian journals describe many delightful days in her employers' country house. Nelly Weeton was happy enough so long as her employers remained decently civil, which they quite often did. Whenever Anna Leonowens forgot to be sternly Christian, her memoirs reveal how much she enjoyed Bangkok. Anna Jameson's descriptions of accompanying her charges across Europe contain many moments of pure pleasure.

The conclusion might be that these are atypical cases – if, indeed, there existed such a thing as a 'typical' governess. But their actions tell a different story. Mary Wollstonecraft became famous for proclaiming the horrors of the system governessing underpinned, in which a girl's only career was to catch a husband. Claire Clairmont never ceased to proclaim her hatred of being forced to spend her life among people with whom she had nothing in common. Nelly Weeton found the job so uncongenial that, even several years into her appalling marriage, she maintained that it was better than the 'freedom' of the schoolroom. And in Anna Jameson's writings on mothers and governesses, despite her own apparently happy experiences, employers are always portrayed as oppressors, governesses as the oppressed. Even in the best circumstances, no one liked governessing.

Nevertheless, it was often the only possibility. As one of the many governesses' advice manuals put it, 'I hate teaching but I must do something, and there is no other occupation for a lady.'[5] And teaching could indeed be a trial, especially if the hours were very long, and the governess and her charges did not get on. But once again, this was not, on the whole, true of the women discussed here. On the contrary, most of them seem to have had a real aptitude for that part of their duties. If they disliked governessing, the fault did not chiefly lie with the teaching.

The real problem was subtler and more insidious: the change that occurred the moment the governess took up her first 'situation'. Until then, she had possessed the recognized status every middle-class woman enjoyed: she was in charge – at least of her own life. Henceforth, however, she would be nothing but a minor appendage in someone else's household – and also, by a bitter irony, something less than a lady. That she had been born one went without saying; it was the job's basic requirement. But a lady's defining characteristic was that she did not work for a living. So the mere fact of seeking paid employment instantly relegated the governess from middle-class respectability to an ambiguous limbo between upstairs and downstairs. As between those who employed servants and those who served, it was obvious to everyone – including herself – on which side of the fence she now stood. When W.M. Thackeray, in his 'Book of Snobs', makes his governess Miss Wirt drop names, he reveals not just her pathetic social yearnings but the ever-gnawing consciousness of her fallen situation:

Do you know Lord Castletoddy, Mr Snob? – round towers – sweet place – County Mayo. Old Lord Castletoddy (the present Lord was then Lord Inishowan) was a most eccentric old man – they say he was mad. I heard his Royal Highness the poor dear Duke of Sussex – (SUCH a man, my dears, but alas! addicted to smoking!) – I heard His Royal Highness say to the Marquis of Anglesey, 'I am sure Castletoddy is mad!' but Inishowan wasn't marrying my sweet Jane, though the poor child had but her ten thousand pounds POUR TOUT POTAGE![6]

Governesses' insistence upon their lofty connections might (and did) become a joke; but that insistence was not surprising. It was the sole tenuous link between what they were and what they might have been.

For the governess, this uncomfortably ambiguous status amounted to a sentence of social death. For novelists, however, it was a heaven-sent gift, affording a matchless entrée into Victorian society's guilts, resentments, fears and taboos; so that in the first great governess paradox, this marginal figure became central to her society's literature. Charlotte Brontë's Jane Eyre, Thackeray's Becky Sharp, Henry James's Miss Jessel, could not be more different, yet all are governesses and are not merely memorable but among the most memorable characters in nineteenth-century fiction. And through the novels that they inhabit – not just *Jane Eyre*, *Vanity Fair* and *The Turn of the Screw* but Anthony Trollope's *The Eustace Diamonds*, Wilkie Collins' *No Name*, Anne Brontë's *Agnes Grey* and countless others – the details of governess life have become familiar to us all: part of our shared cultural consciousness.

Indeed, the governess's career might have been expressly designed for fiction. Her fall from bourgeois comfort, and her long journey to its eventual restitution, provided both an instant dramatic structure and a plethora of plot possibilities. How had she come to find herself in this position? How would she cope with the distress of sudden relegation to the servant class? What were the tensions of sharing a house with employers whose equal she once had been, but now so markedly was not? Where would the children's loyalties lie? Would she succumb to sexual temptation and, if so, what would transpire? When would the legacy arrive that might rescue her from her plight? Would she find the husband who represented her only way back into decent middle-class life and, if so, where? Should she stay single? Was there any alternative to governessing? And, if not, how was she to live once she got too old to work?

Questions like these were the stuff of fiction. But – crucially – they were not themselves fictional. Quite how closely they followed real life becomes clear from a passage in Charlotte Brontë's *Shirley* in which Mrs Pryor, who has spent her life governessing, spells out the job's painful consequences in a curious mix of direct and reported speech:

> I was early given to understand that 'as I was not their equal,' so I could not expect 'to have their sympathy.' It was in no sort concealed from me that I was held a 'burden and a restraint in society.' The gentlemen, I found, regarded me as a 'tabooed woman,' to whom 'they were interdicted from granting the usual privileges of the sex,' and yet who 'annoyed them by frequently crossing their path.' The ladies too made it plain that they thought me 'a bore.' The servants, it was signified, 'detested me:' *why*, I could never clearly comprehend. My pupils, I was told, 'however much they might love me, and how deep soever the interest I might take in them, could not be my friends.' It was intimated, that I must 'live alone, and never transgress the invisible but rigid line which established the difference between me and my employers.'[7]

In fact the views set between inverted commas were not invented by Brontë, but were taken verbatim from a long article by the critic and art historian Lady Eastlake in the influential *Quarterly Review*, discussing governesses' lives in the light of *Jane Eyre* and *Vanity Fair*, both then recently published – the former in 1847, the latter in 1848.[8] Brontë, who had herself been a governess, evidently thought this summation of the governess's plight not just accurate but eloquent – so much so that she herself could do no better.

That the miserable embarrassment Lady Eastlake described arose from British snobbery, rather than governessing as such, becomes clear if it is contrasted with Meg March's experience in Louisa May Alcott's all-American *Little Women*, published in 1868. Here are all the familiar ingredients of Victorian fiction: the absent father who has lost his money; the girls who must help out by earning what they can; the eldest sister who finds a job as a nursery governess – in America as in Britain, then the most usual employment for a middle-class girl. We know that Meg does not much enjoy her job, because it is tiring and because the children she supervises have elder sisters 'just out' in society who possess all the pretty things that Meg would like, and who constantly remind her of her own poverty. But there the matter ends. Alcott's America, a product of the optimistic Enlightenment, had not yet developed the intricate social demarcations that defined nineteenth-century Britain. In America, poverty was not shameful, but simply something people must work their way out of. What Lady Fawn in Trollope's *The Eustace Diamonds* considers 'the embarrassing necessity of earning bread'[9] may be a necessity, but the Marches do not find it embarrassing. If the only way to earn that bread is to be a governess, then a governess Meg will be.

However, when an English friend, Kate Vaughn, visits, it is clear she sees the whole thing quite differently. When Meg confesses that, far from *having* a governess, she *is* one, there is a crushing response: '"Oh, indeed! . . . We have many most respectable and worthy young women, who do the same; and are employed by the nobility, because, being the daughters of gentlemen, they are both well-bred and accomplished, you know," said Miss Kate, in a patronizing tone that hurt Meg's pride, and made her work seem not only more distasteful, but degrading.'[10]

Of course Meg is not degraded, and all the March girls end up happily settled – Beth in heaven, the rest with good loving husbands: *believable* husbands unlike anything to be found in the pages of Charlotte Brontë, whose wives will lead useful, hard-working, American lives. America would have no equivalent to British governess fiction until Edith Wharton's *The House of Mirth*, published in 1905. Wharton's Lily Bart inhabits a society of snobbish exclusion consciously modelled on England;[11] and although she is not a governess, the problems that she faces, as an impoverished young woman from an old family in a society fixated upon wealth, are comparable to those outlined by Lady Eastlake in England sixty years earlier.

Yet even as society swept the governess to one side, she frightened it. Nothing else can explain the shrill and insistent cruelty detailed in Lady Eastlake's litany of social exclusion. 'Tabooed', 'detested', a 'burden' and a 'bore' – what had the insignificant governess done to merit such violent distaste? Unlike the segregation of servants into their traditional 'downstairs' domain, which though resented by some was taken for granted by all, this smacked of panic; not just snobbery, but a closing of ranks against a perceived threat.

To most governesses (Mary Wollstonecraft, in this as in almost every other aspect of her life, was an exception), the notion that they might inspire panic in their employers would have seemed laughable. On the contrary, the word that everywhere crops up in their writings, summing up all that made them most miserable, is 'dependance' [sic]. Most relied on their employment not just for a living, but for a roof over their head; when the choice lay, as it often did, between humiliation and homelessness, humiliation almost always won. 'Egalité sounds so pleasing to poor *dependants*!'[12] sighed Wollstonecraft's governess sister Eliza Bishop, desperate to give up her job yet too frightened to do so, and looking enviously across the Channel to possibilities that in Britain had become treasonous even to mention.

Employers, however, perceived things rather differently. For them, the governess represented not just one threat but several, ranging from simple sexual competition to an undermining of the Victorian social order's fundamental premise: that women could not function independently of men.

The sexual threat was obvious. In most middle-class houses, the governess and the family lived at very close quarters indeed, and the arrival of an unattached young woman might easily lead to complications. Husbands might stray, sons fall unsuitably in love. The advice manuals instructed their readers to 'give up all thought of love . . . while in the position of governess', for the result was 'seldom matrimony'.[13] Nevertheless, many such affairs inevitably occurred; and although it was true that they rarely ended in marriage, horror stories circulated among employers about lower-class girls who became governesses in order to insinuate themselves into families who would otherwise be far above their station (and who, in doing so, deprived deserving middle-class girls of work that was rightfully theirs).

But other, darker jealousies were also in play. In a school, the interactions of teachers and pupils were diluted by numbers. Governesses, on the other hand, usually had only one or two charges, and all accounts – whether by pupils or governesses, whether of pranks played, discipline meted out, or simply of long hours spent eating meals together or going for walks – make it clear that they were expected not simply to teach but to supervise their charges' every waking hour. And this enforced intimacy at once raised a visceral question. To whom did those children really belong: the person who gave birth to them, or the one with whom they spent their lives?

This impossible situation is still familiar today, as working mothers frantically balance the demands of career and family by employing a nanny. If the nanny leaves, the household cannot function; if she stays, the children may grow too attached to her.* Of course, there are important differences. Governesses were often financially exploited, while modern nannies are well paid;[15] nineteenth-century mothers employed governesses because in a society where caste was flagged by conspicuous idleness they had to be seen to do nothing, while modern parents hire help because today's work culture requires them to spend ever longer hours at the office. Nevertheless, both were and are entirely reliant on the paid help, and the underlying tensions and jealousies remain the same.

Of course, friendship between mother and governess (or nanny) was (and is) possible: my first subject, Agnes Porter, and her employer, Lady Ilchester, were devoted to each other. But this could only really happen where the mother was secure enough emotionally not to see the governess as a rival, and had the social assurance not to feel her position compromised if she treated her as a friend. That was a comparatively rare combination: rare enough for the feminist journalist Harriet Martineau, in her essay on governesses, to declare 'friendship . . . with the mother out of the question, from their irreconcileable positions in regard to the children'.[16]

This hostility might manifest itself in a thousand ways, but one of the most common battlegrounds was discipline. When the governess first arrived in the family, she was usually assured that she must keep the children in order, and that the mother would support her in doing so. The reality was that in this, as in other aspects of the job, independence was in practice frowned upon. Mothers did not like the

---

*As work pressures increase, the parallels with governesses grow ever closer. A recent survey (by gumtree.com) of British families with nannies found that 65 per cent rated fluency in a second language, a knowledge of first aid and the ability to teach creative drawing and art more important than a professional child-minding qualification, while 10 per cent also sought the ability to play and teach a musical instrument. In the twenty-first century, the governess lives again.

governess to punish their children, however badly behaved. 'I soon found ... they are to do as they like. A complaint to Mrs Sidgwick brings only black looks upon oneself, and unjust, partial excuses to screen the children,'[17] observed Charlotte Brontë on first taking up a governess post.

Yet when she got on well with her charges, this too was ill received. Her biographer Mrs Gaskell described an occasion when Charlotte had been left to look after the children while the parents went out for the day; against their express instructions, an older boy enticed his little brother, aged three or four, into the stable yard. When she followed they threw stones at her, one of which cut her forehead.

> The next day, in full family conclave, the mother asked Miss Brontë what occasioned the mark on her forehead. She simply replied, 'an accident, ma'am,' and no further inquiry was made; but the children (both brothers and sisters) had been present, and honoured her for not 'telling tales' ... One day, at the children's dinner, the small truant of the stable-yard ... said, putting his hand in hers, 'I love 'ou, Miss Brontë.' Whereupon the mother exclaimed, before all the children, 'Love the *governess*, my dear!'[18]

Here, clearly, is the seed of a scene in *Jane Eyre* in which Lady Ingram and her snobbish daughter Blanche discuss Jane, and the governess question in general, as though she were not present, even when they know she is seated only a few feet away. They are making it clear, among other things, that as far as they are concerned a governess has no social existence. The main message of Charlotte Brontë's own story, however, is maternal jealousy. That the child might love the governess – a situation objectively to be encouraged – was in reality the mother's great fear.

This unspoken and inadmissible hostility often expressed itself as an inability to let the governess get on with her duties. 'It is presumed that you visit your children's study daily; not injudiciously to meddle, and dictate, and interrupt; but to encourage and to observe. ... Do not rashly interfere,' sternly enjoined the mid-century feminist writer (and one-time governess) Anna Jameson in her advice to mothers.[19] But they did rashly interfere; they did meddle, they did dictate, they did interrupt. It was one of the things that governesses most resented, because it fatally undermined their authority; which of course is exactly what it was meant to do. The more the children respected the governess, the more the mother felt threatened.

But the governess represented more than just an emotional threat. She also set a dangerous social example, her presence offering an inescapable reminder of two constantly nagging dreads.

The first, in an era of tremendous financial fluidity in which fortunes were easily won and as easily lost, concerned the pupils she was hired to teach. Since no lady would become a governess unless forced to do so, it was safe to assume that her family, if not clerical (i.e. combining poverty and respectability, like the Brontës, whose father was a vicar), had suffered some sort of financial catastrophe: ruination through debt or a bank failure, the untimely death of a father, the collapse of a business. 'Take a lady, in every meaning of the word, . . . and let her father pass through the gazette [i.e., be bankrupted], and she wants nothing more to suit our highest *beau idéal* of a guide and instructress to our children,' observed Lady Eastlake. ' . . . There is no other class of labourers for hire who are thus systematically supplied by the misfortunes of our fellow-creatures.'[20] And since these things might easily happen to anyone, who was to say that your own pampered and loved daughters might not, in their turn, have to become governesses? *Their* governess's presence constantly brought to mind this chilling possibility.

The second fraught question was that of women's place in the world. In Victorian society, where the middle-class woman's sole career was supposedly marriage and motherhood, independent spinsters presented a worrying anomaly. In the words of the social commentator William Rathbone Greg, writing in 1862, 'In place of completing, sweetening, and embellishing the existence of others, [they were] compelled to lead an independent and incomplete existence of [their] own.'[21]

Greg believed that God had made men and women different but complementary. In this view – shared by many in the reactionary post-Enlightenment years, which were dominated by a peculiarly narrow form of flag-waving Anglicanism – treating the sexes in the same way, educationally or legally, could never be anything but misguided. And one of the chief differences between the sexes was that while men were able to exist quite satisfactorily without women, the reverse was not true. Not only were most lone women unfitted to earn the living their single status required, but spinsterhood itself defied God's dispensation, in which man supported and woman sweetly depended. In this view, the notion of an independent woman was quite simply a contradiction in terms. Yet – ironically, given her own intolerable sense of dependence – the governess was just such a person: undeniably, a respectable woman earning, however exiguously, her own living.

In Greg's ideal world, such a person as the governess had no place. And yet, she was essential to the dissemination of his ethos, along with the strictly limited amounts of knowledge – enough to catch a husband and run a house, but no more – that perpetuated women's acceptance of their subordinate role. Once again, Thackeray's Miss Wirt (governess to the Pontos in the ongoing serial for *Punch* that he called the 'Book of snobs') demonstrates the realities of governess education:

> I asked ... in what other branches of education she instructed her pupils? 'The modern languages,' says she modestly: 'French, German, Spanish and Italian, Latin and the rudiments of Greek if desired. English of course; the practice of Elocution, Geography and Astronomy, and the use of the Globes, Algebra (but only as far as Quadratic Equations); for a poor ignorant female, you know, Mr Snob, cannot be expected to know everything. Ancient and Modern History no young woman can be without; and of these I make my beloved pupils PERFECT MISTRESSES. Botany, Geology, and Mineralogy, I consider as amusements. And with these I assure you we manage to pass the days at the Evergreens not unpleasantly.'
>
> Only these, thought I – what an education! But I looked in one of Miss Ponto's manuscript song-books and found five faults of French in four words; and in a waggish mood asking Miss Wirt whether Dante Algiery was so-called because he was born in Algiers, received a smiling answer in the affirmative, which made me rather doubt about the accuracy of Miss Wirt's knowledge.[22]

But this was the whole point of Miss Wirt: to provide rather the impression of an education than the thing itself. In young ladies like her pupils, inaccuracy was not just tolerated but central to society's workings. Governesses thus constituted a system of education both directed against their own interests as women, and reliant upon a class of person – an independent working woman of the middle class – not supposed to exist. Far from being, as everyone assumed, a minor and marginal by-product of the society in which they lived, they were in fact one of its vital props.

Oddly (since it undoubtedly was one) governessing is not usually considered as an educational system. Perhaps this is because systems imply groups, while the governess's essential state was solitude. In fiction, this was often underlined by making the governess–heroine an orphan (for example Charlotte Brontë's eponymous Jane Eyre and, in *Villette*, Lucy Snowe; Lucy Morris in Trollope's *The Eustace Diamonds*; Becky Sharp in Thackeray's *Vanity Fair*; Jane Fairfax in Jane Austen's *Emma*.)

This device served several purposes. It was a reflection of the frequent literal truth. And it invoked fairytale and myth, in which orphans play so important a role. Jane Eyre – poor but respectable, alone in the world, held back and tormented by a wicked stepmother, mocked by richer and more fortunate girls, picked out and courted against the odds, once again cast down, finally reunited with the prince who always recognized her true qualities – is a figure known to every child by her true name of Cinderella. But this parentless state was also a powerful metaphor. Making the governess an orphan reflected her isolation, both social and emotional.

This loneliness was partly a function of the job's nature. Both Nelly Weeton and Agnes Porter described working days lasting from 7 a.m. until 8 or 9 p.m. seven days a week, and spent almost entirely in the sole company of children. And quite often, when the children had gone to bed, the governess, as Charlote Brontë found, was expected to help with the family sewing.

However, work was not the only isolating factor. The governess, as a lady employed by another lady, theoretically expected to find a home from home in her charges' family, but in practice it rarely worked out quite as this might imply. 'Home' implies a life lived in common; employers, however, preferred not to be faced, every evening across the family hearth, with someone who was at once an awkward social liability, a reproach to their consciences and a constant reminder of everything that they prayed their own daughters would never become.

In this respect, society sided with the employers. Harriet Martineau, expressing her sympathy with 'the employing class, who are at present very unpopular', spoke of 'the sacrifice ... when parents receive into their home a stranger who must either be discontented from neglect, or an intruder upon the domestic party':[23] The anonymous author of *Hints to Governesses*, 'while I would strongly urge no Governess to enter a family where she will be entirely excluded from all society', pointed out that she should 'let [her] pupils be sometimes alone with their parents' and should 'never, unless *invited*, remain with the parents when they are alone'.[24] The result was that governesses' off-duty hours tended to be spent in their own company. When Anne Brontë's Agnes Grey visits her old pupil Lady Ashby, she takes her meals alone in her room even though she is supposedly there as a welcome friend. To do otherwise would be too uncomfortable for all parties.

But where, if not in the drawing room, was the governess to spend her solitary evenings? Agnes Porter and Mary Wollstonecraft, working in the grand houses of the aristocracy, could retire to their own comfortable apartments, but few middle-class houses were large enough to permit anything but the uneasiest separation. Often, like Agnes Grey, the governess shared a bedroom with her charges; if she did have a room of her own, it was almost certainly very small. 'I sit alone in the evening, in the schoolroom,'[25] noted Nelly Weeton. 'Really I should be very glad of some society in an evening, it would be such an enjoyment, but there is nobody in the house with whom I can be on equal terms, and I know nobody out of it, so I must make myself contented.'[26] In schoolrooms up and down the country, thousands of other lonely women did likewise.

Miss Weeton, like most of this book's subjects, was working too far from home for family or friends to visit. Yet even if the governess found a situation near her own home, there was no certainty that visits would be allowed. Charlotte Brontë, though suffering agonies of homesickness and longing to see her friends, worried that visits from them might be 'considered improper'.[27] In fact, unusually, her kindly employers the Whites encouraged her to invite her friends. Many families, however – whether they preferred the governess not to intrude her own life on theirs, or simply because they lacked a convenient space for her to entertain at home – were less accommodating. According to Harriet Martineau, 'a close and equal friendship in the house or neighbourhood is an impossible blessing to a resident governess ... it is practically (and naturally) never tolerated.'[28]

In any case, if you were far from home, where were such friends to be found? Although High Royd, where Nelly Weeton's employers the Armitages lived, has now been swallowed up by Huddersfield, Nelly, writing in 1810, described it as being 'at such a distance from any other house, that Mr and Mrs A. can have little or no company in Winter'.[29] One obvious social focus was church on Sunday, but Nelly, who in any case considered a governess to be 'more a prisoner than any servant in the house',[30] grumbled that she was 'a tenfold closer prisoner than any other governess in this neighbourhood, and am staying home this afternoon (Sunday) for want of a decent bonnet to go to Church in. Mrs A. knows this but neither offers me a holiday, nor a conveyance to Huddersfield to buy one; and I'll stay at home these two months before I ask her.'[31] While we can safely assume that few governesses would have swapped lives with female mineworkers, forced to spend their waking hours half naked below ground and harnessed to trucks of coal, mineworkers and factory workers could at least feel themselves part of a close community. The governess was on her own.

This isolation put her at a particular disadvantage when nego-tiating terms – especially since, by the mid-nineteenth century, she was at the mercy of a buyer's market. 'I wrote to all the Scholastic Agents. I advertised in the *Times* and the *Church of England Magazine*. No answers,'[32] reported one in 1858. It was the experience of thousands.

This oversupply was partly due to a spate of bank failures during the 1830s, which threw large numbers of middle-class women abruptly into the necessity of earning a living. But bank failures were not its only cause. There was also, in this society where marriage and motherhood constituted the only acknowledged female career, a huge pool of spinsters. The 1851 census found that of rather less than 3 million women between twenty and forty, 1,248,000 were unmarried. 'The proportion of women above twenty years of age ... who *must and ought* to be single, being *six per cent*, the actual proportion who *are* single is *thirty per cent*. According to the Registrar-General, "Out of every 100 females of twenty years of age and upwards, fifty-seven are wives, thirteen are widows, and thirty are spinsters,"' observed Greg, whose essay was revealingly entitled not (for example) 'Where are the husbands?' but, starkly, 'Why are women redundant?'[33]

One cause of this imbalance was the different mortality rates of the two sexes. Although more boy babies were born than girls, girls had a better life expectancy – in 1841, 42.18 years as against 40.19 years for boys.[34] A further factor was emigration. A great many single young men, unable to make a satisfactory life in Britain, left to try their luck in Australia or America or one of the other colonies; hardly any single young women joined them.

Both these factors, of course, applied across the board, to all classes. But middle-class girls suffered another disability when it came to finding the husband for whom they had been reared: the reluctance of middle-class men to marry. Between 1840 and 1870, the average age at marriage for clergymen, doctors, lawyers, merchants, bankers, manufacturers and 'gentlemen' was thirty;[35] the 1851 census showed that out of every 100 men in England and Wales, sixteen were unmarried at the age of thirty, eighteen at the age of thirty-five, twelve at the age of fifty.[36]

This state of affairs was facilitated and encouraged by that very British institution, the gentleman's club. As *The Times* remarked in 1861, 'The luxuries which a bachelor can command at his lodgings and in his club on an allowance of £300 a year, are altogether out of proportion to those which a prudent father of a family would afford himself out of a joint income of thrice that amount, and it is not every man who will make the sacrifice.'[37] And as *The Cornhill Magazine* further pointed out, these outlays did not compare with the real expenses of marriage. 'For £100 a judicious man may get a great amount of [champagne, stalls at the opera and expensive dinners]; but if he wants to keep a roomy house, and to provide clothes, food, washing, attendance, change of air, doctors, repairs, and furniture for a wife and several young children, his £100 will go much faster than it would in any prudent and reasonable kind of personal indulgence.'[38] Trollope's Frank Greystock, in *The Eustace Diamonds*, is a successful lawyer and a Member of Parliament, but the notion that he should marry the poor governess Lucy Morris just because he has promised to do so is greeted by his family with horror. Frank's father 'would not for the world have hinted to his son that it might be well to marry money; but he thought that it was a good thing that his son should go where money was. ... Frank had gone out into the world and prospered, – but he could hardly continue to prosper unless he married money.'[39] And that, *ipso facto*, ruled out governesses.

Men did marry, of course, whether they could afford it or not, with the result that many families lived beyond their means. And if one was looking to economize, one's daughters' education was an obvious place to start.

In 1845, if you earned £100 a year (in the view of one observer, 'barely sufficient to provide what is required for the family in the shape of lodging, food and raiment'[40]), you could expect to spend £4 – 4 per cent of income – on domestic help. But if your income was £500, the wages bill rose to £74, or 15 per cent of income. A cook at this period cost £15 a year, a housemaid, £11, a nursemaid, £11;[41] all three were essential in any middle-class household.[42] Boys must go to school and, later, to university, or they would not earn a living, but girls were another matter: earning a living was precisely what (in theory) they were *not* required to do. Why send them to pick up accomplishments expensively at school if they could learn the same things cheaply at home? 'To be under a governess is the safest, the healthiest and pleasantest, the most effectual *and cheapest* form of education,'[43] authoritatively declared the household oracle Jane Loudon in 1840.

No governess would argue about the cheapness, for this buyers' market was inevitably reflected in the salaries on offer.

At the top, these were adequate and, in a few cases, excellent. In 1844, Sir George Stephen found one governess who was paid £400 a year, three who were paid £300, several who earned £200, and many with a salary of £80. But many others earned far less than this. Charlotte Brontë, in 1841, received only £20 a year, which deductions for washing reduced to £16. The unknown author of *Hints to Governesses by One of Themselves*, published in 1856, knew of 'many cases . . . where a Governess has not a salary equal to that of a cook'; she herself 'was once *offered* £6 per annum. The requirements were too many to mention here.'[44] Harriet Martineau reported that she knew some families who paid their resident governess '£12, £10, and even £8'.[45] A letter to *The Times* told how

a daily governess of highly respectable connections called on a lady, living in a splendidly furnished house, not 100 yards from Notting Hill Square, who, it seemed, had four children – the eldest a girl of twelve years of age – requiring tuition in French, German, drawing, and the usual routine of a polite education. After stating that four hours a day – 9.30 to 1.30 – would be requisite, the governess naturally expected a handsome remuneration; but, Sir, you may well conceive her astonishment at the liberal offer of eight shillings per week – one penny per hour per pupil.[46]

A 'common charwoman' at 2s 6d a day, the writer pointed out, earned more than that.

Sometimes no salary was offered at all: 'Wanted, a Governess, on Handsome Terms. Governess – a comfortable home, but without salary, is offered to any lady wishing for a situation as a governess in a gentleman's family, residing in the country, to instruct two little girls in music, drawing and English; a thorough knowledge of the French language is required.'[47] Handsome terms indeed. *Punch* ran a satire on this advertisement, implying that it was particularly outrageous, but for many lone women the only way to find a home was to accept an offer of this sort. Charlotte Brontë, in agreeing to an annual wage of £16, acknowledged the trade-off: 'I have made a large sacrifice in the way of salary, in the hope of securing comfort, – by which I do not mean to express good eating and drinking, or warm fire, or a soft bed, but the society of cheerful faces, and hearts and minds not dug out of a lead-mine, or cut from a marble quarry.'[48] By the 1840s the small ads in *The Times* were full of desperate pleas: 'Superior English Governess – terms 60 guineas, but a comfortable home of more consequence.' 'A permanent home is required for a lady in a highly respectable family, where society and not emolument is an object.'[49]

By no means every prospective governess set so little store by earnings. But even if she was unhappy with the salary offered, the aura of respectability that was her most essential qualification forbade her to argue about money. The special class of posts reserved for respectable women unable to find a man to look after them – traditional female occupations such as the care of the elderly, the nurture of children, dressmaking and millinery – were the kinds of things that women were in any case born to do. To demand pay for them was already a kind of imposition; to haggle about that pay was almost blasphemous. As one advice column put it, 'If a woman allows the cankering consideration that she is underpaid to come between her service and those little ones, she is but a mercenary soldier of the Master Who loved them so well.'[50]

Of course this view of things suited many employers perfectly. But for governesses the result could be near or actual destitution. Unlike (say) doctors, or cooks, or engineers, their working lives were short. Given the choice – and by the mid-century there was always a choice – who would not prefer to share their house with a young girl, still malleable and hopeful, rather than a depressed middle-aged woman, set in her ways? Sir George Stephen pointed out that while men's earning power was at its height between forty and sixty, few governesses could expect to obtain situations after the age of forty. Frances Power Cobbe, as a young journalist detailed to follow up readers' tales of woe, recalled the case

> of a poor lady, daughter of a country rector, who was found (after having been missed for several days, but not sought for) lying dead, scarcely clothed, on the bare floor of a room in a miserable lodging-house in Drury Lane. I went to the house and found it a filthy coffee-house, frequented by unwashed customers. The mistress, though likewise unwashed, was obviously what is termed 'respectable'. She told me that her unhappy lodger was a woman of 40 or 50, perfectly sober and well conducted in every way. She had been a governess in very good families, but had remained unemployed till her clothes grew shabby. She walked all day long over London for many weeks, seeking any kind of work or means of support, and selling by degrees everything she possessed for food. At last she returned to her wretched room in that house into which it was a pain for any lady to enter, – and having begged a last cup of tea from her landlady, telling her she could not pay for it, she locked her door, and was heard of no more.[51]

Naturally all the advice manuals urged governesses to put something by, however meagre their salary; and on the face of it saving should not have been impossible. Since a resident governess lived with the family 'all found', earnings of £80 or even £60 (though of course many earned less) should amply have covered her expenses, with plenty to spare. She would be expected to keep herself provided with up-to-date books and music, but those were no dearer then than they would be now in terms of monetary value; in 1845 'accurate historical works for schools and families' cost 2s 6d for a history of France, 3s 6d for a history of England, while a book of 'new music for the season' cost 1s. And although the governess was required to 'dress like a lady',[52] that did not mean she had to be fashionable. On the contrary, her mistress would almost certainly disapprove of anything too showy. And as in all other aspects of her life, it was the mistress's taste, not the governess's, that mattered. A governess should not 'be offended at being spoken to about her dress; if she comes from some country place it is most probable that the lady of the house knows more about the subject than she does'.[53] In the absence of such advice, 'Dress consistently,' was the recommendation of *Hints to Governesses*. 'It is not necessary for you to have a different dress for every evening in the week; you had much better appear in the same, and a high[-necked] dress is *most* becoming.'[54] Another advice column recommended 'a costume in dark colours', with the reservation that 'some people have a strong objection to black';[55] Nelly Weeton's summer dress was 'very plain, that I may pass unnoticed; a dark print'.[56] For the winter a governess's dress would probably be made, as Jane Eyre's was, of 'stuff' – the kind of coarse woollen fabric that today is used for junior barristers' gowns. If she did not make her own clothes, she could have a dress made up by a dressmaker from her own fabric for 6s.[57]

It was a restricted palette, especially for a young woman in her teens or twenties, but few governesses, even when their salaries were relatively generous, could afford fashionable clothes. Their earnings, during their brief working lives, were usually needed elsewhere, to support other members of the family. In the reports of the Governesses' Benevolent Institution, formed in 1841 because so many were left destitute, case after case reiterated the same story:

> Maintained her mother until her death, apprenticed a brother, took the entire charge of one of his daughters, and assisted him in educating some of his other children ... Materially assisted two cousins ... Began a school at the age of thirteen with an elder sister, to support her mother, deserted, with seven children, by her father – continued to support her mother for twenty years ... Supported her mother, and lent her subsequent savings to a widowed sister in reduced circumstances.[58]

In such situations, even £80 a year did not go far.

It is hard to know how aware employers were of all this. It was probably easier not to enquire – particularly if the governess spent her evenings in the schoolroom. That not only avoided awkwardness, but made it possible to pretend what almost all employers would probably have wished: that outside the schoolroom she did not really exist. Harriet Martineau strongly condemned 'such picture-drawing as the Brontës, and many other novelists, have thrust into every house', declaring that it made governesses 'suffer keenly and indignantly . . . They feel they have their troubles in life, like everybody else, and that they ought, like other people, to have the privilege of privacy, and of getting over their griefs as they may.'[59] But one cannot help feeling that the true embarrassment was that these terrifically successful novels concerned governesses' private lives and thoughts, at a time when society found it more comfortable to assume that on entering the schoolroom they gave up their right to any such luxury.

On a personal level, almost all my subjects had to deal with one or more of these problematic situations. Agnes Porter, seemingly so happily placed, nonetheless keenly felt the subordination of her personal life to the demands of her work and was still desperately angling for a husband – and the independent life that only marriage could bring – until well into her forties. Eliza Bishop, bewilderingly dumped into governessing on the failure of her marriage, found her misery intensified by the realization that, although her employers had once been family friends, the fact that she was now their governess meant that neither she nor her family could hold any further personal interest for them. Mary Wollstonecraft's pupil Margaret King wholly transferred her affections from her mother to her governess; Wollstonecraft so entranced her that she eventually abandoned everything her parents stood for, deserting wealth, high society and respectability – in the person of her husband, Lord Mountcashel, and her five children by him – for a life of unwed bliss compatible with her governess's feminist ideals. Claire Clairmont experienced in an acute form the division of her life into an idealized *before* and a miserable *after*, living her last fifty-seven years in bitter nostalgia for the person she once had been. Nelly Weeton was actively prevented from pursuing the education she craved, because it was thought to make her unfit for the female future that inexorably awaited her. The all-defining straitjacket of class forced Anna Leonowens to invent a completely new ancestry for herself – in vain; the British class system followed her even to Bangkok. Anna Jameson, like Nelly Weeton, made a disastrous marriage because the only alternative was a lonely life in the schoolroom, with no possibility of children of her own.

Unlike all governesses, and indeed almost all women, the pressure group known as the Reform Firm – Barbara Bodichon, Bessie Rayner Parkes and Emily Davies – had money, independent minds and progressive, as well as powerful, connections. So long as their political energies lasted, they, uniquely, had no need to compromise. In Bessie's case those energies were eventually directed into marriage; in Barbara's, they were sapped by increasing ill-health. Emily, however persisted to the end. It was she who finally destroyed the vicious circle that confined women to the elementary level of education, and secondary place in society, that governesses were employed not only to impart but to perpetuate.

Together, these stories form a picture of lone women's lives between the end of the eighteenth century, when Enlightenment hopes came crashing down, and the 1860s, when the first women's college held out new possibilities for those who would otherwise have been condemned to a lifetime as governesses. For although governesses continued to ply their trade until well into the twentieth century, Girton College broke the spell. Despite its tiny student numbers, the mere fact of its existence destroyed the myth upon which governess education, or non-education, was founded: that women were fit only for the confines of domesticity, to be protected by men and subservient to them. How this myth became established, how it was upheld, and how, finally, defeated, is the story of this book.

2

'In these days, there do not exist such people as Miss Porter'[1]

$$\sim\!\!\sim\!\!\approx\!\!\sim\!\!\sim$$

A lone of my subjects, Agnes Porter spent the whole of her working life as a private governess. Born in 1750, she taught two generations of the Earl of Ilchester's family: first, from 1784 until 1797, his daughters and then, after a two-year break, the children of one of those daughters, Lady Mary Talbot, with whom she remained until her retirement in 1806. Like the Brontës and many other governesses, she was the daughter of a clergyman. Poor yet respectable, governessing did not come as a shock to clergymen's daughters. If they did not marry, it was their almost inevitable fate – and even if they did, it could not necessarily be avoided: Agnes' younger sister Fanny, who married a curate, took live-in pupils to make ends meet.

When Miss Porter first arrived at the Ilchesters' house, Redlynch, in 1784, they had three daughters: Elizabeth, aged eleven, Mary, almost eight, and Harriot, five and a half. The month after her arrival another daughter, Charlotte, was born; yet another, Louisa, arrived in 1785. In 1787 came a son and heir, Henry Stephen Fox Strangways, Lord Stavordale, always known as Harry, and finally, in 1790, Susanna Caroline.

In 1791, not long after Susanna's birth, Lady Ilchester died, an event that deeply saddened Miss Porter, who referred to her, in a letter to her daughter Mary, as 'your angel mother'. From then on, it was the governess who chiefly provided love and care for the now motherless family.

Bolted my door till I had said my prayers, then opened it, and in rushed my two children. A thousand things have they to say to Po [her pet name within the family] after a night's separation. Heard them say their prayers ... Saw my darlings at eight o'clock, happily seated over their milk and bread, then left [them] with their maid and took a turn round the shrubbery. Breakfasted at nine, my loves by my side at play with their dolls. Told them if they played very prettily I would certainly allow of their reading and writing a little afterwards as a reward. They soon claimed my promise ... N.B. the grand punishment for misconduct is not to allow them to do their studies. They returned to their play and I practised the harpsichord till twelve, then we walked out in the shrubbery. The weather very rough and cold – made my loves take exercise. We were out till two. Sent them to dress and read an hour in *Peter the Great* ... Dined at three, spoke French all the time at table. After dinner told them a tale, then our little studies, then they played while I was at work an hour. The weather very bad so I made a party with them at 'puss in the corner', found my own spirits rise as I endeavoured to amuse my darlings. Sent them with their maid at seven to supper ... At eight I heard them say their prayers and saw them in bed. Said my prayers, and to bed at eleven.[2]

This cheerful routine, so far removed from the grim picture painted by such writers as Jane Austen and the Brontës, was what every governess, and every parent, aspired to. But although comparably harmonious situations must always have existed, it is noticeable that almost all the writings about governessing that appeared during the nineteenth century inclined to the Austen–Brontë view of things. What was it that enabled Agnes Porter, it would seem so unusually, to enjoy her work? Was it her character, her environment, the times? What happened in the half-century between Miss Porter's governessing years and those of the Brontës, to alter perceptions so violently?

One explanation was the social setting. Private governesses in the eighteenth century were a luxury of the extremely well-to-do. Agnes was undoubtedly a lady: in Edinburgh, where her mother came from, the family was connected with the best society, while one of her closest girlhood friends became Lady Home: in later life Agnes spent many months sharing her lonely life in Scratby Hall, on the Norfolk coast.

The Ilchesters, however, moved on an altogether more elevated social plane. Had she not worked for them, Agnes could never have met them socially. And this sense that she was not their equal made her subordinate position in the household seem natural.

Forty years later, this was not true of the Brontës. Anne's employers, the Inghams and the Robinsons, and Charlotte's, the Sidgwicks and the Whites, were certainly richer than they were. But all that separated them was money. Indeed, in Charlotte's view, the Brontës' social standing was higher than the Whites'. Mrs White had been an exciseman's daughter: Charlotte, who thought she had 'a very coarse unladylike temper',[3] pointedly noted the family's lack of culture and broad Yorkshire vowels.

In Miss Porter's day, families such as these would never have employed a governess. Yet in the half-century between her first arrival at the Ilchesters' and the Brontës' schoolroom experiences, private governesses became a mass phenomenon – often employed, as in Charlotte Brontë's case, precisely because they could impart a veneer of class to the 'wild and unbroken'[4] children of the nouveaux riches. Nelly Weeton, who worked as a governess between 1810 and 1813, noted that for both her employers – the Pedders, who were bankers, and the Armitages, who were clothiers – this was the first time that the family had employed a governess. The Pedders required her not just to teach little Miss Pedder, but to show Mrs Pedder how to run the house and behave in society.

One of the effects of this change was to position the governess and her mistress, both psychically and physically, too close for comfort. Naturally, not all the establishments inhabited by governesses during the eighteenth century were as grand as the Ilchesters', but they were generally spacious enough to allow the governess her own comfortable room. Agnes Porter, Mary Wollstonecraft and Eliza Bishop all worked in great houses (though not, in Eliza's case, for titled people), and all commented on their pleasant quarters. Middle-class houses, however, were smaller. When Agnes Grey's charge Mary Ann emits one of her piercing screams with a vindictive '*Now*, then! *That's* for you,'[5] her mother hears and comes running to find out who is tormenting her darling. Lady Ilchester's daughters almost certainly did not scream in that way, but had they done so, their mother would probably have been too far away to hear.

This inconvenient nearness led to interference and hyper-sensitivity – on one side to any perceived slight, on the other to any overstepping of social or emotional boundaries. And this is perhaps why, of the lives recounted here, only those whose positions were in large and comparatively relaxed aristocratic households formed genuine friendships with their charges. This happened with Agnes Porter and the second Ilchester daughter, Mary; with Mary Wollstonecraft and Margaret King, who modelled her life on her governess's theories; and with Anna Jameson, one of whose charges, Hyacinthe Littleton, remained a lifelong friend.

It is true that in all these cases, either the circumstances or the governess herself were exceptional. With Miss Porter, the friendship was cemented by the fact that, when the first Lady Ilchester died, her daughter Mary was in the throes of adolescence and was gently helped through the crisis by kind Agnes, to whom she ever afterwards turned as to a wise aunt. And both Mary Wollstonecraft and Anna Jameson were outstandingly brilliant and charismatic – the kind of woman that any young girl might look up to in awe, and whose friendship she might cherish. But what really made these friendships possible was that in none of these aristocratic families was the governess demeaned, as those often were who worked in less socially secure, middle-class homes. Eliza Bishop, whose employers had made their money in trade[6] and were at pains to emphasize their superiority to a mere governess, found that the climate of belittlement in which she worked meant that she received nothing but impudence from her charges. By contrast the aristocratic employers of Agnes Porter, Mary Wollstonecraft and Anna Jameson held them in high regard and their daughters, seeing this, treated them accordingly.

There were two other ways in which Agnes Porter was unusually fortunate. The first was her disposition. Unlike those many governesses who took the job unwillingly and because there was 'no other occupation for a lady', she loved children and was a born teacher. She took an interest in the latest ideas on education, had read Richard and Maria Edgeworth's *Practical Education* and had met Madame de Genlis, the celebrated French writer on educational matters. Putting their theories into practice, she taught through play and experience rather than by rote repetition; the result was the delightful atmosphere that she describes. Perhaps, in what one might term a virtuous circle, it was this sympathetic and enlightened approach that drew Lady Ilchester to feel so warmly towards her – which in its turn made the children more biddable and affectionate.[7]

The Brontës, by contrast, were not (as Charlotte's biographer Mrs Gaskell tells us) naturally fond of children, and this absence of natural sympathy resulted in mutual mistrust. Charlotte found her charges 'riotous, perverse, unmanageable cubs', while her employer, Mrs Sidgwick, 'care[d] nothing in the world about me except to contrive how the greatest possible quantity of labour may be squeezed out of me'.[8] And in *Agnes Grey*, a novel clearly reflecting her own dismal governessing experiences (including a low point when, in despair, she actually tied one particularly unruly charge to a table leg), Anne Brontë described her own schoolroom hell:

> Master Tom, not content with refusing to be ruled, must needs set up as a ruler, and manifested a determination to keep, not only his sisters, but his governess in order, by violent manual and pedal applications ... A few sound boxes on the ear, on such occasions, might have settled the matter easily enough: but as, in that case, he might make up some story to his mother, which she would be sure to believe ... I determined to refrain from striking him, even in self-defence: and, in his most violent moods, my only resource was to throw him on his back, and hold his hands and feet until the frenzy was somewhat abated.[9]

Such a scene would have been inconceivable in Miss Porter's gentle, ordered world. But unlike the Ilchester girls, whose behaviour reflected not just their governess's competence but her friendly relations with their mother, Agnes Grey's uncontrollable charges knew that their mother, while not exactly condoning their naughtiness, would not punish it.

Miss Porter was fortunate, too, in her pay: a hundred guineas a year. (A guinea was £1 1s, a way of charging a little more for one's services without seeming to. There were twenty shillings in a pound: Agnes therefore earned £105 a year.) This was less than the £300 that the Edgeworths recommended in *Practical Education*, but more than most governesses could expect. Mary Wollstonecraft, setting off to take up a situation with Lord and Lady Kingsborough in 1786, two years after Miss Porter's arrival at Redlynch, was offered £40, a salary she accepted without demur. That was what a head gamekeeper or a cook earned, while £100 was what an establishment like Lord Ilchester's paid the house steward, the most responsible member of the household. (Reflecting the usual inequality in female pay, the housekeeper, who organized the servants, received only £20.[10])

Yet despite her excellent situation and cheerful nature, Agnes Porter was not really satisfied with her life. Like all governesses she longed for family, friends, and the independence and financial security that could come only if she married. And like all governesses she had drearily to acknowledge that without that financial security, family and friends would inevitably be forced into the margins of her life. 'All the morning with my dear mother. Endeavoured to chear her spirits; was her handmaid in dressing and settled many little conveniencies for her comfort. Had I an independency, how happy should I be to attend on her, but fortune forbids such satisfaction, as I could not give her my company without lessening her provisions and comforts.'[11]

Agnes' devotion to her mother and desire to be with her reflected more than just natural affection. For a single woman – and especially for a private governess, living under someone else's roof in a place where she was often both overworked and routinely humiliated – her parents, and the parental house, embodied everything represented by the word 'home'. Agnes deeply resented her feckless sister Betsey, who lived at home but failed to take proper care of their ailing mother, while Agnes, who asked nothing better than to nurse her, had to live far away, earning money to keep that home going.

It was not that Agnes did not feel at home at Redlynch. Unlike those many governesses who found themselves suspended awkwardly between the worlds of upstairs and downstairs, being welcome in neither, she seems to have been unusually at ease in both. In novels the housekeeper often counterpoints the governess, her comfortable domestic authority acting as a foil to the governess's dangerously unmoored figure. As the chief representative of the servants' hall, her relationship with the governess is often equivocal. 'I don't like them governesses, Pinner,' remarks Mrs Blenkinsop, the Sedleys' housekeeper in *Vanity Fair*, to the maid. 'They give themselves the hairs and hupstarts of ladies, and their wages is no better than you nor me.'[12]

Even where, like Mrs Grose in *The Turn of the Screw* and Mrs Fairfax in *Jane Eyre*, she is benevolent, the housekeeper points up the governess's rootlessness and uncertain social status (a contrast used to particularly chilling effect by Daphne du Maurier in *Rebecca*, where the new wife, her position as ill-defined as that of any incoming governess, is terrorized by the long-established housekeeper Mrs Danvers).

Once again, however – perhaps as a consequence of her warm relations with the mistress of the house, perhaps because of her own unusually sociable and relaxed nature – Miss Porter was the exception. Her relations with the Ilchesters' housekeepers, Mrs Fye and Mrs Hayes, seem to have been friendly and companionable; as single women in positions of responsibility, they evidently felt a mutual bond. (Housekeepers, in real life as in fiction, styled themselves 'Mrs' though they were often unmarried. It was an honorific to which any woman of a certain age and status felt herself entitled. As she moved into her forties, Miss Porter, too, became Mrs Porter. 'I begin to be rather too advanced in life for a Miss,' she told Lady Mary Fox-Strangways, in 1792.[13] But she must have been thinking about it for a while, for Lady Ilchester, who died in 1791, had already christened a favourite spot in the Redlynch grounds 'Mrs Porter's Walk'.[14]

In the nervous calculations that she made as she got older, Miss (or Mrs) Porter reflected bitterly on the fate of Mrs Hayes, who on her retirement had been cheated by a relative and had ended her days in poverty. And well might she agonize; she must often have wondered whether this would be her own fate. For however fondly the governess might establish herself in the family, when her pupils had grown there would be no more reason for her to remain in the house. Then she would be 'let go', often with no more than a reference and at an age when it was no longer easy to find work. Unusually, Lord Ilchester promised Miss Porter an annuity of £30 for life, but died apparently without mentioning it in his will. 'I am resigned, be it as it will!' she wrote in October 1802; but as she was by then fifty-two and crippled with gout, resignation was easier proposed than achieved. A month later the worry resurfaced: 'I have heard nothing of my annuity which Lord Ilchester gave me, . . . I think my right to it is incontestible.' In fact, the annuity, unknown to her, had been increased to £100; but for a long time it was uncertain whether she would ever receive it. 'Very dissatisfactory,' she noted grimly. 'Nothing to be paid until the present earl is of age, near five years hence. I asked the Colonel what I was to do in the interval, and added that should I from ill health be obliged to give up my profession and be reduced to want, I thought it would be a reflection on his noble family. He seemed to think that what I said was *une façon de parler* – but he knows not me.'[15] In the end Agnes got her annuity, but most governesses were less fortunate.

Despite these uncertainties, however, Miss Porter's position must have seemed as secure as it could well be. But, in 1794, when she had been in post for ten years, everything changed. That February her beloved Lady Mary married Thomas Mansel Talbot and left for her husband's house, Penrice Castle near Swansea, in Wales. And in August Lord Ilchester remarried, his bride this time being a cousin, Miss Maria Digby, only two years older than his own eldest daughter.

The news was clearly a bombshell. From Melbury, another Ilchester seat where the earl now preferred to spend his time, Miss Porter poured out her heart to Lady Mary in Penrice:

> I shall begin with what seems to me the most important point alluded to in your dear letter, namely Lord Ilchester's marriage. During our stay in Town I had never heard a syllable of the matter, and never dreamt of such a thing. I was called to Sarum on my dear mother's account, [Mrs Porter died that year] and after a melancholy fortnight arrived at Melbury in such a disposition of mind as to suppose nothing could affect, or rouze [sic] me from, the torpor of spirits I was in. However, I was mistaken . . . Mrs Fye came running up to my room one afternoon in a hurry, with a 'Madam, Madam, what will you give me for news, and a marriage, too? Who do you think is on the point of marriage? It is My Lord himself, I promise you – but law! How pale you do grow – you ben't sick be ye?' . . . This was the manner, my dear Lady Mary, in which I first heard this important event, and I did not recover for some days.[16]

Agnes did her best to put on a brave face: 'His choice is universally approved of, and were you to see her unaffected sweetness, her unassuming manners, you would hold out your generous hand to encourage her'[17] – but she was clearly alarmed at the prospect of a new Lady Ilchester. Playing stepmother to six suspicious children was always going to be difficult; the new incumbent would want to woo them onto her side, and Miss Porter – the current possessor of the children's affections, the old friend to whom they would turn when faced with the incomer – would become a rival rather than a friend. And when a governess had to deal with a hostile mistress, there could be only one winner. The upshot was a sort of guerrilla war, the bitterness of which may be guessed from Agnes' uncharacteristically grudging attitude, two years later, towards her charges' new half-brother: 'Lady Ilchester is quite well, and the little William has reco-vered his health entirely. He is so sweet a child that at *last* he makes *even me* love him, *et c'est beaucoup dire.*'[18] Meanwhile, torn between his new wife and the faithful governess, 'my dear Lord Ilchester's manner altered so much to me that I was afraid I should in time become even an object of his aversion.'[19]

The hostilities came to a head in 1796, when Lady Ilchester decreed that Miss Porter would no longer – as had always previously been the case – have her own parlour in which to receive friends when the family moved to London for the season. These London stays afforded her a rare chance to re-enter her own life, seeing old friends, making new ones, and enjoying dinners and theatregoing. But Lady Ilchester's spiteful prohibition meant that from now on, although she might still go out, she could no longer receive.

It was a direct insult, and a challenge. Miss Porter could either swallow her pride, while knowing that the situation could only deteriorate, or take the hint and stalk off. But now she came up against the governess's curse of 'dependance'. Since her mother's death she no longer had any obvious home of her own. If she left, where would she live, and how? She could stay with her sister Fanny, but the Richardses were not well off and could not afford to support her. Nor was there any guarantee, at the age of forty-six, that she would find a new situation.

She was saved in the nick of time by a recently widowed friend from her Great Yarmouth childhood, Mrs Upcher, who wrote offering her £100 a year 'to live with her as her sister and friend as long as she lives'.[20] Only then, with the assurance of a home to go to, did Agnes feel free to offer her resignation.

Had a conversation with Lord Ilchester on the subject of my leaving his family . . . I proposed six months as notice, asked him if he thought *that* a proper one? He was indeed deeply affected – seemed both surprized and shocked. I made no reflection on any person nor circumstance; said it was probable I might live with a friend, but if I was disappointed and returned to the same *line* of *education*, I should trouble his lordship for a recommendation. I then thanked him for *thirteen* years' protection, and *several* years of happiness. The *thanks*, he said, were *due to me* – he took me by the hand and said I had *knock'd him up*, he could not say a word then on the subject, but if it was for my happiness he must acquiesce. At night I reflected on this conversation, was satisfied in my own mind, as I had not said a single word more than I had resolved to do. ... In the afternoon Lady Ilchester invited me to tea and expressed what she was pleased to term her *sorrow* at my departure.[21]

The only escape from this terrifying cycle of insecurity was marriage, for which, despite her advancing age and homely appearance, Agnes never entirely ceased to hope. In 1792, when she was forty-two, this was one of the factors in her decision to style herself Mrs. 'Do not suppose that being styled *Mrs* will spoil my [chance of] marriage,' she told Lady Mary. 'On the contrary, I may be mistaken for a little jolly widow and pop off when you least expect it.'[22] For as Fanny Burney's 'Mrs' Mittin put it, 'Everybody likes a young widow.'[23] Agnes declared her sister Fanny's Mr Richards to be 'a very amiable man' and reflected that 'just such another man with ten years or more over his age would make me a very happy woman'.[24]

Nor were these hopes as far-fetched as they might appear. While husbands were unlikely to emerge from within the employer's family, it is clear that mid-life marriages between governesses and respectable gentlemen were by no means unheard of. In Jane Austen's *Emma*, the Woodhouse girls' old governess, Mrs Weston – a figure very much in the Miss Porter mould – has found just such a husband, while in Mrs Gaskell's *Wives and Daughters* the widowed Dr Gibson also marries an ex-governess.

At least twice Miss Porter's hopes were raised. On 28 November 1790 she received an 'extraordinary' letter from 'a dear friend', whom her journal two days later revealed to have been a Dr Macqueen, an old friend of her youth now practising in London. She replied to him 'according to my ideas of true friendship' and waited for his response.

In vain; by 23 December she was 'very pensive all day, bordering a little on ill-humour ... At night took myself to task – found it originated in disappointment in not receiving a letter from a particular correspondent.' Two weeks later the letter arrived, but it was not what she had hoped. 'It on the whole vexed and disappointed me: an emblem of all earthly expectations. Resolved to divest my mind of too tender an interest in the concerns of any male friend.' Even so, she still could not persuade herself all was lost. When the family removed to London at the end of January she took the opportunity to write once again to Dr Macqueen, declining a dinner invitation in order to '[stay] at home with some faint chance of seeing a dear friend'. (This, of course, would not have been possible under the parlourless regime dictated by the second Lady Ilchester.) 'As the time was uncertain, chose to wait at home all the day ... [but] Dr Macqueen did not arrive.'[25] A few days later, she was forced to admit defeat. 'He is on the point of matrimony with a lady of fortune and who, by his description, possesses, beside, "an excellent understanding and an angelic disposition". May they be happy together ... I determined to close the epistolary correspondence ... in a gay, chearful style.'[26]

Maintaining the same brave face, she wrote to their mutual friend Mrs Upcher, 'treat[ing] Dr Macqueen's marriage as an event to be wished for – may it prove so in all the consequences'.[27] But on hearing that another old friend had married a French gentleman, she noted gloomily: 'N.B. my acquaintances are marrying very fast off my hands. They will leave me in the lurch, I believe – *n'importe, je serai toujours heureuse en dépit du celibat.*'[28]

Agnes and Dr Macqueen remained friends (in 1803 he prescribed her a remedy for the gout and was always consulted when a friend became ill) and she had the muted satisfaction of noting that the marriage had not worked out particularly well: 'Dr Macqueen called upon me to take leave – his lady is, it seems, no friend to society, and neither makes her own acquaintances nor his welcome – *tant pis pour le mari!* – But he wished for riches – *et le voilà riche.* He told me with a sigh that wealth did not confer happiness.'[29] Whether poverty would have done so was another question; it was fifteen years too late to find out.

A doctor would have been a good catch for a poor governess (this is certainly what Mrs Gaskell implies regarding Dr Gibson's marriage in *Wives and Daughters*). A more likely prospect was a curate, such as Fanny Porter's real-life husband Mr Richards, or Charlotte Brontë's Mr Nicholls. Curates, like governesses, were respectable – the Church was a favourite destination for younger sons – but they rarely had the kind of prospects that might attract a woman with a dowry. Nor could they afford to provide one: clergymen's daughters, like Miss Porter and the Brontës, often became governesses. And so, in genteel semi-penury, generations of governesses perpetuated themselves.

In 1796 just such a possible curate seemed miraculously to present himself when a Revd Mr Griffith became tutor to young Lord Sta-vordale. Clergymen often started their careers in this way, though unlike the governess, who (in George Stephen's words) had 'neither hope nor prospect open in this world, beyond a possible alliance with an inferior',[30] for the curate, tutoring might represent merely a first step in those careers. What tutors could offer, and governesses could not, was the Latin and Greek necessary for entry into such schools as Eton and Harrow and, eventually, the universities. The famous clerical wit Sydney Smith started out in this way and was at this time tutor to a Talbot cousin. In 1799 he and his charge visited Penrice, where Miss Porter was then living, and where (doubtless excited by the rare and welcome presence of a really clever man) she evidently took the opportunity to display her own unusual breadth of culture. Smith, despite liking intelligent women, found such shamelessness on the part of a governess beyond the bounds of decency. 'Miss Porter perhaps ought not exactly to be set up as a model of good breeding, judgment, beauty or talents [he wrote to his employer, Mr Hicks Beach]. She is I daresay a very respectable woman, and may be a much more sensible woman than I think her, but I confess in my eyes she is a very ordinary article.'[31]

Mr Griffith disagreed; he and Miss Porter got on famously. 'Met Lord and Lady Ilchester, who smiled at our *tête à tête*. N.B. I resolved to change my hours of walking, as it particularly behoved me to avoid any particularity, or the least *seeming* indecorum,'[32] she noted coyly. A month later, 'Mr Charles Strangways ... asked me *en badinant* how I did since Mr Griffith's departure – I laughed and answered "As well as could be expected."'[33] But, alas, it turned out that Mr Griffith had been concealing an important detail: he was already married. Agnes met the lady on her next visit to London (where that year's humiliating veto on a personal parlour also meant that she was unable to receive Dr Macqueen for the confidential conversation they both desired).

Mrs Griffith was deeply unsatisfactory. She 'loved her *first* husband dearly' and 'preferred wearing black to any other colour ... When much pleased with Mr Griffith, she told us, she called him Thomas. Mr Griffith's name is Joseph ... Indeed, poor lady her mind seems a good deal weakened and deranged. I do not now wonder at Mr Griffith's not talking about his wife or marriage etc.'[34] However, deranged or not, there she was: a regrettable but unbudgeable fact.

Fortunately, there was the distraction of the move to Mrs Upcher's. However, only two years later, that lady, too, died, and Miss Porter found herself once more in search of a home. Once again, she was lucky. Mary Talbot, with whom she had kept in close touch, had by that time three children of her own: four-year-old Mary; Jane, a year younger; and a baby, Christiana. At some point in 1799 she invited her old governess to Penrice Castle, to help educate and look after them. And at Penrice, Miss Porter remained until her retirement in 1806.

In this congenial and countrified situation Miss Porter's position subtly changed, acquiring a solidity more usual among nannies or housekeepers, who often stayed with a family over two generations. She now effectively became not just a retainer but a de facto family member.

> I go on as usual with the dear children. They come to me at half-past seven, stay near three hours, then I breakfast with their papa and mama. I then am by myself till one o'clock – I walk, work, read and write at pleasure. I again meet my pupils at their dinner and my nunch [the eighteenth-century word for what we now call lunch] at one, and they stay with me till half past four. I then dress for dinner at five. The children come in at desert [sic], and continue in company till eight. I then very often see the two elder young ladies put to bed, and after that return below stairs to the drawing room till ten. Then to bed. I endeavour to be as useful as possible to my dear pupils, and may God bless them here and for ever, amen.[35]

Even in the wilds of Wales, such familiarity on the part of the governess was regarded by some as improper. Miss Porter records one incident where 'Mrs Pryce, who ... is of a most obliging temper, offered to assist me with my cloak. Her husband made her a sign of dis-approbation, and in some confusion she dropt the string and pre-tended to have her attention called another way.'[36] Nevertheless most people presumably took their cue from the Talbots. If the leading local magnate was happy to treat his governess as a social equal, who were they to snub her?

After her retirement, Miss Porter went to live with her married sister Fanny Richards in Fairford, Gloucestershire. But although she loved Fanny and esteemed her brother-in-law, there were constraints. The annuity left her by Lord Ilchester took time to come through, and the Richardses, making ends meet on a curate's small income, evidently expected more from her than she could afford to give. Also, it is impossible to escape the sense that she found life in Fairford unimaginably dull. 'Mr Richards *composes* two excellent sermons a week, which he preaches on Sunday. The saints' days are kept, and there is a sacrament every month. At nine in the evening he reads prayers to his family, and at ten we go to bed.'[37] After a couple of years she began spending long periods of time elsewhere, often returning to Penrice to help out with the children and visit Lady Mary, and eventually settled in lodgings with old friends near Redlynch where she had been happiest. Her warm and intimate correspondence with 'My own dear Lady Mary' and '*our* lovely and good children'[38] con-tinued until her death in 1814, at the age of sixty-four.

In 1846, five years after the death of his wife, Mary Talbot's son Christopher wrote dolefully to his sister regarding the difficulties of finding a suitable governess:

> My poor children want someone that would love them, and feel an interest not merely in 'doing themselves credit' but in seeing their little charge happy. I see and feel this every day more and more, but I know the world too well not to be aware that love and affection cannot be bought for £100 a year, not for £1000. In these days, there do not exist such people as Miss Porter. Formerly servants and dependents remained for half a century in a family, but now these things are changed, and the old feelings of attachment and affection have yielded to a more commercial view of the connection between

employer and employed. I well recollect Emily Murray's advice to me, it was to give a liberal salary which would insure the services of a 'lady'. I let her choose for me, and she sent me a cold hearted self-sufficient fool of a woman, whom I was glad to get rid of, and I will undertake to say that if I were to try fifty governesses, I should not find one that is not more or less objectionable.[39]

Given that this letter was written at a time when the market was flooded with potential governesses, Mr Talbot's despair seems, on the face of it, illogical. The clue, however, lies in his next sentence: 'The fact is, they are not ladies and they cannot be so because, by the very nature of their education, they are compelled to live out of "society".'

Indeed: for what had taken place in the forty years since Mr Talbot's fondly remembered childhood with Miss Porter at Penrice was the evolution of governessing into an educational system for middle-class girls. And this involved not just an increasing awkwardness, as the social boundaries between employers and governesses became less clearly defined and floods of resentful and ill-prepared women were precipitated into a job they hated, but the acceptance of a very different – and much reduced – view of women's capabilities. Miss Porter's breadth of culture (she spoke fluent French, was a good musician, and read widely in English, French and Italian) was doubt-less based upon many childhood hours spent in the library her father, as a vicar, would surely have possessed. That, however, had been during the 1750s and 1760s; twenty years later, when Nelly Weeton was growing up, such freedom was already actively discouraged. A climate of feminine dependence and subordination was arising that demanded a narrowing of young women's mental horizons – and this could not happen unless the teachers were themselves similarly restricted. As Anna Jameson (herself the beneficiary of unrestricted access to *her* father's library) remarked, 'I have heard it said and supported by argument, that to fit a woman for a private governess, you must not only cram her with grammar, languages, dates, and all the technicalities of teaching, but you must ... avoid the cruelty – yes, *that* was the word, – the *cruelty* of giving her any ideas, feelings, aspirations, which might render the slavery of her future life more dreadful than it might otherwise be.'[40] She wrote these words in 1846, the same year that Christopher Talbot wrote his letter, and the year before Charlotte Brontë published *Jane Eyre*, with its description of Lowood, a school based on Charlotte's own experience that was designed to prepare girls for governessing in exactly the way Mrs Jameson deplored.

If the subject of such enforced ignorance was intelligent, the result, as in Nelly Weeton's case, was likely to be a deeply ingrained diffidence. Such a person, doubtless only too aware of her insufficiencies, lacked not merely knowledge but the social ease Mr Talbot sought and that only confidence could provide. As for loving her charges, everything in this new culture militated against it. To become emotionally involved in that way risked not only the jealous wrath of the mother, but additional pain when, inevitably, the position came to an end.

So the lack of Miss Porters was due not, as Mr Talbot supposed, to the decline of faithful retainers, but to the deliberate infantilizing of women. In this new world, Miss Porter might still represent what governesses were ideally supposed to be, but she was no longer typical – if, indeed, she had ever been so.

3

Mary and her sisters:
the problem of girls' education

ᴍary Wollstonecraft's name, anathema throughout the nine-teenth century for her subversive views on female equality, is today widely familiar. She is known both for her feminist manifesto *A Vindication of the Rights of Woman*, written in 1792, and for the extraordinary drama of her life, in which she achieved independence as a writer and journalist, travelled to France to witness the revolution, bore an illegitimate daughter to the American adventurer Gilbert Imlay, tried to kill herself when Imlay deserted her, and finally found happiness with the radical philosopher William Godwin, only to die in 1797 after giving birth to their daughter Mary Godwin, the future author of *Frankenstein*.

Our interest, however, is in her involvement, both practical and theoretical, with girls' education, and the very particular set of experiences that allowed her, almost uniquely, to step outside the mindset of her times. It was Mary's good fortune to inhabit one of those rare hinge moments – the few years just before and after the 1789 French revolution – when real and fundamental change seemed genuinely possible; and this enabled her to live, as well as think, in the revolutionary spirit of iconoclastic freedom.

Mary's parents taught her, by example, that the most mediocre and contemptible of men were able to maintain even the most talented women in a state of near-subjection. Her great aperçu was that the root of this unfairness lay in women's schooling – or, rather, its absence.

To maintain their power, men insisted that women should remain 'innocent; they mean in a state of childhood'.[1] And for this to be possible it was essential that boys and girls be educated separately, girls' education then being confined almost entirely to the superficial 'accomplishments' that would enable them eventually to catch a man.

The solution that Mary proposed in the *Vindication* was universal state-funded co-education. It was implemented in revolutionary France; might it perhaps be adopted in Britain too? For a brief instant, it seemed possible. Had the Enlightenment ideals that gave rise to the American republic and the French revolution taken root in Britain, as Mary and her friends hoped, that would have been the end of the governess.

In the event, all these high hopes came to nothing: Mary's educational vision would not be fully implemented in Britain until after the Second World War. But although she died before it had become clear quite what that would mean for women, the lives of her sisters Eliza and Everina (both of whom long outlived her) were bitterly affected by this failure. Like Mary, they had to support themselves; unlike her, they were not able to escape the usual fate of ladies in this position and spent their whole lives either as governesses or, later, keeping a school together. Their letters, preserved with the Wollstonecraft–Godwin papers in the Bodleian Library, offer a terrifying insight into the lonely realities of life as a governess at the end of the eighteenth century.

In 1784, the year Agnes Porter arrived at Redlynch, Mary Wollstonecraft, her sister Eliza, and their friend Fanny Blood were trying to open a school. Mary was then twenty-five, Fanny twenty-seven, and Eliza twenty-one.

Though members of the respectable middle classes, they were more or less completely without means and knew that, if their enterprise did not succeed, they could not look to their families to keep them out of the gutter. Today this is the situation only of the very poorest. But Mary, Fanny and their sisters took it for granted. Only a few years later, Fanny's younger sister Caroline was found casually prostituting herself on the street. Most contrived to avoid this level of desperation. But life for unmarried women was often a hand-to-mouth affair, in which urgent bills for rent and food were met only thanks to the kindness of friends.

Faced with this heart-stopping insecurity, unmarried sisters looked to each other for support. The fictional Miss Bateses in Jane Austen's *Emma*, the Miss Jenkynses and Miss Browns in Mrs Gaskell's *Cranford*, Diana and Mary Rivers in *Jane Eyre*, echoed thousands of real-life sisterly households – including, eventually, that of Eliza Bishop and Everina Wollstonecraft. Even when Everina and Eliza were apart, small sums of money – £1, £2, five guineas – were constantly sent back and forth between them as needs and urgencies ebbed and flowed. When Mary began earning more substantial sums her first thought was always for her sisters, and they repaid her, clubbing together to provide the money, from their governesses' salaries, that helped keep her in France in 1793.

Schoolkeeping was Mary's second attempt at earning her living. By 1784 she had already spent some years as a lady's companion; two years later, in 1786, she would take a situation as a private governess; eventually she would become known as a writer. She thus tried all the occupations then available to women apart from dressmaking or millinery, which notoriously combined killing uncertainty with long hours, strained eyes and bad pay. She excelled at them all. As a companion, she tamed a notoriously bullying mistress; so long as she was there to supervise it, her school flourished; as a governess she showed both that a truly inspiring teacher may permanently change her pupils' lives and that governesses need not be victims; as a writer, she remains famous to this day. Nevertheless, the narrowness of the available choices never ceased to chafe her. Unlike Agnes Porter, or her sisters Eliza and Everina, or her friend Fanny, Mary did not accept that this absence of possibilities for women was simply the way things were and had to be.

The feminist proclamation on which her fame rests, *A Vindication of the Rights of Woman*, is propelled by fury. On society and its leaders: 'What but a pestilential vapour can hover over society when its chief director is only instructed in the invention of crimes, or the stupid routine of childish ceremonies?'[2] On parents: 'Parental affection is, perhaps, the blindest modification of perverse self-love ... but a pretext to tyrannize where it can be done with impunity.'[3] On women: 'Educated in the enervating style recommended by the writers on whom I have been animadverting; and not having a chance, from their subordinate state in society, to recover their lost ground, is it surprising that women every where appear a defect in nature?'[4]

Mary's drama – the source of this enabling anger – began in 1763, when she was four and her sisters had not yet been born. That year their grandfather died, dividing the fortune he had made as a Spitalfields master-weaver between the daughter of his first marriage, his son Edward, who was Mary's father, and his grandson, Mary's older brother Ned. Edward Wollstonecraft and his half-sister each received £10,000; Ned got £3,000 together with a lease on some land and a share in a merchant ship. For Mary and her future siblings (Henry Woodstock, who may have ended in a lunatic asylum; the two younger sisters, Eliza and Everina; and two younger brothers, James and Charles), there was nothing.

Mary always thought this apportionment unfair and illegal, and she furiously resented it. In fact it seems unlikely that her grandfather deliberately intended to pauperize his small granddaughter and her future siblings. £10,000 was a substantial fortune; any normally energetic man should have been able to convert it into a comfortable living for himself and all his children, including decent portions for his daughters. Mary's real misfortune was that her father was a lazy drunkard. Nonetheless, she preferred to tell herself that she was poor not because of his incompetence, but because men – her grandfather, her father, above all, her brother – had decided that she should be poor.

Ned's bequest, his handling of it, and Mary's reaction to it, showed the Wollstonecraft family poised on the dividing line between two societies. In the earlier world that Mary instinctively inhabited, all siblings could count on receiving some part of any family money, and an unmarried sister, if left otherwise unprovided for, would find a home with one of them. Even if (as often happened) she was treated as an unpaid drudge, she would be guaranteed board and lodging, and would remain part of the family. However, in the coming world of the industrial revolution it was more important to keep fortunes than families intact. In this new world-view, daughters were not equal family members, but burdens to be shifted as soon as possible to some other man's account (which is yet another reason why so many novels were built around orphaned daughters). A daughter's function – and the only way in which she could be sure of a decent life – was to marry well; any family money belonged as of right to her brothers. That was Ned Wollstonecraft's view, as it would be Tom Weeton's a few years later. Fifty years earlier society would have looked askance on such behaviour, but now it went unnoticed. Men were allowed to act in this way, and so they did.

Edward Wollstonecraft, of course, did not set out to lose his inheritance. On the contrary, he hoped to propel himself up a class by abandoning his roots in trade to become a gentleman farmer. He took a farm at Epping; after two years it failed, so he moved to another at Barking, where Mary remembered being left to play happily with the other children in the open air. Three years after that, in 1768, the family moved again, to Beverley, in Yorkshire. Here they stayed for six years, a period of near-normality that Mary recalled with nostalgia. 'Those were peaceful days,' she wrote to her Yorkshire friend Jane Arden in 1779. 'Your's since that period may have been as tranquil, but mine have been far otherwise.'[5]

The Beverley farm, like the others, failed. The Wollstonecrafts moved to Hoxton, in north-east London, where they lived for eighteen months, after which came yet another bout of farming at Laugharne, in Wales – 'a most expensive and troublesome journey that answered no one good end'[6] – followed by another return to London.

The Wollstonecrafts' family life was as unsuccessful as their farms. Although Mrs Wollstonecraft, sickly and constantly pregnant, was wholly reliant on her eldest daughter, she reserved all her affection for Ned. Mr Wollstonecraft, charming when sober, took to drink and, when drunk, became violent. On these occasions Mary tried to protect her mother; her future husband, William Godwin, related that 'She has even laid whole nights upon the landing-place near their chamber-door, when, mistakenly, or with reason, she apprehended that her father might break out into paroxysms of violence.'[7] In her two transparently autobiographical novels, *Mary, a Fiction*, published in 1788, and *The Wrongs of Woman: or, Maria, a Fragment*, begun in 1796 and published posthumously, the cast was the same: the sad heroine; the feeble, dependent but unaffectionate mother; the dastardly brother; the bullying father.

Ned, whose financial independence assured him his freedom, escaped to school, where he prepared to be a lawyer. But Edward Wollstonecraft 'always exclaimed against female acquirements, and was glad that his wife's indolence and ill-health made her not trouble herself about them'.[8] In Yorkshire, Mary attended a day school; in Hoxton she was taken up by a neighbouring clergyman, Mr Clare, who lent her books and made sure she read them. He offered to give her a home, but some 'painful circumstances, that I wish to bury in oblivion' made this impossible.[9] For a while Eliza and Everina attended a school (presumably a boarding school) in Chelsea.

This total absence of anything others might recognize as a normal upbringing was vital in creating the woman Mary became. Most middle-class girls grew up in a settled world where mothers deferred to fathers and women's secondary position was never questioned. But Mary grew up trusting nobody but herself, while for the men in her life – her bullying father, her mean brother – she had only contempt. She had her moments of self-doubt, sometimes so acute that they made her physically ill. But her underlying assurance was unstoppable: a rash, enabling certainty – false modesty's diametric opposite – that set her apart from the rest of her sex. One of her sisters' disabilities was that they wholly lacked this self-confidence. Mary was used to taking charge, Eliza and Everina to being looked after.

Equally importantly, the chaotic Wollstonecraft household also allowed Mary to escape the psychic tyranny of established religion. She was, Godwin tells us, 'accustomed to converse'[10] with her God, but He, like everything else in her life, was self-built, and functioned chiefly as a divine safety valve. He decidedly was not the patriarchally authoritarian Anglican deity in whose name *Hints to Governesses* advised its readers to 'remember Who it is that has placed you in your present position; perhaps you have no home, perhaps you are one of a large family, perhaps you have experienced a reverse of fortune; no matter what! It is God who has willed it so, therefore look to Him for guidance and protection ... To repine against His commands is wicked, and will do no good.'[11] Mary would become famous for this very wickedness.

With such an unsatisfactory experience of family life, it is not surprising that Mary showed no desire to start a family of her own. On the contrary; she declared herself 'on many counts ... averse to any matrimonial tie'.[12] Nonetheless, this left her in a quandary. If she did not marry, she must find work. And as she acknowledged in *Thoughts on the Education of Daughters*, her first book, published in

1786 just before she became a governess, possible occupations for ladies were few and getting fewer. Women did run businesses: selling books; importing and retailing chinaware, silks and tea; making stays, caps, gloves and wigs, but these were mostly inherited. Anne Hogarth, for example, began in the print-selling business as her brother William's agent and inherited his copper plates after his death. Women rarely started a business themselves; that needed capital and goodwill, neither of which they commonly possessed; they were also regularly excluded from the guilds that permitted entry to various trades.[13] 'The few trades that are left, are now gradually falling into the hands of the men, and certainly they are not very respectable,' Mary observed.[14]

Even more gallingly, in the few instances where men did much the same work as women, the mere fact of their maleness enhanced both their status and their pay. The very top salary for governesses was £400; in Sir George Stephen's 1844 survey, he found only one woman who received that amount, and she, we may assume, was fearsomely qualified, teaching not only all the usual accomplishments but many other subjects besides. Yet in 1845 a run-of-the-mill music master charged 7s per lesson. Even if he gave only four lessons a day, that meant (assuming a six-day week) an income of over £400 a year and, if he organized his life sensibly (for instance, by spending two or three days a week giving his lessons in a school, and so cutting down on time wasted travelling between clients), he might earn much more. Similarly, when Lord Ilchester increased Agnes Porter's lifetime annuity from £30 to a hundred guineas, this represented unheard-of largesse for a governess. But the unsatisfactory Mr Griffith, who tutored Ilchester's son, received livings to the tune of £500 a year, each of which probably included an excellent house. Miss Porter, despite her respectable retirement income, had no house of her own, having to spend her last years shuttling between her sister's house, the homes of various friends and lodgings.

In 1778, when she was nineteen, Mary reluctantly settled for one of these unsatisfactory female possibilities. She took a position as companion to a widow, reputedly such a difficult woman that no previous occupant of the post had been able to stand it for more than a few weeks. Mary swore she would subdue this gorgon, and both she and her employer agreed that she succeeded. Perhaps, like many bullies, Mrs Dawson respected those who stood up to her.

47

But although her letters from this period were comparatively cheerful – Southampton was pleasant, Windsor in summer delightful, Mrs Dawson a good conversationalist – eight years later, in *Thoughts on the Education of Daughters*, Mary wrote feelingly of the horrors of being 'an humble companion', chief among them the indeterminate social status she shared with the governess:

> It is impossible to enumerate the many hours of anguish such a person must spend. Above the servants yet considered by them as a spy, and ever reminded of her inferiority when in conversation with the superiors. If she cannot condescend to mean flattery, she has not a chance of being a favorite; and should any of the visitors take notice of her, and she for a moment forget her subordinate state, she is sure to be reminded of it.[15]

At least Mary, unlike many girls in her situation, did not miss the pleasures of home. However, in 1781 she had to return there. Her mother had fallen dangerously ill and needed her attentions – her father, tired of living with an invalid, having some time since taken a mistress.

Mrs Wollstonecraft died the following year. Mary's posthumously published novel *The Wrongs of Woman* contains a revealing scene in which the dying mother 'solemnly recommended my sisters to my care, and bid me be a mother to them';[16] it is clear that Mary did think of herself in this way and took her responsibility very seriously. But where Eliza and Everina always instinctively looked to one another for support – 'my heart's best friend', Eliza called Everina[17] – their relationship with Mary was more complicated. Set apart by age and also the knowledge, shared by all three, that Eliza and Everina wholly lacked Mary's brilliance and charisma, the instinctive camaraderie that existed between the two younger girls never extended to their older sister. 'I have no creature to be unreserved to,' Mary complained after the departure of her friend Fanny Blood for Lisbon and marriage in 1785. 'Eliza & Averina [sic] are so different, that I could as soon fly as open my heart to them.'[18] Burdened by a sense of her duty towards them, she chided her sisters for not appreciating as warmly as they should the efforts she made on their behalf: 'I should like to be remembered in a kinder manner.'[19] 'Your affections are not sufficiently warm, or lasting, to enable you to keep up a regular correspondence

. . . Can I suppose that I am loved when I am not *told* that I am *remembered*.'[20] 'I ought *not* to have expected from *you* that kind of affection, which can only gratify *my* heart.'[21] 'If I had not cared for my sisters who certainly do not adore me – the last two years of my life might have passed tranquilly not embittered by pecuniary cares.'[22] But should they feel so very grateful? They were never quite sure.

Immediately his wife died, Mr Wollstonecraft married his mistress. Meanwhile Ned, freed from his mother's restraining influence, 'discovered a flaw in the settlement [of their mother's property] made on my mother's children, which set it aside, and he allowed my father, whose distress made him submit to any thing, a tithe of his own, or rather our fortune'.[23]

This was too much for Mary: she quit her father's house and moved in with the family of her friend, Fanny Blood. Eliza, too, escaped. By common consent the best-looking of the three sisters, she married Meredith Bishop, whom Mary declared 'a worthy man whose situation in life is truly eligible'.[24] She was soon pregnant and in August 1783, aged nineteen, gave birth to a little girl.

Following the birth, Eliza slipped into what sounds like a severe bout of post-natal depression. Mary, happy to escape the Bloods' cramped quarters and do what she most enjoyed – take charge – eagerly rushed to her side. What followed was so extraordinary that only some irrational compulsion can possibly account for it. Something in Eliza's situation – perhaps the all-too-familiar conjunction of a woman in tears, a squalling infant and an irritable man – evidently sparked in Mary an irresistible need to act: to do something, *anything*, to bring this insupportable drama to a close. The solution, she concluded, was to end the marriage. Everina, then seventeen or eighteen, was her confidante.

Poor Eliza's situation almost turns my brain – I can't stay and see this continual misery – and to leave her to bear it by herself without any one to comfort her is still more distressing – I would do anything to rescue her from her present situation . . . In this case something desperate must be determined on – do you think Edward will receive her . . . do speak to him . . . but you must caution him against expostulating or even mentioning the affair to Bishop for it would only put him on his g[ua]rd and we should have a storm to encounter that I tremble to think of – I am convinced this is the only expedient to save Bess – and she declares she had rather be a teacher than stay here . . .

Those who would save Bess must act and not talk.[25]

Act she did. In January 1784, poor Bess, so overcome that as they rode in the coach she bit her gold wedding-ring to bits, was spirited away from her Bermondsey home to lodgings in Hackney that Mary had taken under a false name.

Since Mary's letters to Everina constitute the only account of all this, it is impossible to know the real truth of the matter. Was Meredith Bishop cruel, or rejecting? On the contrary, he seems to have pleaded with Mary to let things be: 'my heart is almost broken with listening to B. while he *reasons* the case'.[26] Or perhaps he was simply trying to persuade Eliza that things would not be this way for ever, that she would get better, that he would be kinder. Either way, he was no match for Mary. Neither was poor prostrated Eliza in any state to withstand her sister's irresistible combination of tender concern, steely determination and absolute conviction that she knew best.

What would seem to us, now, the drama's central tragedy was that Eliza was compelled to leave not just her husband but her baby. Children, like everything else in a marriage, belonged by law to the man; if Eliza had taken the child, she would have been not merely a runaway wife (which was quite bad enough as far as society was concerned) but a felon. 'Bess is tolerably well she can't help sighing about little Mary who she tenderly loved – and on this score I both love and pity her – The poor brat it had got a little hold on my affections – some time or other I hope we shall get it.'[27] They did not. The baby died just before her first birthday and was given a lavish funeral by her father. Whether Eliza ever saw her again, we do not know. Neither do we know whether Mary ever repented her hasty action. Significantly, she did not tell Godwin about this episode; in his memoir of her, which contemporaries found so scandalously full and frank, Eliza's marriage is dismissed in two oblique words.

Having removed Eliza from what had been her life, Mary was now in honour bound to construct her another. This was how the two of them, with Fanny, came to start their school.

At first, when 'the MONIES [for a school] did not answer',[28] Mary thought they might have to support themselves by working from home. Fanny had recently sold two drawings for five guineas; Mary reckoned that 'with oeconomy'[29] they could live on a guinea a week; between Fanny's art and some needlework, this could easily be earned. However, Fanny had already tried and failed to support her family in this way. As she well knew, there was no chance they would earn that amount.

> In my eagerness to enjoy the society of two so dear to me, I did not give myself time to consider that it is utterly impracticable [Fanny wrote to Everina]. The very utmost I could earn, one week with another, supposing I had uninterrupted health [she was in the early stages of consumption] is half a guinea a week, which would just pay for furnished lodgings for *three* people to pig together. As for needle-work, it is utterly impossible they could earn more than half a guinea a week between them, supposing they had constant employment, which is of all things the most uncertain. This I can assert from experience . . . As for what assistance they could give me with the paints, we might be ruined before they could arrive at any proficiency at the art.[30]

Mary's old friend Mrs Clare, the wife of the clergyman from Hoxton, suggested that they might keep a haberdashery shop; if Ned agreed to help, they could stock it for £50. But Ned had no time for Fanny and, in any case, shopwork was physically beyond her.

Eventually, a school it was. A Mrs Burgh, the widow of a well-known educationist – perhaps an acquaintance of the ever-supportive Clares, and from then on a staunch friend – came up with a loan that enabled them to rent a house in the village of Islington. But no pupils came; and the threesome decided that they would move a little way out of London, to Newington Green, where Mrs Burgh herself lived, and start their school there.

In *Thoughts on the Education of Daughters*, Mary held little brief for schools, declaring that 'A teacher in a school is only a kind of upper servant, who has more work than the menial ones,'[31] and that 'If a mother has leisure and good sense, and more than one daughter, I think she could best educate them herself.'[32] Nevertheless, keeping school had several attractions. No qualifications were needed. The only essentials were to know more than your pupils and to have a house large enough to receive them. The result, if it could be made to work, was an independence otherwise almost unattainable for single women. In 1783, after leaving Redlynch (where she had, by an odd coincidence, been Agnes Porter's predecessor), Mary's friend Jane Arden opened a school with her sister in Beverley; it was there when Mary visited the town in 1795, and its descendant (it had by then moved to Lincolnshire) still flourished in 1834. Miss Richmal Mangnall made little money from her famous *Historical and Miscellaneous Questions*, which doubtless originated in her own lesson preparations and which she sold outright for a hundred guineas to her publishers, Longmans, thereby setting them up for a generation. But she made such a success of her school, Crofton Hall near Wakefield, that when she died in 1820 she left £13,000, independent of the goodwill. At the very least a school might offer an excellent outlet for Mary's qualities of leadership.

Schools at this time were unregulated, and varied enormously. There were bad schools for boys, and good ones for girls. Among the very best must have been the one run by Erasmus Darwin's illegitimate daughters, Mary and Susan Parker, whom he had prepared as teachers and set up in a boarding school of their own. The *Plan for the Conduct of Female Education*, which he wrote for them, was published in 1797. His recommendations ranged from 'Taste' – Addison's *Spectator* papers, and Hogarth's analysis of beauty – through 'Heathen Mythology' and 'Polite Literature' (but 'the excessive study of words is universally an ill employment at any time of life') to Botany, Chemistry and Mineralogy, all using the latest texts, to which he added sports (he regretted that skating, swimming, acrobatics and tightrope walking were 'not allowed by fashion' but nevertheless recommended 'theatrical marching, dancing and singing'),[33] as well as ball, shuttlecock and swinging. In his capacity as a medical man, he offered strictures on care of the shape, deportment (he advised lying down horizontally for an hour in the middle of the day) and the correction of lisping and stammering. This regime was supported by a diet of full-cream milk, meat, puddings and fruit pies, with short intervals between meals and not too much slimming: a programme that, if properly adhered to, would have turned out some formidably learned and healthy young ladies. Very few boys, let alone girls, can have had such an education as this.

Miss Mangnall, by contrast, was more concerned (as one would expect from the author of the *Questions*, whose emphasis was all on lists of facts) with rote learning. 'My Governess told our class of Geography if we did not know the rivers off we might go away . . . they all went but myself though some of them know them,'[34] recorded Elizabeth Firth, a pupil at Crofton Hall, on 13 May 1812. And a few days later, 'Several of the Ladies were sent to bed for losing at spelling. I was one of them.'[35] Life was not all lessons; there was plenty of outdoor exercise and fruit-picking in season. And although there is no mention in Elizabeth's diaries of being taught arithmetic, we know that she could add up because she kept meticulous accounts: in May 1813, frock-washing cost her 6d, rug needles 2d, gingerbread 6d, gloves 4s 6d, postage 5d, a plate 1d, more frock-washing 6d, a comb 2s, a sash 2s 6d. With 13s 3d carried forward from the previous month, this amounted to £1 4s 5d. Miss Mangnall was known as the governess: 'The mistress of the school is called *governess*, for the word *mistress* has a vulgar sound with it.'[36]

But since the guiding principle of education for both boys and girls was that pupils should be taught strictly with an eye to their future lives, girls' schools were often concerned less with book-learning than with turning out perfectly finished young ladies. The most fashionable was Mrs Devis's in Queen Square, 'the female Eton', where backboards, dancing masters, music masters and drawing masters were much in evidence, and where the diminutive Maria Edgeworth was 'swung by the neck to draw out her muscles and increase growth'.[37] (The treatment failed.) A Mrs Cooper, who taught there in the 1790s, wrote disapprovingly of the distorted moral values Mrs Devis enforced: 'To become amiable elegant and accomplished, punishments are set before them for the most insignificant of faults, and they undergo the same penance for mislaying their gloves or dirtying their frocks, as for telling untruths, or being guilty of deceit, and they are to be incited to diligence by working on their vanity and self love.'[38] Mrs Devis might have replied that this was merely a realistic reflection of society's priorities.

These hatcheries for marriageable young ladies embodied everything that Mary most hated. She railed against their product when in

1787 she moved briefly in Dublin's fashionable drawing rooms, despising their priorities and conscious that their perpetuation of ignorance contributed to women's subjugation. In 1791, her *Vindication of the Rights of Woman* would expose this vicious circle and try (though fail) to break it. However, her own establishment seems to have concentrated more on character than academic attainment, which was probably wise. Mary's own education, as she was painfully aware, had been extremely sketchy – her lack of French in particular was a real disadvantage – and Eliza's, Everina's and Fanny's had been no better. She declared in *Thoughts on the Education of Daughters* that 'The forming of the temper ought to be the continual thought, and the first task of a parent or teacher,' adding, perhaps from rueful self-knowledge, that 'Half the miseries of life arise from ... a tyrannical domineering temper.'[39]

Despite this, her magnetic personality evidently proved as irresistible to her pupils as to everyone else. That she was the school's kingpin is clear: when she was there, it flourished; as soon as she left, it failed. Godwin remarked on her affinity for children; with them she was 'the mirror of patience ... I have heard her say, that she never was concerned in the education of one child, who was not personally attached to her, and earnestly concerned not to incur her displeasure.'[40] Soon her students were doing so well that Everina came to join them, prompting Mary to take a bigger house with more room for boarders.

Newington Green is still an intimate space. In the eighteenth century it was some way from London; any new arrival would soon get to know the neighbours and these were very special neighbours. For Newington Green had long been a centre of Unitarianism, a variant of nonconformism marked by a spirit of searching and tolerance that extended beyond religion to politics, education and every manner of intellectual enquiry. In all of these, Unitarians were active: some, such as the pioneering chemist and Unitarian divine Dr Joseph Priestley, were active in all of them. And here, too, Mary found herself on the dividing line between two possible societies. In one, the old prejudices dominated, along with the old values. In the other – whose template was the newly independent American republic and which would shortly find its European expression in France – everything was open to debate. At Newington Green, and ever after, she threw in her lot with Dissent, France and America.

Newington Green's pretty Unitarian chapel still stands, flanked by handsome houses. Its minister, Dr Richard Price, was an old friend of Priestley (though they had at this time fallen out), a brilliant mathematician and a fiercely radical politician who, having supported the American revolution, naturally welcomed the one now brewing in France. Price and his wife were childless; perhaps his attachment to his new neighbour had something paternal in it. Whatever its roots, he recognized her quality and introduced her to his friends – poets, physicians, Fellows of the Royal Society.

Until then Mary had known only the arbitrary male ascendancy typified by her father and brother, but at Dr Price's house everything could be discussed and everyone, male or female, was accepted purely on his or her merits. And this new vision of what life might be quite simply enchanted her. In *Mary, A Fiction*, written four years after her arrival at Newington Green, several passages clearly recall her happy times with Price and his friends. 'The society of men of genius delighted her, and improved her faculties. With beings of this class she did not often meet; it is a rare genus; her first favourites were men past the meridian of life and of a philosophic turn.'[41] By a happy chance, she had fallen into the one milieu that suited her perfectly.

The Newington community was education-minded: in 1824 the poet and children's author Mrs Barbauld noted that 'I think nothing flourishes more in Newington than schools.' Mary's did well until February 1785, when Fanny Blood left for Lisbon to marry her long-standing suitor, Hugh Skeys.

Given the choice between running a school with female friends or getting married, Fanny did not hesitate. But without her friend, Mary pined. 'I try to smile,' she told Fanny's brother George, '– but somehow or other my spirits are fled and I am incapable of joy.'[42] When Fanny became pregnant, Mary determined to journey to Lisbon to be with her for the birth in November. It was a deeply impractical proposition, both financially – she had no money – and also because the school seemed unlikely to survive her absence. One neighbour gave a foretaste of what might be expected, threatening to discourage three potentially lucrative boarders if Mary refused to abandon her plans. Nevertheless she persisted, and was sped on her way by a loan from the faithful Mrs Burgh – money which, according to Godwin, 'she always conceived came from Dr Price' and which she 'faithfully repaid'.[43]

Mary arrived in Lisbon in time to see Fanny delivered of a boy, but a few days later, after a short rally, both mother and baby died. Mary, bereft, stayed in Lisbon for a few weeks before returning home in December; when she got back to Newington Green, she learned that her school had foundered. The boarders, having quarrelled with Eliza and Everina, had flounced off; she was deep in debt; the rental on the too-large house was very heavy ... Depression alternated with resignation: 'Yet I may be a tedious time dying – Well, I am too impatient – The will of Heaven be done!'[44]

In this desperate situation, John Hewlett, one of the new friends she had met at Dr Price's, came to the rescue. He had often urged her to try her hand at writing; she now set to. The result was *Thoughts on the Education of Daughters*. Hewlett took the manuscript to his friend Joseph Johnson, London's leading radical publisher. Johnson – whether on Hewlett's recommendation, or because he genuinely thought the author promising, or perhaps because he was introduced to her and, like the other members of his set, was simply swept away by the force of her intelligence and personality – bought it for ten guineas. The rapids had once again been negotiated, and the rower flung, exhausted but safe, onto the banks of what would be (though she did not yet know it) a new life.

Once the school had failed, it was every woman for herself. Mary was heartily tired of living with her sisters, while Eliza and Everina were constantly galled by the way everyone preferred Mary's company to theirs.[45] Everina was despatched to an unwilling Ned, now married and living at St Katharine's Dock; Mrs Burgh, whose husband's work had left her well connected in the educational world, found a place for Eliza in Leicestershire with a Mrs Tew, a fellow Dissenter.

Eliza detested it. She wrote miserably to Everina:

I can no longer indulge the delusions of fancy, and the phantoms of hope are for ever, ever flown; – you can have a fellow feeling for a luckless wretch, shut out from all society or conversation whatever, I can not make myself understood here; had I an inclination to do so, praying is the only amusement, not forgetting eating, and *mourning*, and so on – The idea of parting from a *husband* one could never make them *comprehend*, I could much *sooner* persuade them, that a stone might speak, indeed they have some notion of churches moving. – Oh! hale hale [sic] all *those delightful little elegances of life*, those smoothers of the rugged path could I but now and then meet with them.

. . . Oh! that you had a good *Husband*, to screen thee from those heart-breaking disagreeables . . . But alas to have no-one to express those transcendent feels to – not *no-one* [sic] to talk it over with.[46]

Eliza's constant underlinings of the word husband suggest that she looked back longingly to the time, only three years distant, when she had been a wife and mother, but Mary, having settled her, had no more time for complaints. 'You have not many comforts it is true – yet you *might* have been in a much more disagreeable situation at present – but it is not the evils we escape which we dwell on,'[47] she reminded her sister bracingly.

Mary thought for a short time of continuing with a day school at Newington Green, but experience had shown that the combination of no French and a total absence of funds would probably prove fatal. The only serious possibility was governessing. Dr Price and Mrs Burgh knew a Mrs Prior, the wife of a housemaster at Eton, and had some time previously recommended that Mary write to her on Eliza's behalf, presumably on the chance that some Eton boy's aristocratic family might be looking for a governess. Now that letter bore fruit; with Eliza safely in Leicestershire, Mary decided to take up the offer herself. 'I have had two offers of being received as a governess in reputable families – The one in Wales and the other in Ireland,' she told Fanny's brother George Blood in July 1786. She rejected the Welsh job, although she was 'very much pressed'[48] to take it. Perhaps it was the one that Eliza took some years later, at Upton Castle near Laugharne, which was arranged through a clergyman who knew both families (Mr Wollstonecraft having now moved permanently to Laugharne). However, the Irish post, Mary thought, was too good to turn down. It was with Lady Kingsborough, whose son George King was at Eton in Mrs Prior's house, and who was offering a salary of £40 a year.

Mary did not like the idea of governessing; her experience as a companion to Mrs Dawson had given her only too clear an idea of the anomalous social position it would entail. 'I should be shut out from society – and be debarred the *imperfect* pleasures of friendship –

as I should on every side be surrounded by *unequals*.'[49] Nevertheless, there were strong arguments in favour: an important payment from one of her old boarders had failed to materialize, she hated being in debt to her Newington Green friends, and for the moment the necessity of a secure income outweighed the pleasures of independence. If fifty guineas a year would have been enough to support 'with oeconomy' herself, Eliza and Fanny, £40 all found was riches. She reckoned that she could live on half her salary; board and lodging were provided; clothes held little interest for her; the rest would be used to pay her debts. 'I owe near eighty or ninety pounds,' she told George Blood, 'and some of the debts I would give the world to pay.'[50] She might also be able to help Eliza, who continued to weigh on her conscience.

The Kingsboroughs' offer was not particularly generous. Lord Kingsborough was the richest man in Ireland; at this same period Lord Ilchester was paying Agnes Porter the highly respectable annual salary of a hundred guineas, while in 1804 Lord Lucan offered double that to the learned Miss Hamilton, authoress of the successful *Memoirs of Agrippina*. (She did not stay long: it transpired that he was more excited by her recent subject matter, and the stimulating possibilities it suggested, than her doubtless excellent intellectual abilities.) However, Mary accepted the post gladly enough, and by October 1786 was at Eton, staying with the Priors until various members of the Kingsborough family should feel ready to make the trip to Ireland. Meanwhile she was working on her first novel, *Mary, a Fiction*. 'I have had so many new ideas of late, I can scarcely arrange them – I am lost in a *sea* of thought,'[51] she told Everina.

The Kingsboroughs were by no means unenlightened. Lord Kingsborough wanted to turn his estate at Mitchelstown, near Cork, into a model settlement, and to this end had hired the distinguished agriculturalist Arthur Young and established a plantation of mulberries in order to set up a silk industry. Mary later conceded that 'Lady K is really charitable – the poor about here bless her.'[52] However, although they were in some ways a model couple, he with his good intentions, she with her intellectual preferences and charitable work, the Mitchelstown household was riven with gossip and scandal. There were rumours that Lord Kingsborough had had an affair with Miss Crosby, the previous governess, who had been given notice and granted an annuity of £50, possibly in recognition of her unjust dismissal. This had entailed much coming and going between Young, the slandered lady and Lord Kingsborough. Rumour-mongers whispered in Lady Kingsborough's ear that Young was acting as a go-between for the lovers; others insinuated to his lordship that Young was in love with her ladyship. The upshot was the departure of Young as well as Miss Crosby, and the arrival of Mary. 'I entered the great gates with the same kind of feeling as I should if I was going into the Bastile,'[53] she dramatically announced to Everina from graceful Mitchelstown Castle, with its Italian plasterwork, French pictures and views of cloud-capped mountains. 'I hear a fiddle below . . . the servants are dancing – and the rest of the family diverting themselves – I only am melancholy and alone.[54]

In *Thoughts on the Education of Daughters*, Mary had observed that the mother was the key to every governess's happiness – and 'it is ten to one if they meet with a reasonable [one]'.[55] Her own experiences would bear this out. However, Mary's problems with Lady Kings-borough were rather different from those usually experienced by governesses vis-à-vis mothers. Usually it was the mother who dictated, the governess who trembled. But Mary's brief year with the Kingsboroughs provided a dramatic demonstration of the power that governesses might – occasionally – wield, and the unnerving situation that was liable to arise when they did so.

Lady Kingsborough promised well. She had told Mrs Prior that her daughters' education had so far been very unsatisfactory, that their minds had been neglected in favour of 'the ornamental part of their education, which she thinks ought ever to be a secondary con-sideration – These things,' Mary declared, 'prejudice me in her favour.'[56]

The Kingsboroughs had twelve children, but their mother – being, in the words of her eldest daughter, of 'that rank of life in which people are too occupied by frivolous amusements to pay much attention to their offspring'[57] – seemed blithely uninterested in them. In true upper-class style she was far more concerned with her dogs, which she petted with babytalk. Mary, unaccustomed to aristocratic behaviour, was shocked. 'To see a woman without any softness in her manners caressing animals, and using infantine expression – is you may conceive very absurd and ludicrous,' she told Everina.[58] Meanwhile the situation had its compensations, chief among them that it left her a free hand regarding her pupils.

Of the three girls committed to her care, she particularly took to the eldest, Margaret.

> Fourteen – by no means handsome – yet a sweet girl – She has a wonderful capacity but she has such a multiplicity of employments it has not room to expand itself – and in all probability will be lost in a heap of rubbish miss-called accomplishments – She is very much afraid of her mother – that such a creature should be ruled with a rod of iron, when tenderness would lead her any where – She is to be always with me.[59]

Hitherto, the girls' education, though far from neglected, had been hedged around with prohibitions – things that they were not allowed to read or do, and after which they naturally hankered. Although they understood several languages and had read '*cart*-loads of history', Mary found them quite uncultivated, with no topics of conversation other than dress, dogs and marriage. Even the latter was discussed 'not in a very *sentimental* style – alas poor sentiment it has no residence here – I almost wish the girls were novels [sic] readers and romantic, I declare false refinement is better than none, at all.'[60] From this we may deduce that novel reading had been one of the forbidden pastimes. On Mary's arrival all these caveats were at once lifted, with the result that all the girls instantly wanted nothing better than to do and to read whatever their governess positively approved.

Clever Margaret, Mary's favourite, felt particularly liberated by this new regime. Had she not met Mary, she told William Godwin, she would have become 'a most ferocious animal'.[61] Intellectual by preference, 'no expence [had been] spared to make me what was called accomplished'. But now for the first time someone understood and encouraged her true nature – and to this 'extraordinary woman['s] . . . superior penetration and affectionate mildness of manner' she later attributed what virtues she possessed. Although Mary was in Ireland less than a year, this brief acquaintance would shape and alter her pupil's whole life, instilling values that years of conventional overlay failed to dispel. In 1818, explaining herself to her two youngest daughters, Margaret would write of her 'unbounded admiration [for Mary] because her mind appeared more noble & her understanding more cultivated than any others I had known – from the time she left me my chief objects were to correct those faults she had pointed out & to cultivate my understanding as much as possible'.[62] When Mary's own daughter, another Mary, and her stepsister, Claire Clairmont, decided in their turn to reject convention for a life of Romantic freedom, Margaret King, by then calling herself 'Mrs Mason' after a character in one of Mary's books, would be their staunch friend and guide – a sort of avatar of her old governess, by then long dead.

'I go to the nursery,' wrote Mary, '– *something like* maternal fondness fills my bosom – the children cluster about me – one catches a kiss, another lisps my long name – while, a sweet little boy, who is conscious that he is a favorite, calls himself my son – At the sight of their mother they tremble and run to me for protection.' This 'renders them dear to me'.[63]

Mary tried to resist the growing attachment, but although she in no way identified with the family – as, for example, Agnes Porter identified with Mary Talbot's family – she was too warm-hearted to remain as detached as she might have wished, and was unavoidably drawn into the emotional dance.

> I grow too much interested for my own peace. Confined almost entirely to the society of children, I am anxiously solicitous for their future welfare, and mortified beyond measure, when counteracted in my endeavours to improve them. – I feel all a mother's fears for the swarm of little ones which surround me, and observe disorders, without having the power to apply the proper remedies.[64]

We do not know what Lady Kingsborough felt about the burgeoning affection between the new governess and her charges. Her awkwardness with her children and inability to express her feelings, at which Mary so scornfully wondered, were probably more a matter of habit than hard-heartedness. And no mother, unless carved from stone, could feel anything but dismayed to see her children reject her for someone else. However, far from being angry, it is clear that Lady Kingsborough, too, fell under Mary's spell. Mary continually repeated (to both her sisters as well as to George Blood) that she was treated 'like a gentlewoman', 'with civility – nay, even with kindness'.[65]

This did not mean that the usual social embarrassments were absent. Mary grumbled to Eliza shortly after her arrival at Mitchelstown that

'I cannot easily forget my inferior station – and this something betwixt and between is rather aukward [sic].'[66] However, far from her being isolated in the schoolroom, Mary's problems arose because the Kingsboroughs insisted that, governess or no, she must join in the party. Godwin records her mentioning 'the ludicrous distress of a woman of quality ... that, in a large company, singled out Mary, and entered into a long conversation with her' and her 'utter mortification' when she found that the person to whom she had been talking was Miss King's governess.[67] Far easier to be a servant and know where you stood: 'I went into the steward's room, the other day, and felt something like a sensation of envy.'[68]

Doubtless Lady Kingsborough assumed that no one in Mary's position could be other than dazzled by such treatment. But unlike Eliza, who had 'a *sneaking* kindness ... for people of quality',[69] for Mary the aristocracy held no glamour.[70] Compared with the society she had known in London (and perhaps already hoped, via the novel she was writing, to rejoin), anything they had to offer was poor stuff. 'If my vanity could be flattered, by the respect of people, whose judgment I do not care a fig for – why in this place it has sufficient food – though rather of the grosser kind; but I hate to talk all myself, and only make the ignorant wonder and admire. Confined to the society of a set of silly females, I have no social converse.'[71] As for Lady Kingsborough, the leader of this social set, she was soon dismissed. 'Lady K. is a *clever* woman – and a well-meaning one; but not of the order of being that I could love,'[72] Mary concluded within a week of arriving.

The result was predictable. Sensing her indifference, and fascinated by this brilliant and charismatic young woman whose politeness clearly concealed depths of thought to which her employers had no access, Lady Kingsborough began to court her governess.

We can follow the progress of their relationship in Mary's letters. 'Lady K. is very civil, nay, kind – yet – I cannot help fearing her,' was her first reaction to her employer.[73] This grandee's life was something wholly new to her: 'a fine Lady is to me a new species of animals';[74] she also worried that her qualifications, particularly in French and 'fancy works &c &c',[75] would be found insufficient.

Soon, however, she gained confidence. No one queried her capacities, and she was getting the measure of her opponent. Lady Kingsborough's 'animal passion fills up the hours which are not spent in dressing . . . I think now I hear her infantine lisp – She rouges . . . I am almost tormented to death by dogs.'[76] No one, however, guessed her real feelings. On the contrary, they thought her temperament 'angelick'. 'I make allowance – and *adapt* myself – talk of getting husbands to their *Ladies* – and the *dogs* – and am wonderfully entertaining and then I retire to my room, form figures in the fire, listen to the wind or view the Galties a fine range of mountains near us – and so does time waste away in apathy or misery.'[77]

It was not long before Mary was 'a GREAT favourite in the family';[78] when they removed to Dublin, she was much in demand. Lady Kingsborough invited her to balls, dinners, masquerades and theatre outings, and would not take no for an answer. When Mary pleaded that she had no clothes suitable for such occasions, she was lent a black domino in which she made a splash at a masked ball.

But then the social veneer began to crack. Lady Kingsborough – perhaps feeling that this fraternizing was getting out of hand, perhaps reacting to insufficient gratitude on the part of her protégée, perhaps from sheer whim – delivered a series of snubs:

Next week . . . there is to be a Ball . . . and a masquerade – and as it is impossible for a fine Lady to fix, in time, on her dress, when the day arrives many necessaries are wanted and the whole house from the kitchen maid to the governess are obliged to assist . . . You know, I never liked Lady K., but I find her still more haughty and disagreeable now she is not under [her stepmother's] eye. Indeed, she behaved so improperly to me once, or twice, in the Drawing room, I determined never to go into it again. I could not bear to stalk in to be stared at, and her *proud* condescension added to my embarrassment, I begged to be excused in a civil way – but she would not allow me to absent myself – I had too, another reason, the expence of hair-dressing, and millinery, would have exceeded the sum I chuse to spend in those things. I was determined – just at this juncture she offered me a present, a poplin gown and petticoat, I refused it, and explained myself – she was very angry.[79]

Whatever the genesis of this episode, there can be no question of its insulting nature. First, along with the rest of the servants, Mary was required to act as an impromptu lady's maid. The scenes in the drawing room were studied exercises in humiliation. And the offer of a gown was particularly demeaning. Ladies customarily passed on gowns to their maids as one of the perks of the job; governesses were expected (and were paid) to dress themselves. At this point Lady Kingsborough's stepmother, Mrs Fitzgerald, arrived; she took Mary's side and made her stepdaughter apologize, following which 'she has endeavoured to treat me with more propriety'.[80]

Despite these social complications and Mary's often-stated dislike of superficial bustle, she clearly enjoyed the amusements Dublin offered. Above all, after Mitchelstown's '*host* of females ... Mrse's and *Misses* without number',[81] in Dublin they were surrounded by the company Mary always preferred: that of cultured men. Even Lord Kingsborough acknowledged her: 'He bowed respectfully – a *concatenation* of thoughts made me out *blush* her ladyship's rouge.'[82] But whatever the blush-making thoughts – and later the gossip, perhaps recalling his supposed affair with the previous governess, did link Mary and Lord Kingsborough, adducing a supposed affair as the reason for her sudden departure from Mitchelstown – it is clear that her preferences lay elsewhere. Her chief beau was a Mr Ogle, MP for Wexford and a keen amateur poet, 'between forty and fifty – a *genius*, and *unhappy* – Such a man, you may suppose would catch your sister's eye.'[83] He complimented her and showed her his verses; Mary, clearly attracted despite the fact that she and Mrs Ogle were good friends, passed them on to Everina. Unfortunately, Lady Kingsborough, too, had marked down this fascinating gentleman for her 'flirt' and was thoroughly jealous. However, by now Mary was regaining the upper hand:

> Miss Moore and Mrs Ogle paid me a visit – and her Ladyship followed – Her father-in-law had dined with her, and she repeatedly requested me to come down to the drawing-room to see him ... I at last consented – and could perceive that she had a guard over herself – For to tell you a secret she is afraid of me – Why she wishes to keep me I cannot guess – for she cannot bear that any one should take notice of me. Nay would you believe she used several arts to get me out of the room before the gentlemen came up.[84]

A couple of months later, relations between Mary and her employer had changed yet again. 'Lady K. and I are on much better terms than ever we were,' Mary reported. ' . . . Though the conversation of this female cannot amuse me I try to entertain her – and the result of my endeavours worries *me* for I have more of her company . . . To tell you a secret she is afraid of me,' she added, repeating her phrase of two months before. As for her charges, 'Margaret is . . . so much attached to me I govern her completely.'[85] Within a few months of her arrival at Mitchelstown, Mary had become the emotionally dominant figure in the household.

However, for the governess to entrance the children and overawe the mistress was not a sustainable social situation. Its complex dynamics were expressed with revelatory unselfconsciousness nearly a hundred years later, when Olive Schreiner, who like Mary would become famous as a writer and feminist, was working as a governess in her native South Africa. Olive was then twenty-four; as with Mary and Lady Kingsborough, her brilliance and magnetism both bewitched and appalled her employer, Mrs Cawood, who in the end felt she could deal with them no longer and wrote her the following letter:

My dear Olive – I . . . no longer love you, and cannot act hypocritically. If you needed friends, I could not have allowed my heart to turn against you. You are rich in intellectual, influential friends. And I am quite sure you only valued my acquaintance because you thought I loved you. And I have *loved* you, at times almost with an idolatrous love. I have sometimes found it in my heart to say, Olive Schreiner, I love you so, that for your sake I could become anything. That is why God in his goodness and wisdom used you as a means to show me what an awful, soul-destroying thing freethinking is . . . Richard and I have both, while pointing out to the children that they owe you gratitude, told them you are God's enemy and they cannot love God and you at the same time. I tell you this, so that you shall be spared the pain and humiliation of expecting more from them, than they have been taught to give.[86]

Lady Kingsborough neither could nor would have written such a letter. But it seems clear that Mary Wollstonecraft inspired feelings of love, awe and insupportable discomfort in her, very similar to those felt by Mrs Cawood for Olive Schreiner. When Mary left Mitchelstown after less than a year, in the autumn of 1787, gossip, inevitably, put her departure down to scandal – the supposed affair with Lord Kingsborough. But according to Mary, 'The regret Margaret shewed, when I left her for a short time, was Lady K's pretext for parting with me.'[87] That sounds altogether more convincing. It is only too easy to see how some such scene, crystallizing a mass of unspoken jealousies and resentments, may have precipitated a departure that by then had become inevitable.

Mary's and Olive's experience shows that, even given their usual social and financial insecurity, the powerlessness that most governesses found so intolerable could be avoided. However, it also shows that that powerlessness was no accidental side-effect. On the contrary, it was essential to the functioning of the governess system. Even in an enormous establishment like the Kingsboroughs', with all the advantages of wealth and position stacked in the employers' favour, an overwhelming personage like Mary Wollstonecraft could not long be tolerated. In the far smaller and more intimate middle-class house-holds that over the coming century employed the vast majority of governesses, the governess had to be weak if she was not to be threatening.

By the age of twenty-eight, Mary had run through all the occupational possibilities listed in *Thoughts on the Education of Daughters*. Companion, schoolteacher, governess – she had tried them all and had found them all unsatisfactory. But there remained one other category of work, requiring no capital outlay, no apprenticeships, no entry fees, no tools, no special space, and as open to women as to men: what Harriet Martineau described as the 'departments of art and literature from which it is impossible to shut women out'.[88]

In Miss Martineau's view (despite the fact that she herself made an excellent living from her pen) 'These are not ... to be regarded as resources for bread.'[89] Mary, however, had been careful to maintain her contact with Joseph Johnson and evidently their brief acquaintance had been enough to convince him that Miss Wollstonecraft was an exceptional person. When she told him of her dismissal – which, inevitably for a governess, meant the loss of both income and home – 'he insisted on my coming to his house, and contrived to detain me there a long time – you can *scarcely* conceive how warmly, and delicately he has interested himself in my fate.'[90]

Her gratitude to him was boundless. In *Thoughts on the Education of Daughters* she had written, 'How earnestly does a mind full of sensibility look for disinterested friendship, and long to meet with good unalloyed.'[91] Now, against the odds, she had found it. 'You are my only friend – the only person I am *intimate* with,' she told Johnson two years later. 'I never had a father, or a brother – you have been both to me, ever since I knew you.'[92]

Assuring her that if she worked hard she could make a 'comfortable maintenance',[93] he settled her in a little house near Blackfriars. There she lived happily, finishing her novel *Mary, a Fiction*, working on a children's book, *Original Stories from Real Life* (little morality tales that, in the fashion of the day, starred an ideal governess, whom she called Mrs Mason after a faithful and beloved servant from Newington Green days), and compiling, on commission from Johnson, a volume of extracts in prose and verse for the improvement of female readers.

'Whenever I am tired of solitude,' Mary confided rapturously to Everina (who, immured in an unpleasant teaching job in Henley, must have received these interesting outpourings with mixed feelings), 'I go to Mr Johnson's, and there I met [sic] the kind of company *I* find most pleasure in.'[94] Benjamin Franklin, Joseph Priestley, Tom Paine, Henry Fuseli and William Godwin regularly met around Johnson's table; he published them all, as well as William Cowper and William Blake. In future years to these would be added William Wordsworth, Samuel Taylor Coleridge and Percy Bysshe Shelley besides. More importantly from Mary's standpoint, he also appreciated clever women. Indeed, two of his leading authors were women. Mrs Barbauld's *Lessons for Children* and *Hymns in Prose* were two of his most successful publications, and Sarah Trimmer's *Sacred History Selected from the Scriptures* and (most recently) *Fabulous Stories* were then outselling even Mrs Barbauld. Mary spent a day with Mrs Trimmer, finding her 'a most respectable woman'.[95]

It was at Johnson's house that Mary met the complex and glamorous Fuseli, by then a celebrated painter, though once a Protestant priest. She fell passionately in love with him and would remain obsessed with him for the next five years. Unfortunately for her, however, he had recently married and (if his portraits of her dressed as a courtesan are anything to go by) found his wife highly alluring. In despair, Mary suggested that she might move in with them, but Mrs Fuseli not surprisingly declined and forbade her the house.

With the austere Johnson, however, there was never any question of a physical relationship, and if we had only her then-published works to go on and not (as we do) her letters, his enthusiastic adoption of this new entrant to his circle would be something of a mystery. *Thoughts on the Education of Daughters*, though not without its deeply felt moments, has little new to say; *Mary, a Fiction*, if interesting from a biographical point of view, is wooden and uninvolving (though Godwin admired it); the *Original Stories*, though illustrated by Blake, are at best mildly uplifting. On such a basis, no one – not even the most clairvoyant and experienced of publishers – could have predicted the irruption of the *Vindication of the Rights of Men* in 1790 and, supremely, the *Vindication of the Rights of Woman* in 1791.

In Mary's correspondence, however, we can see what it was that so deeply interested and attracted Johnson. The moment that her published work attained the quality of her letters, she became unstoppable. Passionate, headlong, indiscreet, perceptive and bold, they showed us, as nothing else could, what she must have been like – how her company might charm; how amusing, observant and erudite she had become; above all, how completely she was her own woman. Her peculiar circumstances and explosive nature had made her into a true original.

Johnson saw her potential, worked her hard, and transformed her into a competent journalist. Together with his friend Thomas Christie, he was about to launch a new review, the *Analytical*, and Mary, as well as working on book translations, was to be one of its jobbing reviewers. Her letters at this time brim with the pleasure she took in her wonderful new life. 'I have lately been translating a work of importance,' she excitedly told George Blood (it was Necker's *On the Importance of Religious Opinions*) 'and have made a very advantageous contract for another besides, I have had a variety of other employments, in short, my dear Boy, I succeed beyond my most sanguine hopes.'[96] She expected to clear more than £200 that year – enough to pay her way and also to send Everina to France, where she would be able to use Johnson's contacts while possibly picking up the good French that would make her more employable.

In fact she did not earn that much – far from it – but Everina was sent anyway and spent two years in Paris. Eliza was retrieved from darkest Leicestershire and placed as a parlour boarder at Mrs Bregantz's school in Putney, near Johnson's country house in Fulham. Their young brother James, who had already been to sea, was sent to the naval academy at Woolwich and was shortly after made a lieutenant. And Mary's favourite brother Charles, at one time learning law in Ned's office but since removed by Mr Wollstonecraft because of a quarrel about money, was sent first to another lawyer, which he hated, then to learn farming, after which he intended to leave for America and make his fortune. Mary also, as far as she could, helped keep her father in funds: however much she despised him, she could hardly let him starve. With her family off her conscience, her thrilling new existence could begin.

Her life now was as free and independent as any man's. She lived in her own little apartment, with a servant to look after her – even at her worst moments, there was always a servant; without one, in those days before household gadgets, her entire life would have been occupied with housework. (In the little book of lessons written for her baby daughter Fanny in 1794, Lesson IV reads: 'Let me comb your head. Ask Betty to wash your face.'[97]) She mixed on equal terms with great men. She was poor, but not hopelessly so; and although she had written bitterly that 'Love and friendship fly from poverty',[98] in the circles that she now inhabited poverty was of little consequence. Life was not perfect: her hopeless infatuation with Fuseli was debilitating and sometimes interfered with her work. But great events were in progress. The revolution then taking place in France was at the forefront of every mind, with Mary's friends among its English cheerleaders. And she was about to earn her own place of eminence among them.

In November 1789, when Mary was thirty, her old friend Dr Price preached a sermon 'On the Love of Our Country' to the London Revolution Society, a club of liberal Whigs named for the Glorious Revolution of 1688, the bloodless coup by which the Dutch Protestants William and Mary succeeded the Catholicizing James II on the English throne. The hundredth anniversary of this event had been widely celebrated – celebrations that, as in this case, often extended to the present events in France.

Price was by then old and frail, but his views remained as uncompromising as ever and their expression was as fiery. 'Why,' he demanded, 'are the nations of the world so patient under despotism?'

> Why do they crouch to tyrants, and submit to be treated as though they were a herd of cattle? Is it not because they are kept in darkness and want knowledge? . . . Happy is the Scholar or Philosopher, who at the close of life . . . has reason to believe he has been successful, and actually contributed, by his instructions, to disseminate among his fellow-creatures just notions of themselves, of their rights, of religion, and the nature and end of civil government.[99]

He characterized this institution as 'little better than [a] contrivance for enabling the *few* to oppress the *many*'.[100]

Unsurprisingly, not everyone agreed with these fine words. The following November, Edmund Burke, the conservative orator, rebutted them with savage eloquence in his *Reflections on the Revolution in France*. 'Am I to congratulate the highwayman and murderer who broke prison on the restoration of his natural rights?' Burke wanted to know. He dismissed the revolution as 'this strange chaos of levity and ferocity', vesting 'new power in new persons of whose principles, tempers and dispositions they have little or no experience'. With a nod to Priestley and his discovery of oxygen – 'The wild gas, the fixed air, is plainly broke loose' – he turned his fury on Price, dismissing his sermon as 'the public declaration of a man much connected with literary caballers and intriguing philosophers, with political theologians and theological politicians . . . wholly unacquainted with the world in which they are so fond of meddling'.[101]

For the past year Mary's unrequited passion for Fuseli had depressed her and distracted her from her work. Now Burke's tirade, with its intemperate reference to 'the swinish multitude',[102] its extolling of the rights of property, and its fulminations against her old friend and benefactor, broke through her block. It appeared on 1 November 1790; by the 29th of the same month, Mary's reply, the *Vindication of the Rights of Men*, was on sale. Johnson printed it as she wrote it, but about halfway through the flow dried up. Johnson, instead of scolding her, told her not to worry – 'he would cheerfully throw aside' the sheets already printed 'if it would contribute to her happiness'. Intentionally or not, this was a master stroke: Mary, 'piqued . . . immediately went home; and proceeded to the end of her work, with no other interruptions but what were absolutely indispensable'.[103]

Mary's pamphlet did not approach Burke's magisterial scorn and withering wit, let alone his force of argument; considered exposition was never her forte. But in it she finally achieved a freedom of expression previously unseen in her published work. Although her more abstract paragraphs remained comparatively undistinguished, where her personal feelings were most engaged – above all in her coruscating defence of Dr Price – she became truly eloquent:

> In reprobating Dr Price's opinions you might have spared the man; and if you had had but half as much reverence for the grey hairs of virtue as for the accidental distinctions of rank, you would not have treated with such indecent familiarity and supercilious contempt, a member of the community whose talents and modest virtues place him high in the scale of moral excellence ... Granting, for a moment, that Dr Price's political opinions are Utopian reveries, and that the world is not yet sufficiently civilized to adopt such a sublime system of morality; they could, however, only be the reveries of a benevolent mind.[104]

When writing pamphlets, which unlike books relate to events of the moment, timing is all important. There were many replies to Burke, including Thomas Paine's immortal *Rights of Man*, but Mary's was the first. It sold rapidly and soon moved into a second edition, which carried its author's name, as the first had not. Suddenly she found herself not merely a member of Johnson's circle, but one of his most celebrated authors.

She hugely enjoyed the sensation; indeed, it distinctly went to her head. William Godwin, invited to dinner at Johnson's house to meet Paine, was piqued to find the conversation monopolized by an intolerably forward and wearisome female. He hardly spoke, and left the gathering frustrated and annoyed.

In this rush of energy and confidence, Mary could not wait to begin another pamphlet. There was one topic upon which life had made her expert, the source of all her fury, the repository of her dearest dreams: women's subjugated place in the world. She had already broached it in the *Vindication of the Rights of Men*, which despite its title had a distinctly feminist slant. Unlike her friend Paine, Mary assumed that universal suffrage would also include women. Other paragraphs, too, foreshadowed the work on which she would now embark.

> Girls are sacrificed to family convenience ... Women of fashion take husbands that they may have it in their power to coquet, the grand business of genteel life, with a number of admirers, and thus flutter the spring of life away, without laying up any store for the winter of age, or being of any use to society ... Affection in the marriage state can only be founded on respect – and are these weak beings respectable? ... A woman never forgets to adorn herself to make an impression on the senses of the other sex, and to extort the homage which it is gallant to pay, and yet we wonder that they have such confined understandings.[105]

These observations were only distantly connected to *Reflections on the Revolution in France*, but for 51 per cent of the human race – the 51 per cent that had never until now written political pamphlets – they embodied life's urgent realities. Mary, revelling in her new-found powers, now saw the possibility of changing these realities. The moment was hers.

A Vindication of the Rights of Woman was published in January 1792. The new work was influenced not just by the events in France but by one Frenchman in particular: Jean-Jacques Rousseau. Rousseau, whose philosophical ideas would influence the French revolution, had in 1762 published a book on education, *Emile*, that put schooling firmly on the radical agenda. In it, he advocated the abandonment of rote learning in favour of an education that succeeded because it worked with the child's natural interests and inclinations. He recommended learning from the natural world (he considered *Robinson Crusoe* the ideal textbook); introduced varied studies and separate subjects: encouraged the pupil to read widely so that he would eventually learn to think for himself; emphasized character building; and preferred discipline through 'raisonnement' to corporal punishment. It was revelatory and has influenced the shape of education ever since.

All Mary's instincts were with Rousseau. However, in one important respect she sharply differed from him. The basis of her argument was equal educational opportunities for both sexes, but for Rousseau this was unthinkable. In his writings, the gender of the pupil was invariably masculine. Women, he declared, were fit only for the household arts. It was a question of hormones: eunuchs were no better; even a whole man became suspect if he worked at a womanish employment such as tailoring. This was not to denigrate women – a good mother who involved herself practically in her children's upbringing was essential to the eventual production of a good man. (*Emile* gave rise to an upper-class fad for breastfeeding in France during the 1770s.) But as to their education, 'All women's education must be relative to men.'[106] Women's main concern must be to learn how to please men and be useful to them, because although men could do without women, women could not do without men.

Mary was not convinced. She acidly attributed Rousseau's anti-feminist views to his love life:

Who ever drew a more exalted female character than Rousseau? though in the lump he constantly endeavoured to degrade the sex. And why was he thus anxious? Truly to justify to himself the affection which weakness and virtue had made him cherish for that fool Theresa [his common-law wife, the semi-literate seamstress Thérèse Levasseur]. He could not raise her to the common level of her sex; and therefore he laboured to bring woman down to her's.[107]

Meanwhile, as she pointed out, 'How women are to exist in that state, where there is to be neither marrying nor giving in marriage, we are not told.'[108] Presumably in the same old way: as governesses, milliners, dressmakers, servants or whores. Mary's aim was far more radical: to create a world in which no woman need ever again work as a governess (or, indeed, a whore). Her new work not only discussed the best way of doing this, but showed that, when emancipated women did marry, they made better wives and mothers.

'Educate women like men,' says Rousseau, 'and the more they resemble our sex the less power will they have over us.' This is the very point I aim at. I do not wish them to have power over men; but over themselves . . .

We shall not see women affectionate till more equality be

established in society, till ranks are confounded and women freed, neither shall we see that dignified domestic happiness, the simple grandeur of which cannot be relished by ignorant or vitiated minds; nor will the important task of education ever be properly begun till the person of a woman is no longer preferred to her mind. For it would be as wise to expect corn from tares, or figs from thistles, as that a foolish ignorant woman should be a good mother.[109]

Mary was not the only radical to take up the cause of women's education at this moment. Among her own acquaintances, both Priestley and Laetitia Barbauld advocated equal educational opportunities for boys and girls. But they could not see, or did not want to see, that by excepting as clearly irrelevant for girls those topics (such as Latin, Greek, science and mathematics) necessary for entry into the universities and professions, they were simply perpetuating the existing state of things.

There were, however, two writers who proposed truly equal education for both sexes. One was a Frenchman, the Marquis de Condorcet (with whom Mary would soon find herself working on a 'Plan of Education' for the Committee of Public Instruction, of which he was a member before committing suicide during the Terror).[110] In his essay *Sur l'Instruction publique*, published in 1791–2, he pointed out, with irrefutable French logic, that it would be 'absurd' to exclude girls from a public education system. Not only should women oversee their own children's education, but uneducated women made for inequality within the family, which militated against happiness. In any case, he pointed out, women had the same right to education as men. The main reason for not educating the sexes together, he concluded, was greed and pride.

In England, meanwhile, in her *Letters on Education* published in 1790, the Whig pamphleteer Catherine Macaulay had also recommended that boys and girls be brought up and educated together. In December of that year, Mary had sent Mrs Macaulay a copy of the *Vindication of the Rights of Men*, with an accompanying note: 'You are the only female writer who I coincide in opinion with respecting the rank our sex ought to endeavour to attain in the world.'[111]

Although its conclusions were similar to those of Condorcet and Macaulay, *A Vindication of the Rights of Woman* did not, as they did, proceed by succinct and sober analysis. Impetuous, disorganized, opinionated, full of verve and generosity, it in every respect mirrored its author. Drawing on the familiar cast of characters – the grasping elder brother, the irresponsible parents, the frivolous lady of fashion – Mary's indignation, like her arguments, flowed from her own experience, pulling the reader headlong by its sheer energy and emotion. 'Rousseau exerts himself to prove that all *was* right originally: a crowd of authors that all *is* now right: and I, that all *will be* right,'[112] her opening salvo declared. The writing, Godwin tells us, took a mere six weeks.[113]

That education, or its lack, lay at the root of women's disabilities, Mary did not doubt: 'The neglected education of my fellow-creatures is the grand source of the misery I deplore.'[114] If old habits of family responsibility were to be abandoned – as her own grandfather, father and brother had abandoned them – in favour of capitalist accumulation, then women as well as men must be equipped to earn an independent living. To this end she proposed nothing less than a universal, state-funded system of co-educational day schools in which all boys and girls would be taught together from the age of five onwards. From five to nine she advocated primary schools for all classes and abilities, in which a school uniform would obviate all distinctions of wealth, and with plenty of room for outdoor play.

After the age of nine, girls and boys, intended for domestic employments, or mechanical trades, ought to be removed to other schools, and receive instruction, in some measure appropriated to the destination of each individual, the two sexes being still together in the morning; but in the afternoon, the girls should attend a school, where plain-work, mantua-making, millinery, &c. would be their employment.

The young people of superior abilities, or fortune, might now be taught, in another school, the dead and living languages, the elements of science, and continue the study of history and politics, on a more extensive scale, which would not exclude polite literature.

... As life advanced, dancing, music, and drawing, might be admitted as relaxations, for at these schools young people of fortune ought to remain, more or less, till they were of age. Those, who

75

were designed for particular professions, might attend, three or four mornings in the week, the schools appropriated for their immediate instruction.[115]

One of the questions that had to be tackled, if co-education was proposed, was of course that of sex. What would happen when adolescent hormones started to make themselves felt and the pupils fell in love?

> Girls and boys still together? I hear some readers ask: yes. And I should not fear any other consequence than that some early attachment might take place; which, whilst it had the best effect on the moral character of the young people, might not perfectly agree with the views of the parents, for it will be a long time, I fear, before the world will be so far enlightened that parents, only anxious to render their children virtuous, shall allow them to choose companions for life themselves.
>
> Besides, this would be a sure way to promote early marriages, and from early marriages the most salutary physical and moral effects naturally flow ... In this plan of education the constitution of boys would not be ruined by the early debaucheries, which now make men so selfish, or girls rendered weak and vain, by indolence, and frivolous pursuits. But, I presuppose, that such a degree of equality should be established between the sexes as would shut out gallantry and coquetry, yet allow friendship and love to temper the heart for the discharge of higher duties.[116]

Interestingly, this view – that passion was to be deplored, and that growing up together would render boys and girls all but immune to love's wilder excesses – was shared by Mrs Macaulay, who stated that if boys and girls are brought up and educated together 'friendship may be enjoyed between them without passion'.[117] Even when two young people married, Mary thought 'it would, perhaps, be happy if some circumstances checked their passion; if the recollection of some prior attachment, or disappointed affection, made it on one side, at least, rather a match founded on esteem. In that case, they would look beyond the present moment ... by forming a plan to regulate a friendship which only death should dissolve.'[118] It was a stance utterly at odds with the impulse that would shape her own life during the years that followed.

Mary had recently taken spacious new lodgings in Store Street, Bloomsbury, half an hour's walk from Johnson in St Paul's Churchyard. She now also paid more attention than previously to her appearance – if his biographer is to be believed, in hopes of pleasing Fuseli. Whether she succeeded in this or not, as the *Vindication of the Rights of Woman* raised her to ever greater fame, her pleasant apartment and careful toilette must also have seemed more in keeping with the distinguished personage she had now become.

The next few months were not productive. Perhaps the *Rights of Woman* had for the moment exhausted her; and she was still – more than ever – obsessed by Fuseli. Nevertheless, she had triumphed, and the prospect was brighter than she could ever have imagined. 'Tranquillity does not fly from my quiet study, and the pictures, which fancy traces on the walls, have often the most glowing colours.'[119]

By luck, talent and force of character Mary had carved out an independent life for herself. Eliza and Everina, on the other hand, possessed none of these attributes, and for them governessing remained the only prospect. Dutifully (she was always dutiful) Mary sought out 'positions' for them and provided a bed when all else failed; 'should I succeed,' she assured them when starting to work with Johnson, 'my dear Girls will ever in sickness have a home.'[120] Wherever she found herself – in Ireland, in London – she tried to secure positions for her sisters; that she met with so little success says more about supply and demand than lack of effort. Everina's eventual situation in Ireland may have resulted from Mary's Irish acquaintance, whom she continued to badger for possible openings; when Everina returned from France, she even tried to get her some translating work from Johnson. Nonetheless it was still a hand-to-mouth existence, which would not lead to a place of their own, such as Mary had now and Eliza had once possessed.

At first we can trace their comings and goings only indirectly, through Mary's letters. In 1787, George Blood, after vainly adoring Mary, was for a while in love with Everina. However, it came to nothing; he had been, she declared, too long a quasi-brother for her to think of him as a lover.[121] After Everina's hated teaching job in Henley – 'The inhabitants are vulgar,' Mary wrote sympathetically after visiting her there, 'and would they condescend to take notice of a Teacher, their acquaintance would not be very desirable'[122] – came her stay in France, following which she joined Eliza in Putney at Mrs Bregantz's school. By 1792, when Mary was in France, Mrs Bregantz's school had collapsed, as schools so often did, throwing the 'girls' – as Mary always called them – onto the employment market again. Eliza took a position in Wales, teaching the three teenage Woods girls at Upton Castle near Mr Wollstonecraft's home at Laugharne; Everina, after staying a while in Store Street with Mary, fetched up in County Waterford, Ireland, with the Boyce family.

It is only in 1791, nearly eight years after Mary kidnapped Eliza, that their lives become visible at first-hand through Eliza's letters to Everina. (Only one from Everina to Eliza survives, an indicator, perhaps, of Eliza's chaotic life.) Stranded in discontent amid the families into which their shipwrecked lives had washed them, they comforted each other with the assurance that each had at least one friend. Eliza was by then twenty-seven, Everina a little younger. As their penurious youth drained away it became clear that they would almost certainly spend the remainder of their lives as lone women, uncertain, childless and poor.

Money, or its absence, was a continual worry. On her way to Wales, Eliza, presumably to save on travelling expenses, walked seven miles before giving in and taking a passing mail coach, 'for in reality I thought my soul would soon go aloft I was so exhausted in body and mind'.[123] Physical exhaustion did not last, however, and the rigours of a tiring journey were as nothing to the terrifying prospect of the unknown at the other end, where their happiness would be entirely dependent on other people's whims. 'It is a very strange sensation to inexperienced youth to feel itself quite alone in the world, cut adrift from every connexion, uncertain whether the port to which it is bound can be reached, and prevented by many impediments to that it has quitted,' reflects Jane Eyre[124] – the feelings, no doubt, of a thousand young governesses-to-be as they rattled through unknown countryside to confront the strangers whose lives they were about to share.

Upton, to Eliza's relief, seemed comfortable and welcoming. It was a Norman castle, or fortified mansion house, that until recently had remained in the hands of the family that built it. Lately it had been bought by a Mr Tasker who had made a fortune with the East India

Company – one of the new breed of self-made men for whom a governess to educate their daughters would henceforth be de rigueur. Eliza's new charges were Mr Tasker's nieces; he was childless and they would inherit the estate.

The house was cluttered and old-fashioned, but her room had an armchair and a big bed, and the adjoining drawing room looked onto woodland. She soon acquired a pet dog and a horse. Most important of all, 'I seem to be a great favourite with the family,' she wrote in relief. The effect was immediate: 'My health is much better, I impute it to the sight of haven [sic].' She sent words of encouragement to Everina, then suffering from the after-effects of a rough passage across the Irish Sea: 'I do hope, from the slight sketch you give of Mr and Mrs Boyce, that you (poor sick girl) have at last found a haven!' With any luck they would turn out 'an amiable couple, capable of attachment for their children but of wishing to see you happy'.[125] It was the most a governess could hope for.

The Boyces did prove kind – or at least satisfactory. Everina stayed two years with them, until the elopement of her eldest pupil, Miss Boyce, brought that position to an abrupt end. Eliza's stay at Upton was longer – three and a half years – but her relations with the family, so promising at first, soon cooled. Despite their wealth she was not given a fire in her own room until November, and then only after making a scene. After that, since 'we are less social',[126] she no longer spent the evenings with her charges, who preferred to sit with the two upper maids and tell ghost stories.

With June's warm welcome now nothing but a memory, Eliza found herself in that social limbo that all but the most fortunate governesses had to endure. Her familiar complaint – 'I never lived with any people who felt so totally uninterested about me'[127] – was doubly poignant in that her employers had been friends, or at least acquaintances, of her family. However, 'Your name is never mentioned and Charles they have quite forgot. Even our father they met with a degree of coldness that turned me sick.'[128]

It was generally agreed that Eliza was the sweetest-tempered of the Wollstonecraft sisters. Nevertheless as time went on her letters became little more than a litany of slights and small miseries. Her pupils drank gin and nothing she could do would stop them; nor was she offered so much as a glass of wine. The diet was meat, meat, meat, with never a pudding, pie, nor egg. The children tortured her in the usual ways: they laughed at her healthy appetite; stopped whispering and hissed 'It's Mrs Bishop!' whenever she approached; they declared her dog mad and threatened to shoot it. More painful still, being a governess nullified even the few social opportunities that presented themselves. At a dance she overheard a young man enquire who she was 'and I believe discovered that I was not the uglyest [sic] woman in the room ... yet on being satisfyed exclaimed Oh! – and was repelled from begging the honour of my hand. Be wise Everina and feel not those things that make dependance the bitter draught it is. Be wise, like Eliza, and banish hope.' She concluded that it was 'quite as mad, to expect a <u>home</u> in a state of <u>dependance</u>, as the thought of finding a *friend* when friendless'.[129] Her one consolation was her horse, which followed her about the field and nuzzled her for apples. Her charges, though, refused to accompany her when she went riding – 'they <u>hang over the fire</u> the <u>whole day</u>'.[130]

Everina, it seems, fared little better: Eliza 'couldn't help smiling at the similarity of our pictures'. They differed in temperament, though: Eliza might be depressed by circumstances, but Everina was congenitally sour. 'But my dear Everina,' Eliza gently enquired, 'are there not moments when you greet and follow a tune with pleasure? And when your children seem fond of you?"[131] Seemingly there were not. Perhaps Charles Blood had more of a deliverance than he realized when Everina rejected his suit. 'I love Aunt Bishop as much as I hate (you must not read that word) Aunt Everina,' William Godwin would confess a few years later.[132]

Given their miserable circumstances, it was hardly surprising that despite Mary's real efforts to help her sisters, they remained ambivalent about her. Neither Eliza nor Mary ever referred directly to the reckless kidnapping episode that had ended Eliza's marriage and torn her from her child, but of course it was not something that either of them could have forgotten. Although at first Mary had done her best to make amends by including Eliza in her life, she had never, after that, felt wholly easy with her. She wrote often to Everina but less frequently to Eliza, guiltily afraid that the absence of positive news might induce depression. To make things worse, the worlds they inhabited now were so disparate as to seem almost different planets. 'I never think of <u>our sister</u>,' Eliza sighed from her lonely outpost, 'but in the light of a friend who had been dead some years, and when all here is asleep, and naught is to be heard but the screech-owl, I sigh to think we shall never meet, as such again – though perhaps, in a better world, <u>the love of fame cannot corrupt the soul</u>.'[133]

Eight months later, after the *Vindication*'s publication had made Mary truly famous, the bitterness of Eliza's feelings was even more abundantly visible:

Charles informs me that Mrs Wollstonecraft is grown quite handsome. He adds likewise 'that being conscious that she is the wrong side of thirty she now endeavours to set off those charms she <u>once despised</u> to the best advantage' this entre nous for he is delighted with her kindness and affection to him –

So the author of the Rights of Woman is going to France – I dare say her only motive is to promote her poor Bess's comfort, or thine my girl – or at least I think she will thus reason – Well in spite of <u>Reason</u> when Mrs W reaches the Continent she will be but a woman – I cannot help painting her in the height of all her wishes at the very summit of happiness for will not ambition fill every chink of her Great Soul? (for such I really think her's) that is not occupied by <u>Love</u> . . . And you actually have the vanity to imagine that in the National Assembly, personages like M and F[useli] will bestow a thought on two females whom nature meant to 'suckle fools and chronicle small beer'.[134]

The trip that Eliza mentions here, with Johnson and the Fuselis, was in the end abandoned. Nonetheless, Mary, like many other English radicals, was eager to experience the revolution in person and, if possible (since distraction might allow her to forget Fuseli), to 'lose in public happiness the sense of private misery'.[135] In December 1792, she therefore set out again, this time alone. She was nervous, and not without reason: the political situation was threatening, and a few weeks later England and France would be at war. Still, she had plenty of friends in Paris – Tom Paine was there, and Thomas Christie, and various other members of the Johnson circle. When she first arrived, she stayed at a fine house in the rue Meslée belonging to Mrs Bregantz's daughter, Madame Filliettaz, who had married a rich merchant. Meanwhile she needed funds to live. Rather than draw yet again on Johnson, she asked Everina, whose stay in France she had financed, and Eliza, for whom she promised to seek a situation, to help with money. They did so, eventually sending £30 with more or less good grace. 'I am fearful my manner of writing prevented your sending twenty pounds to Mary, I am sorry if I influenced you,' Eliza told Everina; she would contribute £10, and the result would 'be equal to fifty in Paris, owing to the exchange rate being greatly in favour of the English'.[136]

From the Filliettaz grand house in the Marais, Mary watched, on the morning of 26 December, as Louis XVI rode to his death:

> About nine o'clock this morning, the king passed by my window, moving silently alone (excepting now and then a few strokes on the drum, which rendered the stillness more awful) through empty streets, surrounded by the national guards, who, clustering round the carriage, seemed to deserve their name. The inhabitants flocked to their windows, but the casements were all shut, not a voice was heard ... Once or twice, lifting my eyes from the paper, I have seen eyes glare through a glass-door opposite my chair, and bloody hands shook at me. Not the distant sound of a footstep can I hear. – My apartments are remote from those of the servants, the only persons who sleep with me in an immense hotel, one folding door opening after another. – I wish I had even kept the cat with me!'[137]

It is a measure of her sense of duty (or guilt) that despite all this she did not forget about her sisters, assuring Eliza three weeks later that 'I will not leave P. till you are settled, so let the hope, or rather the moral certainty, keep you warm this cold weather.'[138]

Eliza, trapped in her miserable situation at Upton, hoped fervently that Mary would indeed find something for her in Paris. However much she might from time to time resent her sister personally, she still stood in awe of her. She also, which did not make life any easier, unreservedly shared her politics. Radical views were not generally welcomed in a governess. William Godwin was at this time mentoring a young man called Thomas Cooper, who would go on to make his name as an actor in America; his sister Elizabeth, who was a governess, lamented in a letter that she was never able to express her own opinions because her employer had no notion that 'a young person, a woman, and above all a Governess should ever meddle in politics'.[139]

The problem, of course, was that for obvious reasons governesses' politics were often not those of their employers. Elizabeth Cooper grumbled that she was 'perpetually a witness to speeches, dictated by principles so false and fundamentally erroneous, that it is with difficulty I can forbear declaring them so'.[140] Yet forbear she must, or else her situation would be at an end. Eliza, it seems, felt no such constraint; matters reached such a head that whenever she mentioned politics the family left the room. Her connection with Mary (which of course was known to her employers, even though she no longer bore the name Wollstonecraft) placed her in a particularly difficult position in this respect. Tom Paine's effigy was burned in the square at nearby Pembroke, and there was talk of 'immortalyzing Mrs Wollstonecraft in the like manner; but all end in Damning all Politics: what good will they do men? And what rights have men that three meals a-day will not supply? So argues a Welshman.'[141]

As 1793 progressed, possibilities that Mary might find Eliza a situation in France receded, though even as late as June she did not give up the prospect 'should peace and order ever be established in this distracted Land'.[142] However, her thoughts, as well as those of her sisters, were now turning further afield, to that other liberal haven across the ocean: America.

The American project was always close to the heart of Johnson's circle. He had supported the American side during the war of independence and had many American connections. The most notable was of course Benjamin Franklin; another was Joel Barlow, who had come to Paris to sell American land, then moved to London, where Mary got to know him and his wife Ruth. She and the Barlows became close; she hoped that when they moved back to America they might take her brother Charles under their wing. There was even some question that they might adopt him (the Barlows were childless). However, this came to nothing, as Joel Barlow became increasingly taken up by the French revolution – both its ideas and the business opportunities it offered.

Barlow was not the only American attracted to revolutionary Paris by the intoxicating possibility of making money. Another was an adventurer called Gilbert Imlay, whom Mary met at Thomas Christie's house in Paris. According to Godwin, she did not much take to him on first acquaintance, but by April 1793 the two had fallen in love – an event that transformed, and eventually almost destroyed, Mary's life.

Now thirty-four, she had never before known what it was to love and be loved in return, and the effect on her passionate nature was overwhelming. She certainly overwhelmed the unfortunate Imlay; in Virginia Woolf's phrase, 'Tickling minnows he had hooked a dolphin, and the creature rushed him through the waters until he was dizzy and only wanted to escape.'[143] Experiencing sensual fulfilment for the first time in her life, she became a quite different person. During her hopeless infatuation with Fuseli she had constantly complained of headaches and malaise; now her letters brimmed with life and joy. By June, she and Imlay were planning to leave France for America as soon as he could accumulate sufficient funds, with the intention that there the family might be reunited once more. 'I will venture to *promise* that brighter days are in store for you,' Mary assured Eliza, adding, 'I cannot explain myself except just to tell you that I have a plan in my head, it may prove abortive, in which you and Everina are included.'[144] However, nothing came of this. Communications between England and France became ever more problematic; if letters reached their destination at all, it was (at least in France) at great risk and probably months after they had been written. 'The French are, at present, so full of suspicion that had a letter of James's, improvidently sent to me, been opened, I would not have answered for the consequence,' Mary told Everina the following March, adding: 'Are you well? But why do I ask, you cannot reply to me.'[145]

By then she had other preoccupations, being seven months gone with Imlay's child. Their daughter Fanny was born in France on 14 May 1794, and Mary's entire being over the coming years would be devoted to fending off the growing realization that Imlay, far from being the loving father and husband of her fantasies, in fact had no intention of fulfilling either of these roles.

Meanwhile Eliza's thoughts were still concentrated upon America. For Mary was not the sisters' only correspondent; their brother Charles also kept in touch. In April 1794, a letter arrived to say he had reached Pennsylvania and was at the utopian settlement on the banks of the Susquehanna where Joseph Priestley and his sons were also then living. (Priestley, burnt out of his Birmingham house in anti-French riots, had left for America in 1793 and would spend the rest of his life there.) Eliza, still hanging on miserably at Upton, longed to join him in the

New World. At first it seemed as though this might really happen: three months later Charles wrote again, this time from Philadelphia, to say he was doing very well and offering his sisters the prospect of a home. 'Can this be a dream . . . ?' Eliza wondered to Everina. 'I would I could fancy these things [a] matter of fact. I mean the poor fellow's wonderful good luck in so short a time.'[146]

America, then, with or without Mary, became the great project, the escape hatch through which the sisters would free themselves from the lives to which they otherwise seemed irrevocably condemned. In America, teachers were respected members of society; in America, there was no place for 'accomplishments'; in America, there was equality.

Eliza could not wait to embark for this promised land. Her hopes were particularly urgent, since Upton had by now become more or less intolerable. But although she ached to leave, what alternative did she have? Upton might be hateful, but it at least offered a roof, and she had no prospect of another. Mary was in France; their father, living in squalor on his farm, was in no position to accommodate her. She spent consoling weekends in Pembroke with two French refugees, an aged bishop called Graux and his brother, who had washed up in mid-Wales, and who declared themselves worse off there than if they had been in Paris, since England and France were now at war, and despite a letter to the government they were treated as enemy nationals. Eliza was taking French lessons with them, in preparation for the position she still hoped Mary might find for her in France. She found their company infinitely more sympathetic than that of the dreaded Uptonians. 'At fifty, it is dreadful to be snatched from the lap of abundance, for M. Graux had his carriage and every elegance of life, and to feel all the horrors of dependence in a strange country,' she observed sympathetically.[147]

Like Agnes Porter, she hung on in hopes that something would turn up. However, she was less fortunate than Miss Porter; by November 1794, her situation had become impossible. After one insult too many she offered her resignation, declaring she would remain only 'till my quarter was up'.

The Miser wept – hoped I was not angry with him – Molly . . . declared 'She should quit the house immediately' (meaning the

Governess) that I should be paid and <u>turned out</u> – to compleat the inimitable farce the good old <u>Parson</u> gave me a Kiss of Peace – and ordered the frantic Molly to hold her tongue – I was determined to stay till next Friday as I wanted to get rid of my old complaint (and have my clothes washed) for I have been very unwell of late with that said malady that in days of yore you have so often heard me complain of.[148]

Eliza finally left Upton on 1 December. Her employers, she told Everina, were so furious that on the day of her departure they left the house before she was up, so as not to have to say goodbye. Yet unhappy as she had been there, her pleasure at leaving was marred by sadness. Although she had never liked the teasing girls who had been her official charges, she had become extremely fond of their little brother. And 'to part with my dear dear John cost me many a tear, for I never had before <u>nor</u> shall again the like affection for a child – He had become a part of myself, that it was like losing a limb to leave him <u>behind</u> . . . This is the <u>last</u> child I ever <u>love</u>! While I have the power of loving!'[149] She was right: governesses indulged such feelings at their peril.

Eliza took lodgings at nearby Pembroke, where she could be near M. Graux, to whom she had evidently formed something of an attachment. Despite her dire situation, or lack of one, she nevertheless sent a five-guinea bill to help out her father, who was as usual penniless and improvident. It is noticeable how often these women, living as they did on the edge of absolute poverty, nevertheless contrived to help needy friends and relatives – and it is noticeable, too, that if they were helped in return, it was always by sisters, never brothers. Men, who legally owned anything their wives might earn, seem to have felt themselves entitled to their sisters' earnings as well. Thus, although at this point James Wollstonecraft finally quit his naval career – to the expensive establishment of which all the sisters had contributed – he did not pay back what they had loaned him, claiming he would need everything he had to set himself up in France, where he intended to live cheaply. (He eventually fetched up in Australia.)

So Eliza sat in Pembroke, waiting. The year turned and 1795 arrived; she passed the dreaded milestone of her thirtieth birthday while watching her money melt away. One possibility would be to join

Everina in Ireland, but she could either travel to Ireland *or* afford the clothes she needed if she was to find another situation, not both. Besides, her Frenchman was in Pembroke. And where was Mary, now that her sister really needed the oft-promised roof? Still in France – which might as well have been at the other end of the earth.

In fact, Mary and Fanny were just then on their way back to London and Imlay. He had left France for England on business, and although he was being remarkably uncommunicative, it had become clear even to the disbelieving Mary that he did not mean to return to his 'wife' and daughter. Nevertheless, when he suggested they join him, however hard she tried, Mary could not wholly quell her hope that this might be a new beginning.

She arrived on 11 April; ten days later she sent a note to Eliza from lodgings in Charlotte Street, offering the possibility that should Imlay's current business succeed, he might be able to finance her and Everina to the tune of £500–600. 'As to myself,' the note continued,

> I cannot yet say where I shall live for a continuance it would give me the sincerest pleasure to be situated near you – I know you will think me unkind – and it was this reflection that has prevented my writing to you sooner, not to invite you to come and live with me – But Eliza it is my opinion, not a newly formed one, the presence of a third person interrupts or destroys domestic happiness – Accepting this sacrifice there is nothing I would not do to promote your comfort. I am hurt at being thus explicit and do indeed severely feel for the disappointments which you have met with in Life.[150]

If this letter sounds strained, that is not surprising. Mary, too, was in an impossible position. She did undeniably have a baby and a home – of both of which, as that last sentence acknowledges, she had deprived her sister. Nonetheless, her current situation left her in no state to cope with another dependant. Imlay's cool reception, so different from her fond hopes, had made it clear that, although they were once again in the same city, their relationship, as far as he was concerned, was at an end.

When a full realization of this dawned on her, Mary decided to kill herself. But Imlay either found her and brought her round, or talked her out of it; at any rate, 'she determined to continue to exist.'[151] She took refuge in action: within six weeks she, little Fanny and their French servant girl had left London for Hull, where they embarked for Scandinavia, there to try to retrieve some of Imlay's assets from a swindling Norwegian sea captain.

Of course Eliza knew none of this. As Mary had foreseen, she was deeply hurt by her sister's seeming selfishness. Copying Mary's letter for Everina's edification, she burst into a lament:

> My Everina, what I felt, and shall for ever feel! It is childish to talk of. After lingering above a fortnight in such cruel suspense. Good God! what a letter! How have I merited such pointed cruelty? When did I wish to live with her? At what time wish for a moment to interrupt their <u>domestic</u> happiness? Was ever a present offered in so humiliating a style? Ought the poorest domestic to be thus insulted? Are your eyes opened at last, Everina? What do you say now to our goodly prospects? I have such a mist before my lovely eyes that I cannot now see what I write. Instantly get me a situation in Ireland, I care not where. Dear Everina, delay not to tell me you can procure bread, with what hogs I eat it, I care not, if exactly the Uptonian breed.[152]

Two weeks later she wrote again, even though, as she herself admitted, it was impossible that Everina could possibly have had time to answer her previous letter. Even Upton, however unbearable, had been better than this dreadful, doom-laden waiting.

> I am so eager for you to say you have procured me a situation in Dublin. I now have only ten days to spend in Pembroke, yet am quite uncertain what 'poor Bess's' future fate is to be ... Nine days have now elapsed, and here I am waiting for your letter, my dear Everina ... If it is impossible to procure me bread immediately, perhaps George [Blood] would permit me to remain with him until you succeed. Recollect I value not what situation you get me – agreeable or disagreeable will be equally acceptable to the sister of the author of the 'Rights of Women'.[153]

As Eliza's situation deteriorated, so, too, did her handwriting. By the end of May it was all but illegible, great scrawls galloping blindly across the page. Her every hope had shattered. Charles, who had promised to send money to pay the sisters' passage to America, wrote to say that in fact he had no money. And to cap everything, she had fallen out with her Frenchman, Graux, who was 'dreadfully embittered ... very ill, and thoroughly hurt at my sublime sister'.[154] Perhaps he, too, had been hoping for help from Eliza's famous relative.

George Blood does seem to have offered Eliza a temporary home with himself and his mother in Dublin, and eventually she found a situation. Everina, meanwhile, moved from the Boyces in Waterford to a family called Irwin outside Dublin, and then to another situation in the city itself. However, at the start of 1797, she found herself once more unemployed.

By then Mary had finally done with Imlay. She survived a second suicide attempt in October 1795, when she was pulled out of the Thames only half drowned, and after several final, final letters, at last, in March 1796, she ceased to correspond with him. And then, when it was least expected, happiness crept up on her in the shape of William Godwin, who four years earlier had so emphatically not liked her. They met again in April, became lovers in August, and by February 1797, when Everina came to stay between situations, Mary was already a few weeks' pregnant with his child. But the pregnancy would not yet have been visible, and she does not seem to have told her sister about this new relationship.

The position to which Everina was in transit – with the Wedgwood tribe at Etruria in the Potteries – was probably obtained through Godwin's friendship with Tom Wedgwood. But Godwin's own first meeting with Everina was evidently disastrous. She used the excuse of a bad cold to go up to bed early, confessing herself unable (which is perhaps not surprising) to keep up with the conversation between the austere philosopher and her brilliant sister. After that he did his best to avoid her, the lovers timing their meetings to coincide with her absences. Altogether her presence was a trial for all concerned – not least, we may imagine, for Everina herself, no doubt spikily conscious that she was not really wanted. 'My Sister talks of going to Miss Cristall's tomorrow or next day,' Mary told Godwin on 21 February. 'I shall not then expect you this evening – I would call on you this morning, but I cannot say when – and I suppose you will dine at Johnson's. The evenings with her silent, I find very wearisome and embarrassing ... Well, a little patience.'[155] Finally, on the evening of 6 March, Everina departed. 'I will be with you about nine,' Mary wrote in relief, 'or had you not better try, if you can, to while away this evening, those to come are our own.'[156]

This visit seems to have been the last time that the two sisters met, although Godwin saw Everina in June, in the course of a journey that took him to Etruria. They went on a tour of the famous Wedgwood factory, on which Godwin found her 'in high spirits, for Everina'.[157] Three months later Mary was dead, of septicaemia following the birth of her daughter, who was named after her.

Everina received the news in December, in a letter from Mary's friend Mrs Fenwick. 'No woman was ever more happy in marriage than Mrs Godwin. Who ever endured more anguish than Mr Godwin endures? ... The children are both well, the infant in particular. It is the finest baby I ever saw ... Mr Godwin requests you will make Mrs Bishop acquainted with the particulars of this afflicting event. He tells me that Mrs Godwin entertained a sincere and earnest affection for Mrs Bishop.'[158]

We have just one more intimate glimpse of the sisters, this time in a letter from Everina to Eliza, written some time after Mary's death. She was writing to console her sister, who had just been turned down – 'excluded' was Everina's word for it – by some potential employers, evidently on account of her unsuitable connections. 'The motive that excluded you was a mean one I am sure at least an illiberal one; your relationship to poor Mary,' Everina wrote.

> The whole family are violent Aristocrates, and as violently religious. I am not indeed sorry that you do not go there, and shall rejoice to hear that you are settled in, or near Dublin. We have not given up on our American plans yet, – and when we are obliged to relinquish them, what necessity is there for us to be banished from Dublin? Let the present storm pass over, and the prejudices against me may die away, and I may be able to settle myself in Dublin. – Dependance is ever an evil, but different situations under it less or more evil. We may still be near each other; indeed, we may ... My paroxism [sic] of despair is over and I have regained strength enough to combat my feelings, and to determine to act wisely; I feel I am with humane, good people, and will bear the evils that are unavoidable, I believe,

in this country with patience, depend on it I will. I am studying to avoid dwelling on what is disagreeable and rejoice at having found a temporary asylum; which rely on it I will not leave rashly, or hastily.[159]

The circumstances of this welcome asylum were basic in the extreme: three or four beds to a room, and two miles to the nearest source of water, which was sometimes little more than yellow mud. But, Everina assured Eliza, 'This is the bad side, the other presents much good.'[160] For if they had learned one thing from these wandering years, it was that luxurious, or even comfortable, conditions mattered far less than the temper of their hosts. And on those terms Everina had fallen on her feet. 'I never saw people who appeared so perfectly good-natured . . . They are entirely unaffected, hospitable and cordial . . . You are always in my mind. ps. Have you read "The Wrongs of Women".'[161]

The sisters never did make it to America. Instead they stayed in Dublin, where they kept their heads above water by running a school in which Everina taught the boys, Eliza the girls. An acquaintance remembered Everina as 'an overbearing, disagreeable, ill-tempered woman, very sarcastic and very clever', while Mrs Bishop, who could always be relied on for a smile and a sugar plum, 'had beautiful brown eyes, most winning gentle manners, and [her] whole bearing gave the idea of a perfectly lady-like and refined person'.[162]

When she chose to describe herself on first taking up Johnson's offer of employment, as one of 'a new genus', Mary aligned herself firmly with modernity. This was the terminology of the new scientific modes of thought that were transforming the world. Her attitudes to education, independence, love, work and friends, are ours. By contrast, Everina and Eliza lived in another age.

Partly, this was a question of communications. Mary, in London, lived at the centre of events, within walking distance of a network of influential friends; her sisters' lives were spent on the periphery. However, Everina and Eliza were also vulnerable in ways that middle-class people are rarely vulnerable now. Blown here and there at the mercy of an arbitrary and uncertain market, they knew that without employment they were lost. Hence Eliza's panic in Pembroke, as she sat waiting for letters that failed to arrive, while her savings ran out and the rent fell due, and she had to choose between spending what was left on the fare to Ireland or the decent clothes that might secure her another situation. For who would employ a governess in rags? And without employment, what would become of her? At Upton she had at least been sure of clean clothes and regular meals. What had been absent was respect, without which there could be neither self-respect nor professional satisfaction. However, respect required an interest in her as a person. And that, as generations of governesses would discover, was not part of the employer–governess contract.

All governesses found this hard to endure. But for Everina and Eliza it must have been doubly unbearable. Mary's life, constantly before them, demonstrated that another way might be possible; yet for them it remained inaccessible. It was not simply that they could not hope to live, as she did, by writing, nor to contract, as she finally did, a happy marriage between equals; they could not even, as she had, make a success of governessing. Mary had shown, in her brief time with the Kingsboroughs, that the governess did not have to be subservient. On the contrary, it had become clear that, given a strong enough personality, the mother–governess balance of power might be subverted, and the governess might set her own terms. But unlike their all-conquering sister, Everina and Eliza were just ordinary young women, and if their experiences were anything like the norm – and there is little reason to think them exceptional – it is unsurprising that by the mid-nineteenth century, governesses, along with maids-of-all-work, constituted 'by far the largest classes of insane women in asylums'.[163]

A Vindication of the Rights of Woman suggested how education might create a new sort of woman: an equal citizen of the world. But the euphoria that produced it vanished almost as soon as it appeared. In 1792, the year of its publication, the bright ideals of the French revolution deteriorated into the bloody nightmare of the Terror, and in 1793 war was declared between France and England. For a brief moment France had exemplified the pattern of civilization and its possibilities; after 1793 it represented everything that decent Britons wished to avoid. France was egalitarian, secular, experimental; for the next fifty years Britain clung obstinately to hierarchy, religion and tradition. It was not Mary but Everina and Eliza who would typify single women's lives in the coming century.

4

Claire Clairmont: after the fall

'I am unhappily the victim of <u>a happy passion</u>,' Claire Clairmont
mused to her friend Jane Williams apropos her affair with Lord
Byron. 'I had one like all things perfect in its kind, it was fleeting and
mine only lasted ten minutes but these minutes have discomposed the
rest of my life.'[1]

Claire wrote these words in 1826, ten years after she had first
inveigled Byron into her bed. In 1822, their four-year-old daughter
had died. So, a few months later, had Claire's dear friend, the poet
Percy Bysshe Shelley. With Shelley's death, Claire's first life – the
period against which all else was measured – had come to an end. She
was then twenty-five. Compared to that vivid, tragic, intensely lived
time, her remaining fifty-seven years – of which twenty were spent as
a governess – would always seem a kind of limbo. Twice in the diaries
she kept during her governess years, Claire noted a passage from
Dante's *Paradiso*:

> [Tu] proverai siccome sa di sale
> Lo pane d'altrui e a come è dure calle
> Lo scendere e 'l salir per l'altrui scale.

(How bitter is the taste of other people's bread, how hard the road
that leads by other people's stairs.)

Many – perhaps most – governesses would have echoed her.

*

Claire Clairmont was William Godwin's stepdaughter, the step-niece, after their sister's death, of Eliza Bishop and Everina Wollstonecraft. Her own background – poor but literate – was very similar to that of most governesses. What set her apart (and preserved her papers) was the group of people among whom fate chose to throw her: the poet Percy Bysshe Shelley; his wife, Claire's stepsister Mary Godwin; and Lord Byron – who in Claire's case did indeed prove (in the famous words of his discarded mistress Caroline Lamb) 'mad, bad and dangerous to know'.[2] These brilliant associations led her into a life of extremes and broadened her horizons in ways far beyond the reach of the average poor girl in nineteenth-century England. But her vain efforts to keep up with them led her into almost unimaginable depths of misery.

Claire's mother, Mrs Mary-Jane Clairmont (the 'Mrs', as with 'Mrs' Porter and 'Mrs' Wollstonecraft, was honorific), was probably the daughter of a French merchant, Pierre de Vial, who had settled in Exeter. When her father married for a second time, Mary-Jane set off to visit French relatives in St Etienne. In 1789 she fled the revolution; on her return to England she found that her father had died, leaving nothing but debts. In England she had nothing, and the declaration of war in 1793 had cut her off from her French family.

With no obvious way of supporting herself, she was faced with destitution; and this being so, was not about to turn down the protection of an agreeable man. She met a Swiss, Karl or Charles Gaulis, to whom she bore a son whom she called Charles Gaulis Clairmont (his father, on the birth certificate, was named as Charles Clairmont). Gaulis, however, died in 1796, and Mary-Jane's daughter, Jane, who arrived in 1798, cannot have been his (though later, when she had reinvented herself as 'Claire', she would write to Byron, 'Think of me in Switzerland: the land of my ancestors').[3] She, too, bore the surname Clairmont. We do not know whether there really had been a Mr Clairmont; if so he had vanished, for at some point following Jane's birth Mary-Jane and her family landed in a London debtors' prison. They were released by a charitable subscription that raised money for Huguenot debtors, and took rooms at no. 27, The Polygon, Somers Town, next door to the house that William Godwin had shared with Mary Wollstonecraft at no. 29, and where he still lived with her two daughters.[4]

Legend has it that he was in the street one day just outside his house when an unknown lady leaned over her balcony and uttered the gratifying words: 'Am I addressing the celebrated Mr Godwin?'[5] But whatever gambit she used, it worked. On 13 July 1801, two months after their first meeting, his journal shows that he made love to her. Soon she was pregnant. On 21 December, in Shoreditch church, William Godwin, marriage's arch-enemy, was wed for the second time; the ceremony, as if to make the most of this egregious abandonment of principle, being repeated an hour later at Whitechapel, where Mary-Jane called herself Mary Vial. Perhaps she feared that marriage under an assumed name might not be valid.

One can see how the union must in some ways have seemed ideal. The Clairmont children were much the same age as Fanny Imlay and Mary Godwin; for them the union provided instant playmates. For Mrs Clairmont, it provided respectability and what must have looked like security; for Godwin, relief from the worries of housekeeping and a companion to share his bed. It is clear too, that as far as he was concerned, the marriage worked. 'Be assured ... that I admire you not less than I love you,' he wrote to his 'Dearest Love' ten years later, when they happened to be apart for a few days. 'We are both of us, depend upon it, persons of no common stamp, and we should accustom ourselves perpetually so to regard each other ... God bless you! Good night.'[6]

Others, too, liked Mary-Jane. The American politician Aaron Burr, visiting London and eager to seek out America's British friends, described her in a letter as a 'sensible, amiable woman'.[7] However, what Claire described as her mother's 'commonplace prosy way of viewing all things',[8] though it does not seem to have worried Godwin, jarred with his intellectual friends (who had, of course, also been his first wife's friends). 'The Professor [Godwin] is COURTING,' Charles Lamb wrote unenthusiastically. 'The Lady is a Widow with green spectacles and one child [in fact she had two], and the Professor is grown quite juvenile.' In a footnote he added: 'A very disgusting woman.'[9]

Mary-Jane's stepdaughters, too, compared everything she did or said – to her disadvantage – with the dead mother whose memory they idolized and whose works (and portrait) were constantly before their eyes. Sweet, uncertain Fanny (who alone of the children had no recourse to either of her natural parents) bore her sadness in silence;

but the relationship between Mary Godwin and her new 'Mamma' was bitterly antagonistic; years later, Mary referred to her stepmother as 'that filthy woman'.[10] Godwin's three years as a lone parent had forged an exceptionally strong attachment, both emotional and intellectual, between him and his daughter. Later Mary would write: 'There is a peculiarity in the education of a daughter brought up by a father only, which tends to develop early a thousand of those portions of the mind, which are folded up, and often destroyed, under mere feminine tuition.'[11] She felt not just displaced but, on behalf of her mother, insulted. How could her father ally himself to Mary-Jane Clairmont, after such a woman as Mary Wollstonecraft? In a very real sense, her flight with Shelley was a flight from the hated stepmother, and all she stood for, into the world of her real mother, on whose tomb they first promised themselves to each other.

How Claire felt when she heard Mary talk in this way about her mother, one can only guess, but at the bottom of one of the many loving and admiring letters that Godwin wrote to his second wife, she noted: 'I kept this letter carefully because Mrs Shelley was ever speaking with contempt of my Mother. At any rate Mrs S's father did not share the intemperate prejudice of his daughter.'[12]

However, descriptions of the Godwins at home, and also the letters that the various children wrote to each other, show that despite the various antagonisms and irritations Mary-Jane ran a warm and welcoming home, in which a real family life took place. They soon moved to Skinner Street, Holborn, to a newly built house from whose ground floor they carried on the business upon which they had embarked, of publishing children's books.

There were by now five children: in 1803 the philosopher's only son, William, was born. They led, as Claire recalled,

a lively and cheerful life ... All the family worked hard, learning and studying: we all took the liveliest interest in the great questions of the day – common topics, gossiping, scandal, found no entrance in our circle for we had been brought up by Mr Godwin to think it was the greatest misfortune to be fond of the world, or worldly pleasures or of luxury or money; and that there was no greater happiness than to think well of those around us, to love them and to delight in being useful or pleasing to them.[13]

Godwin saw to it that his children received the best education he could give them, one that would fit them to take their places as citizens of the world – albeit a Godwinian world somewhat removed from that of real life. It helped make Mary the extraordinary person she became; for Jane, it marked her entry into a life to which she would never truly belong.

We can glimpse this wonderful childhood in Godwin's journal. There were outings, with all the children, to dine with friends, and those same friends – the Lambs, Hazlitt, Coleridge, Wordsworth – visited in their turn. In 1808, Coleridge treated the whole family to a reading of *The Ancient Mariner* while Mary and Jane hid under the sofa. There were pleasure parties *en famille*, as in 1802, when peace was proclaimed and the children were taken to see the illuminations, and many visits to the theatre. Aaron Burr, an habitué of the Godwin household whenever he was in London, describes going with them one evening to hear Coleridge give one of his famous lectures. 'Il parlait une heure sans ordre ou suite ou connexion,'[14] noted Burr acidly in the uncertain French he sometimes liked to affect. And revealingly, after dinner one evening, 'William, the only *son* of W. Godwin, a lad of about nine, gave his weekly lecture; one of his sisters (Mary, I think) writes a lecture, which he reads from a little pulpit which they have erected for him ... The subject was, "The influence of governments on the Character of the People".'[15]

Although Godwin's politics had fallen so profoundly out of fashion, his empathy and rigorous honesty, deep learning and radical notoriety continued to attract disciples. He would help and advise them and, provided they acted on his advice, could be relied on to stick by them.

In October 1812, a new young follower arrived at the Godwins' door in the lanky shape of Percy Bysshe Shelley. Shelley was wonderfully gifted – he was then writing his philosophical poem *Queen Mab*, with its Godwinian vision of a happy world of equals, free of kings and religion; he was also rich – or at any rate, potentially so, for he stood to inherit Field Place, the family estate near Horsham, in Sussex. However, he had been kicked out of Oxford at the age of sixteen for distributing, along with his friend Thomas Jefferson Hogg, a pamphlet extolling atheism; shortly afterwards he had met, seduced and married Harriet Westbrook, a girl even younger than himself, by whom he now had a daughter, Ianthe. Shelley's father, disgusted with his behaviour, was keeping him on short financial commons. But although he did not yet have access to the family money, he could borrow against his expectations – what was called a 'post-obit' loan. Godwin – who by then was caught in the spiral of debt that would dog him until bankruptcy finally put an end to his torment – saw in Shelley a potential source of much needed cash. His constant need of ever larger sums of money, and his endless, insistent importuning of Shelley, would eventually poison their relationship. But at first Shelley was only too glad to help the man whom he admired above all others, and Godwin did not hesitate to make the most of this unusually propitious situation.

Shelley, with his tall, stooping figure, fine features and what Claire later described as his 'ardent mouth'[16] and 'beautiful dark blue "marble" forehead',[17] was clearly an irresistible and enchanting young man. In Claire's words, 'Other men had as fair open and commanding foreheads and as dark and luxuriant brown hair to shade them, eyes as full of poetic fire and lips as expressive of gentle serenity, but they wanted that nameless something which touched the heart at every glance.'[18]

However, this entrancing person was also dangerous. Godwin was always prepared to bend principle – as for instance his dislike of marriage – to human necessity. But Shelley's zeal to better the world, and disdain for its rules, was allied to a capacity for extraordinary emotional cruelty on a personal level, nonetheless unbearable for being unintended. Like many progressive idealists – Rousseau, the theoretician of child nurture, who abandoned his own babies, one after the other, at the convent door; H.G. Wells, who devised a philosophical position that allowed him to enjoy, wholesale, the delights of impregnation while declining on principle (as a person designed for greater things) to participate in the boredom created by the ensuing babies; Bertrand Russell, who realized while bicycling that he no longer loved his wife Alys and felt it essential to tell her so forthwith – Shelley used principle to justify behaviour that, while it suited him, inflicted great pain on those close to him. For him, it was a matter of principle to follow his soul's dictates. But as those dictates included a fatal susceptibility to the opposite sex – 'The contemplation of female excellence,' he told his friend Hogg, 'is the favourite food of my imagination'[19] – he was a dangerous lover and a fatal husband.

The two women he married, who not unnaturally hoped for the more exclusive relationship marriage was supposed to entail, suffered continual misery and frustration.

Although Godwin, when they first met, was at pains to introduce all the members of his household to this new and delightful friend, it soon became clear that Shelley was an unsuitable habitué for a household full of adolescent girls. Godwin thought all three of them ('Les Goddesses', as Burr liked to call them[20]) were equally in love with Shelley,[21] and that, despite his married status, he encouraged them.

There is every reason to believe this. When Fanny committed suicide in 1816, Shelley left a verse ('Friend, had I known thy secret grief') that suggests he was aware of her feelings, while Claire's later descriptions of Shelley can leave one in no doubt that she, too, loved him. However, Shelley's eyes, from the moment he met her, were firmly fixed on Mary, with her brilliant mind and nimbus of fine leaf-brown hair. She was unlike any other woman he had met.

> The originality & loveliness of Mary's character was apparent to me from her very motions & tones of voice. The irresistible wildness & sublimity of her feelings shewed itself in her gestures & her looks – Her smile, how persuasive it was & how pathetic! She is gentle, to be convinced & tender; yet not incapable of ardent indignation & hatred. I do not think that there is an excellence at which human nature can arrive, that she does not indisputably possess, or of which her character does not afford manifest intimations.[22]

It was clear to everyone what was happening. Godwin's diary records his having serious talks with his daughter, he wrote reproachful letters to Shelley; yet nothing could stop it – not Mary's promises to her father or Harriet, nor Shelley's assurances to Godwin after meeting with a violent and evidently unexpected rebuff when, naively, as from one idealist to another, he disclosed their plans. That was on 26 July 1814. Two days later, at the crack of dawn, Mary and Jane let themselves silently out of the house to be met by Shelley, and drove away to Dover and thence to France. From this point on, Shelley considered himself Jane's protector as well as Mary's, supporting her financially and including her in his will.

To mark this new life, and the annihilation of her old self, Jane henceforth called herself Claire: Shelley's suggestion, Claire later told the American literary collector Edward Silsbee, 'for her transparency at times'.

This, then, marks the birth of Claire Clairmont. But the larger question remains. Why, since elopement is surely the ultimate duet, was she there at all?

It is true that Shelley and Mary had got into the habit of her company. 'Before his declaration of love,' Claire remembered, 'we both used to walk with him in the Wilderness of the Charterhouse and also to Mary Wollstonecraft's tomb – they always sent me to talk at some distance from them, alleging that they wished to talk on philosophical subjects and that I did not like or know anything about those subjects I willingly left. I did not hear what they talked about.'[23] On those early outings, Jane/Claire was the necessary chaperone, the proof that nothing untoward was going on – a role she was doubtless happy to play, for the sense it gave her, so important to self-respect at the age of sixteen, of being privy to the plot. But the duenna is rarely included in the elopement plans.

Claire herself seems to have taken for granted, then and ever after, her strange presence in Mary and Shelley's great adventure. Asked by a friendly Swiss, three weeks into the journey, whether she, too, had run away for the sake of love, she replied: 'Oh! dear No – I came to speak French,'[24] – a useful legacy from her French mother, but hardly a satisfactory explanation. So since Mary always (and understandably) preferred to have Shelley to herself, and Claire can only have accompanied them because she was asked to do so, we must assume that her presence was Shelley's idea. This is borne out by what took place at Calais when a distraught Mrs Godwin caught up with them there the day after their flight, to reclaim her daughter for the respectable world. Godwin had warned his wife not on any account to talk with Shelley; he knew how seductive Shelley could be. However, no one could stop Shelley from talking to Claire, with the inevitable result that Mrs Godwin, who in the evening thought she had won the argument, had next morning to return to Dover alone.

Given that Shelley was at this time wholly besotted by Mary, there had to be some serious, non-emotional reason why he insisted on assuming this responsibility. The most probable is that as usual he was using principle to underwrite inclination. This expedition was no vulgar desertion of a discarded wife, but a prelude to the ideal community towards which he always strove, of like-minded friends living in harmony, to be established somewhere on the Continent. Claire certainly was not expecting to return. 'As we left Dover & England's white cliffs were retiring I said to myself I shall never see these more,' she recorded.[25] Just a few months later, when they were all back in London, she wrote of talking with Shelley one evening about 'making an Association of philosophical people – of [Shelley's sisters] Eliza & Hellen – of Hogg & Harriet'.[26]

Claire, Mary and Shelley would be together, intermittently, for the next eight years. All the patterns of that turbulent time may be discerned in this first journey: Shelley, borne up by genius, charm and certainty, sheathed in the invincible armour of divine theory; Mary, loving and devoted, yet too perceptive not to be discomfited by the realization, even now on their honeymoon, that he would never be entirely hers; Claire blindly following, welcome and unwelcome in a life where she never quite fitted.

The threesome seems to have worked tolerably well while they were abroad, when three months later they returned to England the strains began to show. Mary had become pregnant, which made her feel tired and ill; Shelley increasingly took Claire to accompany him when he went out walking; Mary, sitting at home, was eaten up with jealousy. Even worse, Shelley's friend Hogg had fallen in love with Mary, and Shelley seemed to indicate that he would not mind if the two became lovers. During this period, Claire told Edward Silsbee, Mary had come to her room and 'putting <u>her head on her [Claire's] pillow & crying bitterly</u> saying <u>Shelley wants her to sleep with Hogg – that he said Beaumont</u> & Fletcher had one mistress'. He had said the same thing to Harriet when he first met Mary, which was not a reassuring parallel. Claire later defended Shelley's behaviour, telling Silsbee she thought that 'Shelley with his Greek ideas & his desire to be superior to the prejudices of the world considered it right to have all in common even wives – not that he was lacking in delicacy in this matter – he treated the matter as a prejudice.'[27]

On 22 February 1815, Mary went into labour. She was not quite seven months' pregnant, and the child, though born unexpectedly alive, died after a few days. In this new misery, Claire's carefree, blooming presence, hitherto merely annoying, became unbearable.

Whenever Claire was not around, Mary noted her relief; almost every day there was talk about 'Clary's going away'.

The Godwins would have taken her back, but Claire had known independence, as few girls of her time had or could, and was not prepared to return to her old role as daughter of the house. 'Nothing settled – I fear it is hopeless – she will not go to Skinner St. – then our house is the only remaining place – I see plainly – what is to be done,'[28] Mary wailed on 11 March; and three days later, 'The prospect appears more dismall than ever – not the least hope – this is indeed hard to bear.'[29]

Things could not go on like this. Claire would have to devise a life of her own and lead it independently.

Her inevitable first thought was governessing. On 17 March, an advertisement appeared in *The Times*, which (although Claire was at this time in London, not France) may have been hers:

TO GOVERNESSES OF SCHOOLS, or LADIES. – An English young LADY, who is now in France, is desirous of obtaining a SITUATION in a respectable SCHOOL, or in a private family, to instruct one Lady; she speaks the French language fluently, and with a good accent; understands the rudiments of Italian, and plays well on the piano forte; she does not require a large salary, but hopes to meet friendly treatment from the family with whom she may engage.[30]

Replies were to be addressed to AZ; on 20 March, Mary's journal recorded 'more letters for A-Z – one from a disconsolate widow'.[31] However when it came to the point Claire found, for the first but not the last time, that she could not – or not yet – resign herself to burial alive as a governess or paid companion. Her current life, with all its tensions, was too exciting and interesting.

It was not until May that the longed-for change occurred. That month Claire left London for Lynmouth, Devon, where she lived in a cottage probably paid for by Shelley, who had finally succeeded in raising some money against his expectations. 'S. and the lady walk out – after tea talk – write greek characters – S. and his friend ~~indulge in~~ have a last conversation,' Mary noted bitterly. The following day she wrote: 'I begin a new journal with our regeneration.'[32]

*

Although Claire greeted solitude and Lynmouth with commendable equanimity, she could not stay there on her own for ever reading books of poetry. It comes as no surprise that after a while she returned to London. However, she would have to find something to do there. And that something was to throw herself at Byron.

Seen from Claire's perspective, the decision had a definite logic. Mary had caught a star; if Claire could catch a star of her own, she could re-establish herself on an equal footing with Mary and Shelley and continue to lead the free life she wanted. And Byron was the star of stars. His poem *The Corsair*, published the previous year, had sold 10,000 copies on the first day of publication; corsair figures, personifying masculine desirability, litter the novels of the time. Becky Sharp in *Vanity Fair* dreams of a 'corsair', as does Lizzie Eustace in *The Eustace Diamonds;* in *Jane Eyre*, Blanche Ingram compares Mr Rochester to a 'corsair'. 'Know that I dote on Corsairs,'[33] she significantly assures him. Had there been Byron posters, every young girl's room would have been plastered with them.

Fate, too, played its part. The landlady of a house the Shelleys had rented on their return from Switzerland, and where Claire now took lodgings, had a sister who was Byron's housekeeper and who could pass on a letter. Admittedly, he was married, but that had not stopped Shelley from running off with Mary – and in any case, London (and certainly Byron's housekeeper) buzzed with rumours that Byron's marriage was all but over.

To elope in a moment of passion is one thing: to offer oneself out of the blue to a man one has never met, quite another. Unfortunately, however, Claire, as so often, had no one to confide in. Many years later she would write, 'I have trodden life alone without a guide and without a companion;'[34] and although this isolation was to some extent self-imposed – she could, after all, have stayed home with her mother – for the most part that was the simple truth.

However, if she had no confidante, she had plenty of examples to follow; and they all indicated that life must be affronted, exactly as she proposed. Mary Wollstonecraft, Mary Godwin, her own mother – all the women whose lives she knew best – had chosen their man, or men, and lived or died with the consequences. Godwin and Shelley, the two men whose opinions she implicitly trusted, admired strong women, declared marriage an outmoded and uncivilized institution, and thought religion, with all its prohibitions, a sham.

Seen in these terms, and bearing in mind her extreme youth, Claire's decision to approach Byron seems not just explicable but almost inevitable. And (for a while, at least) her strategy paid off. As Silsbee noted, 'From that time She running off & Byron's acquaintance taking place Mrs S. was no longer jealous of her.'[35]

In April 1816, Claire finally sent her letter.

An utter stranger takes the liberty of addressing you. It is earnestly requested that for one moment you pardon the intrusion, & laying aside every remembrance of who & what you are, listen with a friendly ear. A moment of passion, or an impulse of pride often destroys our own happiness & that of others. If in this case your refusal shall not affect yourself, yet you are not aware how much it may injure another. It is not charity I demand, for of that I stand in no need: I imply by that you should think kindly & gently of this letter, that if I seem impertinent you should pardon it for a while, & that you should wait patiently till I am emboldened by you to disclose myself.

I tremble with fear at the fate of this letter . . .

Either you will or you will not. Do not decide hastily, & yet I must entreat your answer without delay, not only because I hate to be tortured by suspense, but because my departure a short way out of town is unavoidable & I would know your reply ere I go. Address me, as E. Trefusis, 21, Foley Place, Mary le Bonne.[36]

Byron kept the letter, but for several reasons did not reply. He was in the final stages of obtaining his separation papers from his wife; he was the subject of endless gossip, the object of slander and speculation; he was on the point of leaving the country. The last thing he needed was more complication.

Claire, however, having screwed up her courage to take this terrifying step, was not to be so easily put off. She tried again, requesting him to 'receive a lady to communicate with him on business of peculiar importance'[37] at seven o'clock that evening and signing her note with the initials G.C.B., presumably in the hope that he would take her for a different person. This time he did reply. 'Ld. B. is not aware of any "importance" which can be attached by any person to an interview with him – & more particularly by one with whom it does not appear that he has the honour of being acquainted—He will however be at home at the hour mentioned.'[38]

Claire's affair with Byron lasted from that April until the following August. It was, as he always made brutally clear, never other than completely one-sided. In almost every way, she was just the sort of girl he least liked. Ironically (given that his daughter Ada would become a celebrated mathematician) he preferred his women uneducated and submissive, feeling, with Sir Anthony Absolute, that 'the extent of a woman's erudition should consist in her knowing her simple letters, without their mysterious combinations'.[39] In contrast, Claire was both intellectually pretentious (she unwisely showed him the manuscript of a dreadful novel she had written) and to put it mildly, overbold. The move that she had made – still, almost two hundred years later, a difficult one for a woman – was then the sole prerogative of men and whores. Later, the label of whorishness was one that Byron was happy to use against Claire, even though he must have known – she told him so often enough – that never, throughout those years, did she love anyone but him.

On the other hand, as he himself admitted, bedding her was no hardship. 'I never loved or pretended to love her, but a man is a man, and if a girl of eighteen comes prancing to you at all hours, there is but one way.'[40] Besides, he was nothing if not human – that was part of his singular charm. 'I was not in love nor have any love left for any,' he wrote to his half-sister Augusta Leigh, 'but . . . I had been regaled of late with so many "two courses and a *desert* [sic]" (Alas!) of aversion, that I was fain to take a little love (if pressed particularly) by way of novelty.'[41] Most annoying of all (and much against his will), he found her sexually alluring. So, too, Thomas Love Peacock, whose portrait of Claire as Stella in *Nightmare Abbey*, written in 1818, gives her 'long flowing hair of raven blackness, and large black eyes of almost oppressive brilliancy, which strikingly contrasted with a complexion of snowy whiteness'.[42] When their daughter Allegra was living with him in Venice and Claire proposed a visit, Byron 'declined seeing her for fear the consequence might be an addition to the family'[43] – which, however you read it, does not connote indifference. One of the things that he afterwards held most violently against her, and for which he punished her so bitterly, was his own weakness in succumbing, however slightly and momentarily, to her charms. Each one of those moments of weakness constituted a battle lost.

Yet although he made his position coldly clear, it was inevitable that Claire would be overwhelmed. She was in love with the idea of him before they ever met, and there was never any chance that the real Byron would disappoint. In bed – and, as he himself admitted, they were often in bed – he was doubtless tender and captivating. Furthermore, it was not just the delirium of love that she now experienced, but the indescribable intoxication of actually being Byron's mistress. There was also the triumph (childish, but she was still, after all, a child) of trumping Mary. 'God bless you – I never was so happy!'[44] she truly told Byron, in reply to one of his extremely rare notes.

When she threatened to follow him abroad, however, he forbade it. And so she played her ace: her friendship with Shelley and Mary. She had already, in London, introduced a thrilled Mary (who had 'not the slightest suspicion of our connection')[45] to her new friend; now, as Shelley looked for a haven to escape to with his family following a failed financial lawsuit, she persuaded him to think of returning to Geneva. One inducement was that her friend Byron would be there. He wanted to meet Shelley, whose *Queen Mab* he had admired; Shelley naturally wanted to meet the famous Byron; and Claire could introduce them. So began the expedition that would lead, eventually, to *Frankenstein* – the germ of which, in the shape of general discussion on the question of creator and creature, may be divined from letters and journals they all three wrote.

Once they were in Geneva, a routine established itself. In the morning Byron would send sheets of *Childe Harold*, which he was then writing, to Claire for her to copy; at two in the afternoon Shelley, Mary and Claire would come up to the Villa Diodati to dine with him and his companion Dr Polidori.[46] In the long, rainy evenings of that 'year without summer',[47] when the world shivered in the wake of the Mt Tambora explosion, they sat before the fire at Diodati, talking and weaving fantasies. At these gatherings, Claire took a back seat. All Byron's interest, as he made very clear, centred on Shelley and Mary.

In the course of this stay, Claire realized that she was pregnant. It is impossible to know whether the child had been conceived in England or Switzerland (for she contrived, against Byron's better judgement, to continue the affair: 'I could not exactly play the Stoic with a woman who had scrambled eight hundred miles to unphilosophize me,'[48] he confessed ruefully to Augusta Leigh). Either way, Byron did not dispute his responsibility. 'The (carnal) connection had commenced previously to my setting out,' he explained to his friend Douglas Kinnaird. ' . . . The next question is, is the brat mine? I have reasons to think so, for I know as much as one can know such a thing – that she had *not lived* with S. during the time of our acquaintance – and that she had had a good deal of that same with me.'[49]

Claire doubtless hoped the coming child would constitute a bond between them; Byron, anxious to kill any such notion, immediately barred his house to her. However, Shelley, who knew of both the affair and the pregnancy, persuaded him to receive the two of them just once more, in order to talk over the situation. Byron wanted to place the child with his half-sister and reputed lover, Mrs Leigh (about whom he had spoken freely at the Villa Diodati).[50] Claire objected, saying she felt 'a Child always wanted a parent's care at least till seven years old . . . He yielded and said it was best it should live with him – he promised faithfully never to give it until seven years of age into a stranger's care. I was to be called the child's Aunt and in that character I could see it and watch over it without injury to anyone's reputation.'[51] With that agreement reached, Mary, Shelley, William and Claire prepared to return to England, while Byron continued his journey to Italy.

The Shelleys and Claire settled in Bath, far from the Godwins, while Claire waited out her pregnancy. She passed the time writing Byron numerous letters that might have been especially designed to enrage him, reiterating her undying love for her 'dearest Albé,' nagging about his health and excessive drinking, begging for some sign that he had not forgotten her. However, he had determined never to correspond with her again. Although Shelley did receive a letter from him, which he unwisely showed to her, doubtless after endless pleading, it was not calculated to comfort Claire, and she was desolated. Meanwhile the old tensions had resumed. Claire's pregnancy made Shelley more than ever protective of her; when the baby was born he took a quasi-paternal interest in it. But Mary's irritation increased by the day. All she needed for perfect happiness, she told him, was 'a garden and *absentia Clariae*'.[52]

It was a terrible autumn. On 9 October 1816 Fanny Imlay committed suicide at the Bristol coaching inn, en route for Swansea. She was identified by her mother's stays, marked with the letters M.W., and the small gold watch that had been bought for her by Mary and Shelley at Geneva. Her suicide note indicated extreme depression, though it gave no indication of any one particular precipitating incident. Two months later, Harriet Shelley's body, in an advanced state of pregnancy, was pulled from the Thames. Despite the jury's verdict of 'found drowned', it was obvious she had killed herself – indeed, she left a note telling Shelley of her wishes regarding their children: he could have Charles, the little boy, but only if he left Ianthe with Harriet's sister Eliza, who had brought her up.

Godwin's immediate reaction was that Shelley, now that he was free, must instantly marry Mary. Only the day before Shelley received the news, Mrs Godwin had been discussing the practicability of his obtaining a divorce. Unlike the children, she said, who all supported Mary in what she had done, Godwin 'quite reprobate[d] the act'. As for his anti-marriage declarations in *Political Justice*, 'certainly [he] had forgotten them'.[53] The ceremony took place on 30 December 1816; the previous evening, Shelley and Mary dined at Godwin's house in Skinner Street. Godwin set to work to spread the glad tidings, informing his brother that '[Mary's] husband is the eldest son of Sir Timothy Shelley, of Field Place in the county of Sussex, Baronet. So that, according to the vulgar ideas of the world, she is well married, and I have great hopes the young man will make her a good husband.'[54]

Claire's baby, a little girl, was born two weeks later, on 12 January 1817. Byron was supposed to choose a name for the child, but since he showed no sign of doing so Claire called her Alba – an obvious reference to Albé, which was their usual name for Byron (presumably from LB). In March 1818, the baby was finally christened Clara Allegra: Allegra, a Venetian name, being Byron's eventual choice. Released from exile by the baby's arrival, the Shelleys, after a short stay with Leigh Hunt and his wife Marianne in Hampstead, moved to Marlow, in Buckinghamshire, where they intended to settle. Claire joined them there at the end of March, and the Hunts soon followed with Allegra, supposedly the daughter of friends in the country. The Marlow household, with its tensions, its literary friends and its selection of multi-parented babies (though not as many as there might have been, since

Shelley had failed to gain custody of his first two), must have felt much like the one in which the girls had grown up.

The fifteen months that Claire spent with her child were without question the happiest of her life. 'She is all my treasure – the little creature occupies all my thoughts, all my time & my feelings,' she told Byron (who was not in the least interested). 'When I hold her in my arms I think to myself – there is nothing else in the world that is of you or belongs to you – you are utterly a stranger to everyone else: without this little being you would hold no relations with any single human being.'[55] Although feeding her was troublesome at first, the difficulty soon passed, and Claire found motherhood a source of endless delights. She loved children; a letter that she sent Mary when the Shelleys left her with little William for a few days is full of amusement and fun. No better gift could be imagined than a baby of her very own.

What Claire refused to dwell on, or even admit, was that her idyll with the baby she called 'Itty Ba' could not last. She and Shelley, at their momentous last meeting with Byron, had agreed that the child would be raised by her father; Byron told his friend Kinnaird that he intended to 'acknowledge and breed her myself'.[56] None of Claire's friends, then or later, had the slightest doubt but that this would be the best thing for the child. The case was unarguable: Byron could do everything for her, Claire, nothing. Accordingly, in the summer of 1817, Byron claimed the child, who was now six months old, and asked for her to be sent to him in Italy.

Claire of course knew this had to happen at some point but the thought that she and her baby were really to be parted, and so soon, was so unbearable that she put it from her. Mary, who was once again pregnant – Clara Everina Shelley would be born in September 1817 – and who unequivocally thought Allegra should go to her father, summed up the situation. Claire, wrote Mary, wanted to exact 'promises of writing and sending accounts' before she let the child go. But

promises with Albe! The first object that engaged his attention would put them all out of his head – and negotiated by letter also – why it is the labour of several months to get any kind of answer from him and then if he makes objections and you have to answer the child can never depart – in fact Clare [sic] although she in a blind kind of manner sees the necessity of it, does not wish her to go and will instinctively place all kinds of difficulties in the way.[57]

What Claire would not do under any circumstances was send her baby to Italy, as Byron proposed, in care of a nurse. 'Do you think I would trust her with such a person ... You might as well have asked a miser to trust his gold for a sea voyage to a leaky vessel,' she wrote on Allegra's first birthday, in a letter that swings between exquisite vignettes of maternal love and the terrible dreads that she could not keep down. 'My dear friend, how I envy you. You will have a little darling to crawl to your knees & pull you till you take her up – then she will sit on the crook of your arm & you will give her raisins out of your own plate & a little drop of wine from your own glass & she will think herself a little Queen in Creation.' But then she came down to the nub of it: the

> various and ceaseless misgivings that I entertain of you. Suppose that in yielding her to your care I yield her to neglect & coldness? How am I assured that such will not be the case? ... I so fear she will be unhappy. I am so anxious to be cautious ... Poor little angel! In your great house; left perhaps to servants while you are drowning sense & feeling in wine & striving all you can to ruin the natural goodness of your nature who will be there to watch her ... My affections are few & therefore strong – the extreme solitude in which I live has concentrated them to one point & that point is my lovely child ... We sleep together & if you knew the extreme happiness I feel when she nestles closer to me, when in listening to our regular breathing together, I could tear my flesh in twenty thousand different directions to ensure her good and when I fear for her residing with you it is not the dread I have to commence the long series of painful anxiety I know I shall have to endure it is lest I should behold her sickly & wasted with improper management lest I should live to hear that <u>you</u> neglected her.[58]

Later in the letter she rowed back slightly on these fears. But anyone who knew Byron would know that they were not without foundation.

In the end Shelley, as so often, proposed a practical solution. His health was not good, his doctor had recommended Italy – why should they not all move there? Then at least they would be in the same country as Byron, who had settled in Venice. The house in Marlow was sold; they had a frenetic month of opera-going and theatre in London; finally on 11 March 1818, the party – Shelley, Mary, Claire, the three children, plus two nursemaids, Elise and Milly – set out for Dover. Six weeks later they were in Milan.

Shelley by now felt uncertain about sending Allegra to her father. He had received a cruel letter from Byron, dismissing Claire's out-pourings as 'bad German novels'[59] and implying that he intended, contrary to their agreement, to refuse her all access to the child. Shelley urged Claire to do nothing hasty, to consider the possible consequences before she parted with her baby.* But she dismissed his caveats, taking refuge in her obstinate, sentimental conviction that at bottom 'dearest Lord Byron', when he actually met Allegra, would be enchanted and won over, and would show only that kind and humane side of himself that did, indeed, exist. Making a supreme effort, she sent her 'darling bird' off to Venice with the nursemaid Elise. 'I have sent her off because I love her too well to keep her,' she told Byron. ' . . . She loves me she stretches out her arms to me & cooes [sic] for joy when I take her . . . I assure you I have wept so much to night that now my eyes seem to drop out hot and burning blood. Remember that I am wretched how wretched and for the smallest word of kindness from you I will bless & honour you.'[60]

No such word would ever be forthcoming. Byron's dealings with Claire were extraordinarily cruel. Claire's ten minutes of perfection had been perhaps the only moment in his life when he bowed to someone else's will. Now was his chance to punish her for his weakness, and he took full advantage of it. In the letters she wrote him, the pleasure that he took in her misery was one of her constant refrains; his (though not to her – he never wrote to her) resound with weary self-pity that the magnanimous gesture of acknowledging a natural child should bring him only abuse. His affair with Claire was some-thing he would have preferred to forget; unfortunately, there was a constant reminder in Allegra.

---

* Compare his letter to her of 24 March 1822: 'Remember Clare when you rejected my earnest advice (& treated me with that contempt which I have never merited from you), & how at Milan, & how vain now is your regret!'

His feelings towards the child were therefore full of ambivalence. She was beyond doubt a Byron, and he tried to focus on her Byronic half; it appealed (if nothing else) to his narcissism. As soon as she arrived in Venice he altered his will to leave her £5,000 – a portion large enough to ensure her a decent marriage anywhere but England, where her parentage would in any case count against her. To Augusta Leigh he wrote of her with amused affection, emphasizing her Byronic resemblances: 'much more like Lady Byron than her mother ... is it not odd? I suppose she must also resemble her sister Ada – she has very blue eyes – and that singular forehead – fair curly hair – and a devil of a spirit – but that is Papa's.'[61] A year later, 'She speaks nothing but Venetian – "Bon *di* papa" &c. &c. she is very droll – and has a good deal of the Byron – can't articulate the letter *r* at all.'[62] When in 1819, he proposed returning to England, Allegra was to accompany him; he put off his departure because she had a fever and 'I will not & can not go without her'.[63]

But of course Allegra was not a clone, and those aspects that she took from Claire he found intolerable. Teresa Guiccioli – his mistress and last great love, who was fond of the child – said, 'She was like a perpetual remorse to his sensitive soul, and had it not been for me, the poor girl would have had no education at all. Each time she came into her father's presence, he used to turn away in disgust and exclaim "Enlevez-la; elle ressemble trop à sa mère!" '[64]

In fact, Allegra seems to have been happy enough. Richard Belgrave Hoppner, the English consul in Venice, and his Swiss wife, had agreed to look after her alongside their own small boy. Although at first she naturally pined for her mother, after a while she accepted her new surroundings. The Hoppners were conscientious, although (as Hoppner himself later confessed) they did not particularly like Allegra. However, their rather cold comfort was made up for by the petting she received at her father's house. Mrs Hoppner reported that she sent Allegra to visit him 'as often as possible; but he doesn't get up till 3 o'clock, and that's far too late for her. In any case, when she goes to see her papa, La Fornarina [Byron's notorious Venetian mistress] takes charge, and gives her all sorts of things to eat and drink which make the child ill.'[65] And when Teresa Guiccioli took her back to the family palazzo in Ravenna, she was happily made much of in the warm Italian way.

To his contemporaries, Byron's dealings with Allegra were neither blameworthy nor irresponsible. The blatant way Claire had offered herself – in those days, deeply shocking behaviour – absolved him of all responsibility for any consequences. Even had he taken the initiative, women who agreed to intercourse out of wedlock knew that they were treading a forbidden path. Even more to the point, he was a rich aristocrat, she a poor girl with no connections. Of course, liaisons between upper-class men and lower-class women happened all the time. But society's invariable assumption was that only the upper-class party mattered. Servant girls made pregnant by the master knew they would almost certainly be sacked; governesses, to judge by the advice manuals' reiteration that such affairs' outcome was 'seldom matrimony', fared little better. And Byron unswervingly adhered to this principle. He had many mistresses in Venice, including the baker's wife nicknamed 'La Fornarina', of whom he remarked (perhaps thinking of Claire), 'The best thing about her is that she can neither read nor write. So she can't haunt me with letters.'[66] He dismissed all of them as 'sluts' – all, that is, except the aristocratic Teresa Guiccioli, whom he took seriously because her rank equalled his own.

Nothing, then, obliged him to acknowledge Allegra, let alone take responsibility for bringing her up. That he agreed to do so can only have reflected his affection for Shelley, with whom, that day in Geneva, these arrangements had been agreed. And the child was, as he had promised, well looked after. However – and here lay the rub – there was no way Claire could know this. The nurse Elise sent her own accounts, but how reliable were they? At one point she reported Byron as saying of Allegra, 'She will grow up a very pretty woman and then I will take her for my mistress.'[67] It sounded Byronic enough to be possible. Claire's letters to Byron plead frantically for a word – a glimpse – a hair from her baby's head. None was answered.

Claire and Allegra were reunited just once, in August 1818, four months after the handover, when Allegra was twenty months old. Shelley accompanied Claire to Venice and persuaded Byron to let the child see her mother. To his astonishment Byron not only acceded to his request but said, 'After all I have no right over the child. If Clare likes to take it – let her take it.'[68] But Claire, having once forced herself to let Allegra go, was reluctant to turn back. What she wanted for her child was what had been agreed, the advantages Byron could confer without loss of contact. That, however, was the one combination he would never allow.

Byron offered Shelley and Claire the use of his beautiful villa in the Euganean hills, where Allegra could stay with them for a month or more, and where they spent three idyllic weeks together. Shelley summoned Mary to join them; she obediently set out, bringing William and little Clara, who was not well. As the journey progressed the baby's health became worse and in Venice, on 24 September, she died.

The death of Clara marked a shift in the Mary–Shelley–Claire triangle. Mary, distraught, and not unnaturally feeling that her daughter had been needlessly sacrificed to Claire's interests, began a withdrawal into unreachability that ever after overshadowed her days with Shelley, and that she bitterly regretted after his death. Faced with this icy wall, Shelley turned increasingly to Claire – perhaps not for sex, though that may have happened, but certainly for friendship and comfort: an *amitié amoureuse* that – constantly before her eyes – made Mary's burden even heavier. From now on, in his letters, she was 'dearest Claire' or 'my best girl' – endearments that he kept from Mary's eyes.

Another tragedy followed. The following June, in Rome, where they were then living, William, too, became ill, probably with malaria. 'The misery of these hours is beyond calculation,' Mary wrote to their friend Maria Gisborne, an old flame of Godwin's, now living in Italy. 'The hopes of my life are bound up in him.'[69] Two days later William, too, died.

This final, awful loss – the third of their children to die, and the most loved – devastated both Mary and Shelley. Shelley wept unconsolably, while Mary, who was again pregnant, retreated into a numb misery that was almost impossible to live with. Nevertheless, the forms of life went on: her journal records walks, reading, meetings with friends. In November she gave birth to a boy, Percy Florence, named for the town of his birth. Then they moved on to Pisa, where the climate was less harsh.

By a particularly bitter irony, these deaths allowed Byron to present himself as, by comparison, a model parent. 'I can only say to Claire,' he wrote in a letter to Hoppner, forwarded to Shelley, that I so totally disapprove of the mode of Children's treatment in their family, that I should look upon the Child as going into a hospital. Is it not so? Have they *reared* one? – [Allegra's] health has hitherto been excellent – and her temper not bad – she is sometimes vain and obstinate – but always clean and cheerful – and as in a year or two I shall either send her to England – or put her in a Convent for her education – these defects will be remedied as far as they can in human nature. – But the Child shall not quit me again – to perish of Starvation and green fruit – or be taught to believe that there is no Deity.— Whenever there is convenience of vicinity and access – her Mother can always have her with her – otherwise, no.[70]

At this low point a new, staunch friend entered their lives: Mary Wollstonecraft's old pupil Margaret King, now Lady Mountcashel. True to her mentor (and, unlike Claire, rich enough to do as she pleased, for she had enough money of her own to provide a small annuity), she had decided that she would no longer put up with her unsatisfactory marriage. For some years she had been living in Pisa with George Tighe, generally known as 'Tatty' from his passion for growing new varieties of potato, and their two daughters, Laurette and Nerina. She liked to be called Mrs Mason, after the ideal governess in Mary Wollstonecraft's *Original Stories from Real Life*. And for the Shelleys, and in particular for Claire, this was very much the role she played. For the first time in her life, Claire had a true confidante: a person with whom she could talk openly about her hopes and plans with no fear of being misunderstood or condemned on conventional grounds. 'I made the most terrible mistakes so long as I was with the Shelleys,' Claire said later. 'They were young and I was young – as soon as I got into Lady Mountcashell's hands (who was fifty two) I succeeded in all I undertook – but then I had confidence in her and obeyed her implicitly. God only can tell me from what gulf of ruin, the counsels of that dear Lady saved me!'[71]

Mrs Mason at once established herself as a sort of benevolent aunt to the Shelley household. She was familiar with their story, having kept in close contact with Godwin ever since meeting him in Ireland in 1800. When she left her husband, and most fashionable doors closed to her, he had remained her friend and commissioned books from her. Claire visited her most days and often walked out with the little girls.

Mrs Mason at once saw that the uneasy *ménage à trois* of Claire and the Shelleys was not tenable, viewing Claire's refusal to marry Thomas Love Peacock, who had proposed to her while Claire and the Shelleys were living at Marlow, 'a great mistake':[72] she would never have allowed that to happen. But happen it had; Claire had continued her unsatisfactory life; the situation was what it was. And just then it was particularly fraught. At the end of 1818 a baby girl had been born in Naples and for her brief life (she was born in December 1818, and died in June 1820) was registered under the name of Elena Adelaide Shelley. Rumour (begun by Elise) asserted that Claire was her mother and Shelley her father.

Shelley's biographer, Richard Holmes, thinks Shelley probably was the father, and that circumstances point to Elena's real mother being the nursemaid Elise, who had brought Allegra to Venice and looked after her there.[73] The Hoppners, however, believed Elise's tale and passed it on to Byron, who seized upon it as yet another reason to keep Allegra and Claire apart. When, on her fourth birthday, he placed Allegra (as he had promised, or threatened) in a convent, Claire burst out in a furious diatribe against Italian women – 'all pupils of Convents' – accusing them of ignorance and profligacy, describing them as 'bad wives & most unnatural mothers, licentious & ignorant'.[74] Byron retorted to Hoppner: 'The moral part of this letter on the Italians comes with an excellent grace from the writer now living with a <u>man</u> and his <u>wife</u> – and having planted a child in the Foundling, &c.'[75]

Whatever the truth of the matter, the mud was there and sticky; and Claire's presence more than ever an irritant to Mary. It was obvious to Mrs Mason, who was fond of them all, that for the moment at least Claire must cease to be a member of the Shelley household.

For the first time since she had run away from Skinner Street, Claire's solitary and exposed situation now became apparent. Mary had Shelley. Mrs Mason, though no longer rich, had an income and Tatty. Byron, wealthy enough to do what he liked, had charge of Allegra precisely because he could save her from the fate Claire now faced. But Claire had nothing and no one.

The Godwins, meanwhile, were still treading delicately around the

Agnes Porter: a silhouette found at Penrice. By this time she had clearly lost most of her teeth. From a private collection. © Joanna Martin

Family scene at Penrice. In fact, this was painted some years after Agnes Porter had left, but one can assume that little would have changed from her time. © Joanna Martin

Mary Wollstonecraft painted by John Opie in the year she published *A Vindication of the Rights of Women.* © Tate Britain 2008

Robert King, Lord Kingsborough,
artist unknown.

Caroline King, Lady Kingsborough,
artist unknown.

This letter has so strongly agitated me that I know
not what I say but this I feel and know that if
you value my existence you will comply with
my request for I am positive I will never
torment our amiable friend in Charlotte Street.
Is not this a goodly spring my dear Girl
Alas! Poor Bess can say it is a bountiful
one. — — Alas! Poor Bess! — —

Miss Wollstonecraft
Daniel Cunningham Esqre
Stane Street
Dublin
single sheet

Letter from Eliza Bishop to her sister Everina Wollstonecraft, 21 April 1795. As Eliza's mental
state deteriorated, so did her handwriting. © The Bodleian Library, University of Oxford.

Claire Clairmont, 1819, painted by Amelia Curran. © Nottingham City Museums and Galleries (Newstead Abbey)

Lady Mountcashel, Mary Wollestoncraft's old pupil and Claire Clairmont's Mrs Mason.
(Weidenfeld archives)

Opposite page This early image is thought to be a portrait, or possibly a self-portrait, of Mary Shelley,
done around the time of Percy Bysshe Shelley's death, from an Italian private collection.

Allegra. From a contemporary miniature made for Lord Byron and sent to Claire Clairmont. © Iris Origo

The Children of Karpova A.T. with their Governess in the Yard of the House N 41 at Bolshaya Ordynka Street in Moscow, 1897.

Allegra situation – for despite everyone's attempts at concealment, they had inevitably learned the truth. How far did 'Claire's misfortune' remain a secret? Godwin asked his friend Maria Gisborne 'on the part of Mrs G.'. Was she 'desirous that it be unknown'? Did any attachment still exist between her and Byron? Godwin was amazed that Allegra's father had turned out to be Byron – he had assumed that the culprit must be Shelley. Mrs Gisborne assured him that Claire wished the secret kept, that no attachment now existed, and that 'the tenor of her behaviour was decorous and cheerful'.[76] Despite being disappointed in her daughter, Mrs Godwin had always blamed Mary, not Claire, for what had happened; if Claire wished to return, the maternal bosom was ready to receive her.

This being so, Mrs Mason strongly recommended her to return to it. 'I told her my opinion very candidly,' she wrote later, when Shelley had died and Claire really was on her own, 'and said I would rather be obliged to sit behind Mrs G.'s counter from morning till night than be anyone's *dame de compagnie*; but on that subject we never could agree.'[77]

For indeed, as Mrs Mason recognized, those were the options. Her first freshness gone, possessed (or dispossessed) of a child, with no prospects and no dowry: who would marry Claire now? Her bright looks were already fading; Shelley's friend Thomas Medwin, who met her when she was twenty-two, took her for twenty-six or twenty-seven.

> She might have been mistaken for an Italian, for she was a *brunette* with very dark hair and eyes ... Though not strictly handsome at that time, for she had much to struggle with, and mind makes its ravages in the fairest, most, she was engaging and pleasing, and possessed an *esprit de société* rare among our countrywomen. From her personal appearance at that time, I should conceive, that when Byron formed an intimacy with her at Geneva in 1816, she must have been strikingly handsome.[78]

The implication, of course, was that she was less handsome now. But that did not detract from her considerable accomplishments: she spoke fluent French and Italian, as well as being extremely musical. It all pointed in one direction.

Mrs Mason, still well connected, set out to find her a suitable situation. Claire's presence in any respectable English household would have been problematic, but the Tighes' own irregular situation meant that most of their friends and contacts were Italian. Accordingly, on 20 October 1820, Claire became a paying guest – what today we should call an au pair – with a fashionable doctor's family in Florence, the Bojtis. She was not quite a governess, just as Eliza Bishop, when a parlour boarder with Mrs Tew, had been not quite a teacher. Claire would teach the Bojtis' numerous little girls English; in return they would treat her as part of the family and introduce her to their friends. Since they lived opposite the Pitti Palace and knew everyone – Dr Bojti was personal physician to the Grand Duke Ferdinand – it was an excellent opportunity to make useful contacts; and as Signora Bojti was German, Claire could and did take the opportunity to add another language to her repertoire. Her first post in Vienna, when she fled Italy after Shelley's death, was with friends that she had made during this period.

On the surface, her life remained much what it had always been: cultured, social, cosmopolitan. She soon settled down, cheerfully joining in the Bojtis' lively social round, enjoying the music in various Florentine churches, reading widely from books passed on to her by Shelley and Mary, 'Germanizing', and making friends of her own – in particular among the large Russian émigré population, by whom, said Medwin, she was 'much courted'.[79]

Nonetheless a crucial change had taken place, and she knew it. This was the moment when she first noted in her journal Dante's lines about 'the bread of others'. At the end of her first week with the Bojtis she wrote, 'Think of thyself as a stranger and traveller on the earth, to whom none of the many affairs of this world belong and who has no permanent township on the globe.'[80]

The difficulty, for Claire as for many lone women, lay in the question of home – or, rather, of its absence. Since 1815, when Shelley had taken financial and emotional responsibility for her, home for Claire had meant Shelley and Mary. That, however, had always been a contentious situation, with Shelley welcoming her presence while Mary hated it. Now Mary had won her battle; they would remain her friends on condition of being no longer her guardians. Like any recently orphaned daughter, Claire must henceforth face the world alone and provide for herself. Unlike a genuine orphan, it was still open to her to live with her mother and stepfather. But since she refused to consider that, she must rely on employment to provide her with a roof.

In March 1821, Claire's miseries were compounded when she heard of Allegra's placement in the convent of Bagnacavallo, near Ravenna. The news sent her almost mad with rage. She had not seen the child since their month together in August 1818; although she had repeatedly tried to arrange visits, Byron simply ignored her letters. She wrote a furious letter of complaint, berating him for subjecting his daughter to this inferior education, for breaking their agreement that Allegra would remain with one or other parent until she was seven, and accusing him of injuring Allegra as a way of hurting herself, Claire. She dreamed that Tatty Tighe had snatched Allegra from the convent: 'I rejoiced said to S– now she shall never go back again.'[81]

In fact Bagnacavallo was far from the hellhole of her imaginings. Allegra's entry to the convent there brought it to the notice of the local grandees, who began sending their own daughters to join her; but entry was usually at the age of seven, and as the youngest (and richest) pupil, Allegra remained something of a pet. Shelley visited her that July and found her well.

> The traits have become more delicate, and she is much paler, probably from improper food ... She has a contemplative seriousness which, mixed with her excessive vivacity, which has not deserted her, has a very peculiar effect in a child. She is under strict discipline, as may be observed from the immediate obedience she accords to the will of her attendants. This seems contrary to her nature, but I do not think it has been obtained at the expense of much severity ... [She] led me all over the garden, and the convent, running and skipping so fast that I could scarcely keep up with her. She showed me her little bed, and the chair where she sat at dinner, and the *carrozzina* in which she and her favourite companions drew each other along a walk in the garden. I had brought her a bag of sweetmeats, and before eating any of them she gave her companions and each of the nuns a portion. This is not much like the old Allegra.

Shelley's only worry was the religious superstition with which her head was being filled, and of which he, as a militant atheist, sternly disapproved.[82]

It was a comfort, but it did not make up for the fact that Claire herself was still prevented from seeing her daughter, whom she could not visit without Byron's permission. 'I assure you I can no longer resist the internal inexplicable feeling which haunts me that I shall never see her any more,' she told Byron in February 1822.

> I waited two months in the Autumn, expecting from all you professed to see her every week and when on the sudden you would no longer allow it to be a melancholy fearfulness came over me which has never since passed away ... I shall shortly leave Italy, for a new country to enter upon a disagreeable and precarious course of life; I yield in this not to my own wishes, but to the advice of a friend whose head is wiser than mine ... but indeed I cannot go without having first seen and embraced Allegra ... My dear Friend, I conjure you do not make the world dark to me, as if my Allegra was dead.[83]

This new life was being arranged by the indefatigable Mrs Mason, now combing her acquaintance for a proper paid position for Claire. There had been a possibility in Paris, but 'we hear ... that Clare's reception there, as an Englishwoman, is impossible', Shelley told their friend Maria Gisborne, adding that 'our Irish friend is exerting herself to the utmost to find some substitute'.[84] Claire may already have been contemplating Vienna, where her brother Charles – the only person apart from Shelley and Mrs Mason upon whom she could now rely for support – had a teaching position. Indeed, she may have had this in mind from the moment Mrs Mason began to broach ideas regarding her future; it would explain why she was so keen to learn German. However, she did not leave at once; the Shelleys called her back to Pisa and persuaded her to remain in Italy, at least for a while.

When her desperate plea yielded no reply from Byron, Claire began concocting wild scenarios to rescue her daughter from the clutches of the nuns. One was to enter the convent as a pensioner boarder. It would involve converting to Catholicism, but no matter; she would at least be with her daughter. 'She was all prepared a month before Allegra died,'[85] Silsbee noted, which would have been in March 1822, but the scheme foundered on the difficulty of finance; Shelley was the only source of possible money, and he would never have countenanced it. Another plan, to kidnap Allegra from the convent, was also abandoned. Where, the Shelleys wanted to know, did Claire think of bringing her? Not to their house, they assured her in horror.

What Claire did not know was that Shelley had written to Byron, supporting his decision to place Allegra in the convent and dismissing Claire's opposition as 'the result of a misguided maternal affection'.[86] What she did know, because Mary told her, was that when Shelley, citing Claire's misery, had proposed that, after all, Allegra should perhaps be removed from Bagnacavallo, Byron, infuriated,

> vowed that if you annoyed him he would place Allegra in some secret convent; he declared that you should have nothing to do with her, and that he would move heaven and earth to prevent your interference. Lord Byron [Mary went on] is a man of twelve to fifteen thousand a year, he is on the spot, a man reckless of the ill he does others, obstinate to desperation in the pursuance of his plans or his revenge. What then would you do, having Allegra on the outside of the convent walls? Would you go to America? The money we have not, nor does that seem to be your idea. You probably wish to secrete yourself. But Lord Byron would use any means to find you out.

Mary was terrified Byron might even challenge Shelley to a duel: 'I need not enter upon the topic, your own imagination may fill up the picture.' She advised waiting until Byron left the country, which he would have to do at some point to settle his English affairs. 'Nothing remains constant, something may happen – things cannot be worse.'[87]

With no response from Byron, and seemingly no way to arrange a sight of Allegra, Claire, who had returned to Florence far from either Ravenna or Pisa (where Byron had now arrived to spend some time near the Shelleys), began to imagine terrible things. 'It seems to me some time since I have heard any news from Allegra,' she wrote to Mary on 9 April. 'I fear she is sick.'[88]

Previously, her forebodings had proved baseless. But this time she was right. Allegra was suffering from what the doctor called 'little slow fevers' (possibly typhus or malaria). She was bled and seemed to recover; on 15 April she was considered out of danger. But five days later, on 20 April, Byron – who when told of her illness had authorized all necessary medical intervention – heard that she had died 'after a convulsive catarrhal attack'.[89] He described it as a 'stunning and unexpected' blow.[90]

By the time the Shelleys heard the news, Claire was travelling up the coast with their friends Edward and Jane Williams, looking for a house in which they all might spend the summer. The party arrived back in Pisa two days later, but with Byron still near by the Shelleys thought it best to put off telling Claire the devastating truth. Instead, she, Mary and another friend, the romantic adventurer Edward Trelawny, at once set off for Lerici, where a suitable house, Casa Magni, had been located. When Shelley and the Williamses followed a few days later, Claire still knew nothing. In the end, she learned the truth by accident, coming into Jane Williams' room one evening to find everyone discussing how best to break the news. She asked whether Allegra was dead; Shelley stood up and said yes.

At first he was afraid that Claire might lose her reason. Byron offered her complete control over the funeral, but Shelley replied, 'she now seems bewildered; & whether she designs to avail herself further of your permission . . . I know not. In fact, I am so exhausted with the scenes through which I have passed, that I do not dare to ask.'[91]

Despite his unspeakable behaviour towards Claire, Byron cannot be blamed for Allegra's death. As the Shelleys' bitter experience showed, in those days the lives of children were fragile things, snuffed out by untreatable illness regardless of care or love. One of Byron's reasons for selecting Bagnacavallo had been its healthy situation in the clean air of the countryside, far from the debilitating miasmas of the city. For Claire, however, he was and always would be a murderer. The outburst she sent him was so bitter that he – who kept all the letters he ever received – must have destroyed it, for it has not survived. Byron, predictably, rejected guilt. 'I do not know that I have anything to reproach in my conduct, and certainly nothing in my feelings and intentions towards the dead,' he wrote stiffly to Shelley four days after the event.[92] However, the phrase shows that even he realized that his dealings with the living would be seen in a harsher light.

Allegra's death left Byron unexpectedly bereft. 'While she lived,' he told Lady Blessington three years later, 'her existence never seemed necessary to my happiness; but no sooner did I lose her than it appeared to me as if I could not live without her. Even now the recollection is most bitter.'[93]

It was a reaction in some ways the opposite of Claire's, for after her first terrible outpouring of grief, she became surprisingly and rapidly calm – 'more tranquil than when prophesying her disaster', Mary thought.[94] And perhaps this was not so surprising. In many ways she had already done her mourning. If a disaster is long enough awaited its actual occurrence can seem almost a relief. As the years passed with no word from Byron, no sight of her child and no prospect of seeing her, the loss must have felt very like bereavement. Mrs Mason, unsentimental and clear-eyed as ever, commented, 'Had the child lived she would no doubt have been a constant source of misery, and the first shock being over I have no doubt Claire will be more tranquil in future.'[95] Eight or so years later Claire herself wrote, 'At Lerici I know not how it was, I had a stern tranquillity in me suited to the time – the flame of a deep sullen resentment for unmerited misfortunes burned within me and I bid defiance to the dark visitings of misfortune and to the disastrous hauntings of Fate. I said, You cannot inflict more than I will proudly bear.'[96]

Claire returned to Florence. Then on 7 June 1822 she joined the Shelleys, the Williamses and Trelawny (who was, or thought himself, in love with her) at Casa Magni. Mary, once again pregnant, was on edge, the overcrowded house and Claire's presence having their usual effect. On 16 June she miscarried, haemorrhaging so violently that she would have died had not Shelley had the presence of mind to sit her in a bath full of ice. He, meanwhile, was conducting one of his periodic flirtations, this time with Jane Williams, who had the sweet singing voice that he always found beguiling, accompanying herself on the guitar. Claire, Shelley reported, seemed 'restored . . . to tranquility' by Allegra's death. He found her character somewhat altered – she was 'vivacious and talkative', perhaps as a result of Trelawny's obvious admiration. Although he sometimes found her annoying, he liked her in her present mood. It was certainly a relief from Mary, who – as ever hankering after the one unattainable thing: a calm life alone with Shelley – was nervous and depressed.[97]

The Leigh Hunts arrived at Livorno, bringing their six children and burdened with debt; Shelley and Edward Williams sailed from Lerici to meet them in Shelley's new boat, the *Don Juan*. Shelley managed to persuade Byron to help them out and, on 7 July, Mrs Mason, meeting him in Livorno, found him in better health and spirits than she had ever known him, 'his face burnt by the sun, & his heart light that he had succeeded in rendering the Hunts tolerably comfortable'.[98] The next day Shelley and Edward Williams set out to return to Lerici, were caught in a squall and drowned.

For some days it was not clear what had happened. Mary and Jane clung to the hope that, after all, their husbands might have survived. But on 15 July, Trelawny received a letter saying that the bodies had been found three miles from Viareggio. He passed the news to Claire, who wrote to Leigh Hunt, still at Lerici: 'I entreat you, give me some counsel, or to arrange some method by which they may know it. I know not what further to add except that their case is desperate in every respect, and Death would be the greatest kindness to us all.'[99]

Claire's life had been lived between two triangles, anchored on one side by Shelley, on the other by Allegra (or the thought of Allegra). Now both her anchors were gone and she drifted, directionless and penniless.

In theory Shelley's death should have made her financially independent, for he had left her £12,000 in his will – £6,000 in 1815, an extra £6,000 when Allegra was born. For the moment, however, this meant nothing; his father, Sir Timothy, was still alive and until he died his son's will could not take effect. His death was 'an horizon which retreats as one advances', as Claire despairingly observed to Mary[100] – and until it happened (which would not be for another twenty-two years) she was confined to the life chronicled in so many novels of the time: of present penury and endlessly delayed expectations. She had hoped to earn some money translating Goethe's *Memoirs* (that March, Byron had offered £100 to anyone who would do this for him) but as soon as he discovered who the translator was to be, he lost interest in the project. Unless she could find a husband – and 'I might wait to all Eternity for a party'[101] – she must go a-governessing.

For all these years the prospect had hung over her; only Shelley's kindness, and her own obstinacy, had enabled her to hold out as long as she had. In London, in 1816, she had avoided it first by removing to Lynmouth at Shelley's expense, then by flinging herself at Byron and so defusing Mary's jealousy. The Bojtis had been a halfway house, a step towards the inevitable. There had been the situation in Paris mentioned by Shelley to Maria Gisborne, which had fallen through because of French antipathy towards the English. Claire herself had sabotaged another attempt to place her: Lady Blessington told Medwin she had taken a great interest in Allegra's mother and had all but found her a position as a 'humble companion', but Miss Clairmont 'was too noble to conceal her story from the ear of her intended benefactress, before she entered on her office, and in consequence of her sincerity, the affair was broken off'.[102] Now, however, the days of prevarication were over.

As it happened, a 'party' presented himself almost at once: Trelawny. In the terrible days after the bodies were washed up, he had been a rock of strength, with an unerring ability to judge the appropriate word or action: the ceremonial cremation on the beach and, following it, the only thing that could have been of any comfort to Mary in her agony, a long and unstinting eulogy to Shelley. 'He did not attempt to console me, that would have been too cruel . . . but he launched forth into as it were an overflowing & eloquent—of my divine Shelley – until I was almost happy that I was thus unhappy to be fed by the praise of him.' By contrast Mary found Mrs Mason distressingly cold, 'though she felt his loss keenly, & would be very glad to serve me'.[103] Mrs Mason's clear-eyed appraisals were rarely comforting, however well she meant.

With Claire, too, the uninhibited Trelawny found the needful transforming touch. Just before she left Pisa they spent a single perfect day together – a day that would constitute, throughout the anonymous years that followed, a sort of amulet: a source of hope and a proof that she had truly been who she had been, had truly done what she had done, known whom she had known.

Precisely what happened, neither of them ever made clear. Did they become lovers, in the technical sense of the term? It seems improbable. Claire, of all people, knew only too well what the consequences of that might be. But whatever took place, it became ever after for them both a moment of profound meaning and promise. 'I loved you from the first day – nay, before I saw you,' Trelawny wrote three months later: 'you loathed & heaped on me contumelies and neglect till we were about to separate, – Claire, I love you and do what you will – I shall remain deeply interested in you.'[104] A few days later he added, 'Well I have suffered real and solid pain enough for the few moments of pleasure you granted me.'[105]

Perhaps she was too drained to cope with more emotion so soon; perhaps it was impossible to take seriously such an obvious self-dramatist. Corsairs and giaours, however alluring, rarely make ideal life partners, and perhaps, as with Byron, it was precisely this glamorous untameability that, for Claire, constituted much of his attraction. 'If [Trelawny] had been different . . . I might have been as happy as I am now wretched,' she noted in her journal three years later, on the anniversary of their fleeting epiphany.[106] But if Trelawny had been different, they might never have found each other.

On her own and without income, she decided to make for Vienna, where she would be provided with a family, in the shape of her kind and helpful brother Charles, and where, Mary hoped, she might 'become really attached to some one'.[107] Not least, in Vienna she might hope to avoid the gossip that otherwise seemed inescapable. Governesses and radical politics did not mix. Eliza Bishop's experiences at Pembroke during the days of Mary Wollstonecraft's notoriety showed what Claire might expect in even the furthest-flung corners of Britain, in the unlikely eventuality that she could find someone to employ her. Indeed, she had already lost Lady Blessington's post on account of her connections.

Claire was not alone in hoping to blot out the past and construct a new future, by burying herself in distant lands. A good many young women, finding themselves suddenly removed from comfort and respectability and plunged into the necessity of governessing, preferred the anonymous adventure of life abroad to the miseries of *déclassement* at home. Miss Amelia Lyons, who embarked for St Petersburg after the sudden death of her father, the Senior Examiner of Public Accounts, in 1849, found that 'the Russians are extremely fond of being surrounded by a large society of strangers, especially foreigners, and as English persons are regarded with distinguished favour, I had no doubt that whenever I should propose to accompany any family into the interior, my proposal would be accepted with pleasure'.[108] Miss Lyons did not admit in so many words that she would accompany them as a governess, but there was no other way a young Englishwoman could have travelled to Russia without chaperones, companions or letters of introduction. Only as a governess could an English young lady hope to experience such exotica as a ride in a *vostok*, the supremely uncomfortable, cushioned and enclosed Russian sled, in which the unfortunate passengers spent the journey tossed from side to padded side as their conveyance, pulled by a team of horses, bounced from rut to rut on the appalling Russian roads.

So fascinating (despite these discomforts) did Miss Lyons find Russia, and so insatiable was the demand there for English governesses, that in 1853 her younger sister Juliana decided to follow her. This demand would continue for the rest of the century. The novelist Vladimir Nabokov, writing of the same milieu – fifty years later, but in many respects unchanged – describes 'a bewildering sequence of English nurses and governesses',[109] as well as a French mademoiselle.

Since Claire already knew a good many Russians from her time with the Bojtis, that vast country must already have seemed a potential destination. Nevertheless, Russia, with its unknown language, alien script and unimaginable icebound expanses, represented a daunting leap into the unknown. By comparison, Vienna promised a comparatively gentle introduction to her new life. Charles would meet her off the coach and had made arrangements for her reception. He was earning more than enough to live on as a peripatetic teacher, but did not advise this for Claire, 'for she could not as I do, scamper through the streets in every species of winter weather, so as to squeeze in sometimes 10 lessons a day, from 6 in the morning till 8 at night, without eating'.[110] Much better, he advised, to stay with a family. There were several possibilities, from which he had selected the Henicksteins, whom she already knew from Florence. As for her worries that it would not be respectable for a young woman to journey from Pisa to Vienna all alone, and that she should wait for a family or elderly lady to chaperone her, they could be dismissed; the Viennese would only admire her courage. Viennese society might have its own rigid rules and class distinctions, but they were not English rules.[111]

Claire's stay in Vienna started well. The Henicksteins received her warmly, as a friend rather than a companion or governess, and various members of the household requested English lessons. 'I have made numerous acquaintances, all rich and fashionable and have been received with the greatest politeness and hospitality – I am perpetually in company – at the theatre, the Corso or dinner parties,' she told Jane Williams; and although she lamented the loss of '<u>my dear den</u> that I had with you', these were nonetheless pleasant distractions.[112] It was not long, however, before everything began to fall apart, both within the family and outside it. In the Henickstein house, soon after her arrival, Charles noted that 'the Old grandmother died; an old servant died; Mrs H's sister-in-law dying; one of the daughters extremely ill; the bridegroom of the other, to whom she was to have been married in a week or two, changes his mind and leaves the poor girl in the lurch; so that you may easily suppose poor Claire in the heart of all these gossipping folks has had enough to do & think of'.[113] No doubt English lessons were low on the family's list of priorities.

What was worse, it appeared that, even in Vienna, the names Godwin, Wollstonecraft, Shelley and Byron were enough to damn by association. Following the debacle with Lady Blessington, Claire had taken the greatest pains to keep her story secret. But her new-found discretion was no match for Metternich's police state. Created in 1821 to counter the revolutionary tendencies so distressingly visible elsewhere in Europe, it encouraged informers; one of these sent a note concerning Charles Clairmont to Count Joseph Sedlnitzky, president of the Supreme Police and Censorship Office. The note, which was in English, anonymous and undated, accused 'Claremont' of coming to Vienna ostensibly to teach English but in reality for some subversive purpose. It identified him as 'son of the authoress of the "rights of Women" – his father was prosecuted in England some years ago for sedition – his sister married Shelly – the author of Queen Mab–Shelly was a deist – was deprived of his rights of a father by the Lord Chancellor of England – was the intimate of . . . Lord Byron'. The note went on to claim that 'Claremont' was not Charles's real name.[114]

The upshot was professional and personal disaster for both Charles and Claire. In addition to Charles's papers not being in order, it appeared that there existed an Act specifically 'prohibiting any foreign young woman from entering a Family as Governess, in order to facilitate the placing [of] young officers' daughters brought up at a Pension under the direction of the Emperor'.[115] Charles and Claire were at one point given five days to leave Vienna; the efforts of some well-connected friends, who vouched for them and argued their side of the case, lengthened this, after enormous effort, to four weeks. Fortunately, before that period had elapsed, the matter was more or less resolved. After that, Charles was free to stay in Vienna; two years later Sedlnitzky himself approached him for English lessons. Eventually Charles married an Austrian girl and spent the rest of his life in the city.

However, until the issue was settled they could have no peace; and while they were nervously waiting, Claire became seriously ill. Mrs Mason described her symptoms to her own doctor, who concluded that she must be tubercular and held out little hope; Charles put it down to Glands.

Stranded, sick and penniless in a foreign city where she was forbidden to work, Claire believed that even if she survived her illness she might die of starvation. Mrs Mason was so worried that she even wrote to Byron, asking whether he might help – he did, after all, owe Claire something – but received a refusal so insulting that she was forced to revise her hitherto favourable opinion of him. Mary, who could ill afford it (Shelley's father was refusing to support her or Percy Florence), sent £12; Charles gently declined it on Claire's behalf. Claire should depend on him, if anyone, 'as I am unencumbered & accustomed to pinching & you are the very opposite of both'.[116]

Claire did eventually recover and, ignoring Mrs Mason's urgent advice to return to England, pushed on to Russia, in what Trelawny termed a 'compulsive emigration to the north'.[117] She had, Charles informed Mary, 'almost concluded an agreement with the Countess Zotoff, daughter of Prince Kurakine'.[118] Claire thought the pay low, though at £75 it compared well with what other governesses earned, but the countess was agreeable, if unreliable, and Claire was to be rather a companion than a governess to her two daughters. These were beauties of fourteen and sixteen, and with any luck they would marry early, after which the countess, 'whose health is not robust', might decide to leave for Italy, or some other warm climate.[119] The Zotoffs, with Claire in tow, duly left Vienna on 22 March 1823 and by that July had arrived at their country house in Brody, Galicia, near the border between Poland and Ukraine. In September they expected to leave for St Petersburg, where they would spend the winter in the comfort of the city.

After Claire's departure for Russia no one heard from her for more than a year. We know she got on well with the Zotoffs – one of her charges, Betsy, remained a friend for the rest of her life. However, by the spring of 1824 she had moved on to Moscow as governess to the Posnikov children, nine-year-old Ivan, or Vanya, whom Claire called Johnny, and five-year-old Dunia.

Zachar Nikolaievitch Posnikov was a successful lawyer; like the Zotoffs and all other well-off Russian families, the Posnikovs spent the winter in the city, then migrated to the country as soon as the roads became passable after the thaw.

Claire's days during the winters in town were the unending routine familiar to every governess. 'From eleven till four I teach my children, then we dine – at five we rise from table – they have half an hour's dawdling for play it cannot be called, as they are in the drawing room and they learn two hours more. At eight we drink tea, and then they go to bed which is never over till eleven because all must have their hair curled which takes up an enormous time.'[120] In the country, however, teaching was combined with social and intellectual activities in a pleasant round that bestowed a peace of mind she had never before recorded. The Posnikovs' country place, Islaysky, on the Moskva river, was near enough to Moscow for Zachar Nikolaievitch to travel back and forth, and for guests to visit from the city. It possessed a flower garden, orangeries, guesthouses and broad acres of meadow and woodland, and was surrounded by what Claire calls 'balconies', covered verandas where much of the household's life took place. 'We sit in the Balcony – we go to the dairy and gather strawberries, sit in the Balcony there. When we come home . . . Johnny goes on horseback. Drink tea in the Balcony – then go downstairs and write in the lower Balcony . . . My whole day goes in a stroll from Balcony to Balcony.'[121]

Another pleasure of country life was the Posnikovs' young German-French tutor, Hermann Gambs, who came from Alsace. 'Never any where did quarrelling flourish as in Russia – every house is in a state of civil war – as every child has its governess, and each governess is of a different nation, each pursues her own mode and method, and such a system affords no guages [sic],'[122] Claire told Jane. But despite this description, Claire's relations with Gambs were very far from 'civil war'.

[He] is a great resource to me; in such a country as Russia, Where nothing but the vulgarest people are to be met, a cultivated mind is the greatest treasure ... You may imagine how delighted he was to find me, so different from every thing around him and capable of understanding what had been sealed up so long in his mind as treasures too precious to be wasted on the coarse russian soil.[123]

Claire's journal for the summer of 1825 is full of their joint activities.

Read Wilhelm Meister – After breakfast walk with Dunia, John Mr Gambs, Nicolas Catherine and Helene to the Mills. The country round is only rurally pretty, yet it fills me with delight, and I sat at my window this morning, and listened with melancholy pleasure to the sound of the wind among the neighbouring trees – it recalled to my mind the breaking waves upon the shores of Lerici ... After dinner Dunia digs her garden and I read Wilhelm Meister ... After tea some officers come. Sing with Olga Michailovna and Mr Gambs. Then walk with Catherine on the bank of the river and climb up and down the Hills. After supper long talk with Marie Ivanovna and Mr G. upon astronomy.[124]

Claire and Gambs often combined their charges as well as their efforts into a sort of school. They alternated in giving regular history lectures, which seem to have been attended by the entire household. Claire summarizes one of hers on ancient history: 'Description of Babylon. Floating Garden. Asia Minor. The Kingdom of Troy, Phrygia and Lydia. The Hatred between the Greeks and the Trojans a commercial hatred,'[125] while on another day, 'Miss Kakorchkine gave the Lecture upon History instead of Monsieur Gambs.'[126]

Her friends, hearing of this delightful fellow, wondered whether at last Claire might not have met a suitable husband. But as with Peacock, it seemed Claire could not be seduced by sensible suitors. She told Jane Williams that although 'His attachment to me is extreme ... I have taken the very greatest care to explain to him that I cannot return it in the same degree; this does not make him unhappy and therefore our friendship is of the utmost importance to both.'[127] Mrs Mason, however, did not believe this complex explanation, characteristically regretting that 'the German tutor was not rich enough to marry'.[128]

Alongside this life of cultured pleasure ran another, of restlessness and (to European eyes) outlandish squalor. The daily life of a Russian household was 'always the same scene of bustle, confusion and quarrelling',[129] Claire told Jane Williams. And at night 'they move their beds almost perpetually, roving up and down all the rooms; be it drawing room or cabinet, it is all one to them, the morning is a curious picture – You meet a hundred beds, (that is to say, mattresses, pillows, sheets &c) born [sic] upon so many heads, and returning like sheep to the fold, to their respective rooms.'[130] Yet although these beds might look comfortable, appearances could be deceptive. More than once Claire was driven out of her bed by 'Bugs the torment of Russia' and 'escaped only from them by sitting up the whole night in an armchair'.[131]

Bedbugs, invisible but disgusting, could be seen as a sort of metaphor for Russian life. Both Claire and Amelia Lyons remarked on the contrast between its public elegance and private sluttishness. Although they bathed once a week, Russian ladies saw no need to wash between times and 'will sometimes wear during the whole day a loose dressing-gown in which they have passed the night, their hair in curlpapers'.[132] Meals were copious: soup, then hors d'oeuvres – caviar, pickled herring, radishes – then meat, vegetables, poultry with salted cucumbers, salad, pastry, ices. But as the kitchens were a *verst* from the house, the dinner, on horseback or in a coach, might be espied from afar, trotting towards the drawing-room windows: 'I shall never forget a plumb-pudding they made in my honour, at a country house, coming along in the rain, on an old blind stumbling mare, shaking to pieces, tumbling into bits, into the mud, at every step and two ragged, dirty boys carrying boats of the sauce ... Naturally, only half the pudding and the sauce arrived.'[133] Nor were the cups and plates from which they ate entirely clean. 'Every plate, glass or cup is wiped with as much precaution as though it had not been washed since it had last been used, [but] with all this parade of cleanliness it is impossible to move a single article of furniture without being smothered in a cloud of dust.'[134] The reason for the wiping was revealed by yet another English governess working in Russia, who heard a peasant explain that 'it is a sin to kill [insects], because God has given them to us'. Unless one wiped or washed crockery before using it, this lady explained, one risked swallowing 'a little animal'.[135]

Something Claire found even harder to cope with was the almost total lack of solitude. Given that solitude was precisely what most governesses complained of, this was ironic. Russian households, however, with their constant press and turbulence, were very different from the cold rigidities of English middle-class life. As well as her official charges, there were 'no less than twenty young girls, or children in our house that I have something to do with – Some of them protégées, others relations, some the daughters of some favourite washer-woman, others foundlings – so you may imagine what fights, what quarrels, what disputes go on – they are merciless to you if you are anything less than savage with them.'[136] Once the long day of teaching, from eight in the morning till five in the afternoon, was over, and the daily walk had been succeeded by tea or supper, and Claire had washed out the delicate linen that she couldn't trust to the servants, calm remained as distant as ever. She took refuge, when she could, in the bathhouse. 'Here I was very happy – reclining in the warmth of the soft water; and listening alone to the wind amid the trees; the green shade which the surrounding grove threw upon the room.'[137]

Another distressing aspect of Russian life was that all teaching was assumed to involve beating.

> The only people who are not whipped in a Russian house are the Master and Mistress and the foreigners – for the slightest fault whipping is always threatened, and the same with the children – It is a very lucky day, when boxes on the ear are only given ... I may safely say the Russians and I are always at cross purposes – they pull one way, and I another – they educate a child by making the external work upon the internal, which is, in fact, nothing but an education fit for monkies [sic].[138]

Claire found it particularly distressing to be forced to witness the effects of such treatment 'upon little amiable creatures who, if otherwise managed, would be delights instead of torments'.[139]

This violence was the normal custom of the country. Sufferers, both serfs and children, seem generally to have accepted it, albeit gloomily. The novelist Ivan Turgenev, who was born in 1818 and so must have been an almost exact contemporary of Vanya Posnikov, grew so frightened of his mother's thrashings, administered daily for no reason that he could understand, that he determined to run away. Creeping out of the house at midnight, he ran into his German tutor, who, when the matter was explained, comforted him and gently promised that he would never be beaten again. Clearly, for Russian children at this time, European tutors and governesses constituted a bulwark against native savagery.

Turgenev ever after hated his mother, but at least he did not kill her. A Swiss governess, looking for her charges' parents when they failed to appear one morning, found them almost beheaded in their bedroom, a revenge silently executed during the night by some serfs who had been maltreated once too often.[140]

Despite this violence, Claire seems to have formed a good relationship with Marie Ivanovna, as Madame Posnikov was always known. Like all mothers, she could not resist interfering in her children's education. But without the peculiar social tensions that made mother–governess relations so painful in England, her interference did not carry the resonances of humiliation that made British governesses' lives such a misery. Naturally this interference annoyed her, but Claire was able to joke about it with Marie Ivanovna – something that would have been inconceivable in England.

> The lady with whom I live is of such an extremely weak character, the only good she does me is to make me laugh a hundred times a day – Every minute she changes her opinion; and then she has such an adoration of instruction and Knowledge, that she can't possibly spend a minute without recalling some *souvenir historique*, and she crams her son's head with chronological, typographical and geographical facts to such a degree, that he told her the other day, 'sur mon honneur, Maman, si vous continuez à me persécuter avec la litterature, comme vous faites, Je vous jure ma parole que Je me fracasserai la tête contre la muraille' [I tell you, Mamma, if you go on persecuting me with literature like this, I swear I'll break my head against the wall] ... The time she spent away was the only pleasant time I ever spent in Russia, as the children were entirely under my care – I wrote to her that I had diminished John's lessons, and notwithstanding the friendship I had for her, I was actually cruel enough to allow the poor boy to eat breakfast, without the

aid of historical recollections, and that in the space of two months, he had progressed so much from learning fewer words and thinking more, that ... he could now say a sentence to the person opposite to him, without twisting all the buttons off his waistcoat, or breaking the first thing that might come to hand.[141]

No governess in England could ever have written such a letter to her employer.

It was not that Russian employers saw governesses as equals. But – like serfs, for that matter – they were always fellow human beings, with personal lives and opinions and, as such, worthy of interest. In January 1827, Princess Galitzine, for whom Claire was then working, 'related to me the conversation which had taken place at dinner about me. The Prince Alexander and the Count Rastopchin said my dislike to men was affected, that they were sure I was always falling in love, and that either one or the other had only to make love to me for a day or two and I should become *amoureuse folle*.'[142] In England, in the unlikely event that such a conversation had taken place, no mistress would ever have retailed it to its subject; while any English governess, hearing of such remarks and remembering her ladylike antecedents, would have felt herself honour-bound to take mortal offence. Claire simply found it ridiculous, remarking, 'I must really take great care of my poor heart.'[143]

If she had taken offence, however, she would have been expected to say so. '[The Russians] are so ignorant and vulgar that, at least, I may say what I please, while in England, I should be obliged to follow their opinion, and not my own,'[144] she reported in 1824. For in the Russian approach to personal relations, sincerity ranked far above politeness. In contrast to the meek subservience demanded in England, 'The mark of your dignity here is that you dare dispute and upbraid them.'[145] A French maid who had boxed her mistress's ears after being slapped for pulling her hair while dressing it, far from being dismissed as would instantly have happened in Europe, was given thirty silver roubles and a new gown to buy her silence, and was still employed by the same family several years later.[146]

In October 1825, Claire's pleasant life with the Posnikovs came abruptly to an end, when she helplessly watched little Dunia die of what sounds like diphtheria. Gambs left Moscow for a position in the country; Claire, left alone in Moscow as winter set in and reminded by Dunia's death of her own dead daughter, became increasingly depressed. 'I struggle as hard as I can against the inroads of deterioration,' she sighed to Mary, 'but I feel already as if I were grown a vile common creature; all my faculties are annihilated ... I feel at every step like a person who has lost his way.'[147]

This sense of disorientation was heightened by the constant care necessary to conceal her true identity. Russia, no less than Austria, was a police state; she could not risk another debacle of the kind that had occurred in Vienna. If she used the post, she preferred to send her letters under cover to John Hunt, Leigh Hunt's innocuously named brother; but this was still dangerous, because censorship was strictly enforced, and letters were opened and read. More often she would wait until some member of the English community returned home, and confide her mail to them. Even then she could not always feel secure; she told Jane Williams that she dared not write to either Mary or her mother through one of her letter-carriers because he was 'tho' a tolerably good man, yet a great Aristocrat' and 'I have no inclination to let the name of Shelley and Godwin go thro' his hands.'[148]

Ironically, it was one of these safe carriers who eventually gave away her secret. Claire had sent Jane a letter by a Miss Trewin; Mrs Godwin got wind of it and, naturally agog to hear about Claire's life in Moscow, asked her to dinner. Mrs Mason, unaware of Claire's political difficulties, thought her precautions excessive and was 'glad to hear Mrs G-'s mind has been tranquillized about her daughter by the prohibited visit, in which no doubt she asked ten thousand questions – what would have been the motive for the prohibition?'[149]

When Miss Trewin returned to Moscow, however, the 'motive for the prohibition' became all too clear. The enigmatic Miss Clairmont's scandalous connections were soon a subject of gossip and came to the notice of a stern and much respected Scottish professor whose recommendation – or disrecommendation – was law among possible employers. 'You may imagine this man's horror when he heard who I was; [t]hat the charming Miss Clairmont, the model of good sense accomplishments and good taste was brought up, issued from the very den of freethinkers ... He cannot explain to himself how I can be so extremely delightful and yet so detestable.'[150] Even Moscow, it seemed, had not been far enough.

This fatal news broke just as Claire was looking for a new position. She had been hoping to take over 'the education of an only daughter, the child of a very rich family, where the Professor reigns despotic ... the mother and father had been running after me these two yrs'. But 'now all is broken off, because the scruples of my Professor do not allow of it. God knows he says what Godwinish principles she might not instil ... If this is only the beginning what may be the end!'[151]

Although Claire was always prone to melodramatic exaggeration, this time her dismay was understandable. Without employment, she had no home: a daunting prospect in the Russian winter. Another English governess had the previous year left Moscow for the southern city of Odessa with the notion of setting up a boarding house there; the climate was better, and if it went well it would provide both an income and a home; Claire had been planning to join her. Unfortunately the venture had failed, and rather than return north, the lady committed suicide. Claire wondered whether that would be her fate, too. In the event she dragged out another year in Moscow. 'It is four years that I have lived among strangers,' she noted in February 1827. 'The voices that spoke to my youth, the faces that were then around me, are almost forgotten; and not to be able to remember them augments what I feel.'[152]

She was saved her in her hour of need by the Kaisaroff family, to whom she remained eternally grateful. When she first met Madame Kaisaroff, 'I was a solitary and uncertain wanderer upon the face of the earth ... my mind was in that state of destitution and misery which are the surest roads to Vice ... She gave me a home, she gave me consideration and kindness, and beyond all these sympathy in my thoughts and feelings.'[153] The Kaisaroffs had a sulky twelve-year-old daughter called Natasha who now became Claire's chief charge, though she also taught the numerous children of Princess Galitzine.

The Kaisaroffs offered not just employment, but a way back to the sun. They were off to take the baths at Teplitz, in Bohemia; Claire was to accompany them, all found, in return for giving English lessons to Natasha. She jumped at the offer, hoping (since she had money put by and the trip would involve no expense) to buy some clothes and, at long last, a ticket back to England. However, the arrangement did not work out as everyone had hoped. In the coach Natasha took over Claire's space as well as her own, forcing Claire to travel squeezed into a corner, and this led to a falling-out with the Kaisaroffs. They persuaded Claire to continue on to Teplitz, where she could at least take the cure, although they would no longer pay her expenses. The dispute was later resolved; she remained with the Kaisaroffs, and Natasha, until 1832. Meanwhile, however, paying for her return to England was problematic: could Mary lend her some money? Perhaps she could, for that autumn Claire returned home, for the first time in ten years, in the company of the wonderfully named Miss Esperance Sylvestre, governess to the Duchess of Saxe Weimar.[154]

All this time, Trelawny had been much in her mind. She wrote him many letters, though he rarely replied; she looked out for his name in the papers and often mentioned him in her journal and correspondence. Trelawny, too, cherished the memory of their last meeting. 'Dearest', he wrote, on hearing of her imminent return,

> *... how to reply to such a letter – beautiful it is – but its melancholy strain vibrates on my heart and fills me with sadness! How undeserved is your fate – all goodness yourself you have met with nothing but unprovoked ill – it is ever the fate of the gentle and worthy ... But I will not indulge this baneful feeling of melancholy despondency which you have excited in my bosom ... my dear Claire, rather by shaking it from you encourage me to preserve myself from its baneful influence ... Write to me – my sweet Claire – good night Dear – and remember that I at least am*
> *Your Dear friend E.J.T.*[155]

One of the more bizarre (and counter-productive) aspects of the letters that Claire had written to Byron, during those months of her pregnancy when she was still hoping that he might yet love her, was the bathetically domestic tone they sometimes took – so blindingly inappropriate, considering the addressee, as to be almost comic. 'You should have a nice house to live in; my nice little girl (I hope it will be a girl) to educate ... & we should have nice Poems written by you & copied by little me.'[156]

Now Trelawny, that hardy fighter who had survived the Greek war in a cave near Missolonghi and taken the thirteen-year-old sister of his companion-in-arms for his bride, evoked the same cosy sentiments.

Thus in 1826, when there had been talk of his returning to England, she adjured Jane Williams to 'take care of Trelawney and do not let him get his feet wet'.[157]

They met in December 1828. On 1 January 1829 he sent her the following:

> *Dear Claire,*
>
> *Why will you not dedicate one spare hour to me? – nothing gives me so much pleasure as your letters – I prefer them infinitely to oral communion – particularly as you are becoming so horridly prudish – and sister-like insensible.*
>
> *I consider you very fish-like – bloodless – and insensible – you are the counterpart of Werter – a sort of bread butter and worsted stockings – like Charlotte fit for 'suckling fools and chronicling small beer.'*
>
> *Adieu old Aunt*
>
> *J. Edward Trelawny.*[158]

To Mary he wrote: 'She talked of nothing but worsted stockings and marrying – the only doubt in my mind is which is worse – but if I am condemned to one – I think I must take the former.'[159]

The years of denying her former self had done their work too well. Shelley's girl, freethinking, reckless, heedless of convention, had vanished – if, indeed, she had ever truly existed. The pretence of being a correct lady governess was a pretence no longer. She had become the real thing.

The September after this fatal meeting, Claire returned to the Kaisaroffs, who by then were in Dresden. They spent the winter there, then went on to Nice, still with Claire in tow. She left them the following year and returned to Italy, seeing much of Mrs Mason while tutoring the daughters of English families in Pisa and Florence. Yet even the sun and the proximity of friends could not reconcile her to the relentless loneliness of a governess's depersonalized existence. She had solitude now – enough and to spare – and, as with so many governesses, it filled her with despair.

From Morning till Night, month after month and year after year never to see a person one cares a pin to see; to be ever surrounded by demons who torment you without ceasing; to have one's soul ever full of rage and despair. What a life! Has Hell any thing worse to offer? I frankly confess I am driven to such a pitch of frenzy by it, there is no crime however dreadful, there is no horror I would not perpetrate to deliver myself from my present state.[160]

That was written in 1832; Trelawny, who had seen her the previous year, when she was still with the Kaisaroffs, was shocked by her deterioration. She was still only thirty-four, but 'her spirits are broken and she looks 50', he told Mary.[161] Even so, he asked her to live with him and take charge of his three-year-old daughter Zella by his Greek child bride. Claire refused, then thought better of it; but by that time he had changed his mind. However, she stayed in touch with Trelawny and when she came to live in Italy kept a familial eye on Zella.

By 1838 she was back in England and by 1840, now aged forty-two, was living in London, waiting for Sir Timothy to die ('I can never think of him without seeing his grey hair growing into fine clustering brown locks ... and the most glowing pink creeping over his once aged but now youthful cheek'[162]) while grinding out a living as a daily (rather than a live-in) governess.

The advantage of this arrangement was that the governess could retain her own life and friends; the disadvantage, that rent, food and travel all had to be paid for out of one's earnings. Daily governesses charged by the hour, and as with other itinerant teachers such as music and drawing masters, the greater the number of their pupils, the more they could earn. However, the logistics of travelling around a city like London were peculiarly difficult. Vienna, where Charles Clairmont had spent his days running from one pupil to another, was small and concentrated, but London was far larger and far more spread out. With one pupil in Belgravia and another in Richmond, a disproportionate amount of Claire's time was spent on horse-drawn omnibuses.

This is now my life – I go by nine to Mrs Kitchener's where I give lessons till one – then I rush to the top of Wilton Place and get a Richmond Omnibus and go to Richmond to give a lesson to the Cohen's [sic] – their daughter is going to be married to a Genoese and must have an Italian lesson every day that she may speak Italian when she gets with her husband to Genoa. That vile Omnibus takes two hours to get to Richmond and the same to come back and so with giving my lessons I am never at home before seven – I get no dinner – nothing within my lips from eight in the morning till seven at night.[163]

Within a few years the arrival of railways would transform itineraries such as this; by 1855, for example, trains from Waterloo regularly stopped at Richmond. But by then Claire was no longer a governess, for in 1844 Sir Timothy Shelley at last died, releasing the long-awaited legacy. 'My first emotion was utter disbelief,' Claire confessed to Mary. 'The idea of that man has been my companion so long, it seems tearing half my mind out, to convince me that I have no occasion to think of him any longer.'[164]

An unerring nose for a bad investment ensured that she would never achieve the comparatively easy life that the money might have provided had she been well advised. But at least she had enough to live on, if only in a small way. Eventually she made her home in Italy, whose sunny skies she had so craved during the endless Russian winters.

In their post-Shelley lives, both Claire and Mary became pillars of respectability. Mary turned to Anglicanism and became a literary lioness, revered both for her associations and her achievements; while in the 1850s Claire joined the Roman Catholic Church. Perhaps she should have done so earlier. Atheism was all very well for a Godwin or a Shelley, but it was too much for Claire. In every way it was a bad creed for a governess – unwelcome to employers, unforgiving for the non-believer. Religion, with its words of comfort and resignation, might have eased her suffering.

In the absence of any surviving children of her own, she interested herself greatly in her nephews and nieces – both Percy Florence, Mary's surviving son by Shelley (who did not like her), and also Charles's four sons and daughters by his Viennese wife Antonia, or Tonie. There were two boys, Charles Junior and Wilhelm, and two girls, Clara or Cleary, and Pauline.

In 1864, living in Hungary where her brother had a farm, an unmarried Pauline Clairmont gave birth to a daughter whom she christened Johanna Maria Georgina, adding the surname Hanghegyi – a Hungarian approximation to Clairmont.

Pauline came to Florence in 1870, planning to board with Claire and earn a little money by giving lessons. However, it was not until the spring of 1871 that she told her aunt about her illegitimate daughter. Perhaps she did not know about Allegra: if she had, she might have been less nervous about confessing all to the religious old lady Claire had become. But if she expected a rebuff, she was in for a surprise. To Pauline's dismay Claire – perhaps envisioning a second Allegra, miraculously restored to life – on the contrary proposed to take the child over. 'You will bring the child here and I will adopt her,'[165] she announced.

Pauline hated this idea and bitterly resented Claire's appropriation of Georgina. Georgina, too, was reluctant to come to Italy. Nevertheless, because Claire was now the one with the income – that is, with the power – and Pauline the dependant, she had unwillingly to comply. Claire's will instructed her executor to sell all her letters from Shelley, Godwin and Mary, and invest them in Italian stock at 5 per cent. The interest was to be paid to Pauline and, on her death, the whole amount was to go to 'my dear Georgina Hanghegyi who is living with me'.[166]

Two quite distinct tragedies dominated Claire Clairmont's life. One, the loss of Allegra, made worse by Byron's vindictiveness, was the product of her peculiar personal circumstances. In some ways it resembled, as we shall see, such stories as Caroline Norton's and Nelly Weeton's. But Claire's extraordinary trajectory was unique to her.

The second tragedy, however – the loss of self – was one that plagued almost all governesses. Who was the real Claire Clairmont? Was she the brave, foolhardy innocent who shared Shelley's and Mary's great adventure, or Trelawny's 'old Aunt', the sad spinster fixated on bathetic domestic detail? Circumstances dictated that the aunt prevailed, but was the brave girl wholly stifled? And what did the aunt think of her?

Almost all governesses' lives were split in this way, into a bright beginning and a drab remainder. Some, like Claire herself, must always have been aware that when they reached adulthood they would have to fend for themselves – and that this would mean governessing. Few lives, of course, involved quite such a violent contrast as hers between the *before* and the *after*. More typical, doubtless, were stories such as those brought to light by the Governesses' Benevolent Institution, founded in 1841, which imply a lifelong drabness: 'Devoted all her earnings to the education of her five nieces, who all became governesses'; 'Supported her mother during fourteen years, and educated three younger sisters, who are now governesses . . . '[167]

Of course, not all governesses had been raised in this life-sapping expectation. Many had grown up with every expectation of comfort, only to be forced into the schoolroom by financial catastrophe. But whatever their circumstances, virtually all moved from a youth of material and (even more importantly) emotional security to a lonely life dominated by insecurity of every kind.

The scenario with which we are inevitably most familiar is the one that held the most appeal for novelists: of the well-to-do brought low by financial catastrophe. It appears in its purest form in Frances Hodgson Burnett's *A Little Princess* – though this is not, strictly speaking, a governess novel, since Burnett's heroine, Sara Crewe, is still a child at boarding school in London when the catastrophe occurs. Her father's business partner in India mysteriously disappears with all their assets, and Sara, formerly rich and pampered, finds herself in an instant penniless. She is immediately removed from her comfortable quarters to the servants' bare attic, where she must thenceforth work for her keep, and feel grateful not to be thrown into the street.

Sara accepts her fate with the socially approved resignation endorsed by all the governess advice manuals. And this being a novel, a rescuer of course appears. The rich man next door turns out to be her father's vanished partner, a victim of that uniquely Victorian malady 'brain fever', who has been searching for her to tell her the money is, after all, not lost. Sara, who maintains a philosophic sweetness throughout her trials, thus exemplifies the maxim upon which the whole governess edifice was built: that adversity, cheerfully borne, would get its due reward – if not in this world, then in the next.

In his novel *No Name*, Wilkie Collins subverts this theme. Two sisters, Norah and Magdalen Vanstone, are suddenly orphaned. Their wealthy father is killed in a railway accident; their mother shortly afterwards dies of grief. It transpires that the girls were born before their parents married, making them illegitimate – hence they have 'no name' (and no automatic right of inheritance as next of kin). And since their mother died before she could sign a will naming them as her heirs, they must at once hand over all that has hitherto been theirs to a semi-criminal cousin. Their old governess Miss Garth takes responsibility for them; her sister keeps a successful school and can help them find good posts as governesses. The elder sister, Norah, gratefully accepts; but Magdalen is determined to regain what she sees as their rightful inheritance. *No Name* follows her subsequent seamy adventures.

In refusing passively to accept what fate hands out, Magdalen Vanstone violates the first rule of respectable female adversity. And as with similarly bold heroines – Thackeray's Becky Sharp in *Vanity Fair*, or Trollope's Lizzie Eustace in *The Eustace Diamonds* – it is clear that her creator finds her far more attractive and interesting than her more timid sisters. Unlike Thackeray or Trollope, however, Wilkie Collins not only admires but approves his heroine's bold course of action. Although Becky and Lizzie survive fairly well, it is only in somewhat scabrous circumstances. Magdalen, however, is rescued from the gutter in the nick of time and improbably married off to a good (and prosperous) man.

In a sense, Claire Clairmont's story – beginning with romantic defiance, ending in conformity – is the converse of Magdalen Vanstone's. Having no money of her own, she must always have recognized, in some part of her mind, that she would have to find work should a suitable husband not materialize. But for the eight years of their acquaintance, Shelley's friendship and financial support veiled this reality, cushioning her from it to the extent that she even felt free to turn down the highly desirable offer of marriage from Thomas Love Peacock – who made the offer not only in full knowledge of her unruly past, but while she was actually still living with Allegra, and whom she liked, even if she did not love him. Her poverty, and its accompanying grim realities, began to impinge on her only when she was forced by Mrs Mason to leave the Shelleys and live with the Bojtis. And when Shelley died, those realities could no longer be disguised. The choice then was the choice that all women in her situation faced: governessing – or starvation.

Of course, as Claire was only too aware, this did not apply to all lone women. Her friend and mentor Mrs Mason was one obvious exception; Mary Shelley another. But both had what Claire did not: position, talent, connections, above all enough money. Claire, though intelligent, attractive and musical, had none of these essential worldly attributes. Her fortune – or misfortune – was to have been set arbitrarily among people who had all of them, and who acted accordingly.

Nevertheless, Claire, like many governesses, preserved certain memorials of her earlier self. Vladimir Nabokov's vast Swiss mademoiselle had a picture of just such a person: a photograph in 'a fancy frame incrusted with garnets' showing 'a slim young brunette clad in a close-fitting dress, with brave eyes and abundant hair'.[168] Claire's memories, pre-photographic, were the poems that she had inspired in Byron and Shelley: Byron's 'Stanzas for Music' beginning

> 'There be none of Beauty's daughters
> With a magic like thee;
> And like music on the waters
> Is thy sweet voice to me.

Shelley's lovely ode, 'To Constantia, Singing', that ends with these lines:

> I have no life, Constantia, now, but thee,
> Whilst, like the world-surrounding air, thy song
> Flows on, and fills all things with melody.–
> Now is thy voice a tempest swift and strong,
> On which, like one in trance upborne,
> Secure o'er rocks and waves I sweep,
> Rejoicing like a cloud of morn.
> Now 'tis the breath of summer night,
> Which when the starry waters sleep,
> Round western isles, with incense-blossoms bright,
> Lingering, suspends my soul in its voluptuous flight.

The aunt, too, had her own life: the one examined in these pages. Not famous, of interest to few, but solid stuff, and amply documented. Yet had it not been for the existence of a third Claire, that life, like most governesses' lives, would have dropped into obscurity.

This third incarnation was altogether less substantial than either Constantia of the aunt. To quote the title of her biography, she was *Claire Clairmont, Mother of Byron's Allegra*: a footnote to other people's lives, interesting not for who she was but for whom she had known. And she, too, has her literary memorial: Henry James's novella, *The Aspern Papers*. James describes, in his introduction, how his story is based upon Claire's; he describes, too, his astonishment (so distant did Shelley and Byron seem by the 1870s) on realizing that he had actually visited Florence while she was still living there.

James, like so many others, knew Claire Clairmont only as 'the half-sister of Mary Godwin, Shelley's second wife, and for a while the intimate friend of Byron and the mother of his daughter Allegra'.[169] And like so many others, he got the details slightly wrong: Claire was Mary's stepsister, not her half-sister. But then he was writing fiction, not biography (though based, as he acknowledged, on fact: the American collector Edward Silsbee did visit the aged Claire in Italy; did, unlike James's narrator, go so far as to seduce the middle-aged niece who lived with her; did thereby succeed in interviewing her aunt; and probably did get his hands on some of her papers).[170] Even in supposedly factual accounts, however, Claire tends to be misrepresented. Thus, in his biography of William Godwin, Kegan Paul makes her older than Fanny Imlay, Mary Wollstonecraft's first daughter, whereas in fact she was a little younger than Mary Godwin, her second (Mary was born in 1797, Claire in 1798). Paul goes on to blame Claire, in effect, for Mary's elopement with Shelley. Mary was, he thought, too young at sixteen to be held fully responsible for her actions; but for Miss Clairmont, who accompanied them, 'it is difficult to find excuse'.[171]

Indeed, history has not been kind to Claire. Everyone remembers Mary's reported remark that Claire had 'been the bane of my life since I was three years old' – Mary's age when her father married Claire's mother – while forgetting that the person who passed it on with such glee was Mary's daughter-in-law, Jane Shelley, who bitterly resented Claire because of the substantial legacy left her by the poet, and which had so annoyingly to be paid out of the Shelley estate inherited by her husband in 1844. Claire's presence did indeed drive Mary to distraction; but no one who reads their correspondence can fail to be aware that – so long as they did not have to live in the same place – a real affection also existed between them.

That Claire got on Mary's nerves is understandable. Why she should inspire so much posthumous resentment is harder to explain. Perhaps history never forgave her impropriety and impudence, not just in taking the sexual initiative, but in continuing to thrust her demands upon an unwilling Byron. It was certainly less uncomfortable to load blame onto a commonplace person such as Claire than onto such a golden talent as his, or Shelley's, or Mary's. And perhaps this continuing indignation, along with her twenty years as a governess, are her enduring punishment for taking liberties above her station.

Is it possible for the person one has become entirely to obliterate the person one has been? Silsbee thought not. In April 1876, when she was seventy-eight, he wrote: 'Claire what a dark, subtle, treacherous woman's nature one makes out of her – Her passiveness in youth with Shelley's yet her [?forcemindfulness] as now. Her double ways, mercurial, Byronic nature. Paola insists much on this – her resemblance to Byron – capricious, wilful, stingy, mercenary &c &c.'[172]

Claire died in 1879. She signed her will Claire Maria Constantia Jane Clairmont.

5

Nelly Weeton: the cruelty of men

❦

So violently different are their worlds that it is hard to imagine, reading Nelly Weeton's story, that she and Claire Clairmont were contemporaries: that the primitive melodrama of Nelly's first 'situation' at Dove's Nest happened in the same country, and at the same time, as Claire's idyllic and sophisticated childhood among the London literati; that while Nelly's ghastly marriage was playing itself out in Wigan, Claire was adventuring through Italy with the Shelleys and living her urbane Florentine life with the Bojtis.

That Nelly's story survived at all is even more improbable. In 1925, a local historian poking about a junk-shop in the Lancashire town of Wigan came upon a dusty letter-book. It contained copies of letters sent by a Miss Ellen Weeton to her friends and relatives between 1807 and 1809, together with some journal entries. At the beginning of this period she was keeping a school in the nearby village of Up Holland; by the end she had become a lady's companion in Liverpool.

The letters were so lively and circumstantial that their finder published extracts in a local paper. To his delight, a reader, the descendant of a minister who had known Miss Weeton, came forward with three similar volumes. Originally there had been seven; those that survived covered, with gaps, the years 1807–1825. An additional volume contained 'occasional reflections' for the year 1818, by which time Miss Weeton had been four years married to Aaron Stock, as well as a fragment, 'The History of the Life of N. Stock, 1824', written for her daughter Mary and telling of her family and early years.

Nelly Weeton lived before photographs, but from these restless pages her likeness springs vividly forth: a tall, bony Lancashire woman, usefully able to see over the heads of crowds, slightly stooped on account of her height. She was plain (the Armitage children, whom she looked after in her thirties, called her 'Ugly-face', and she described herself as 'very plain-featured' though 'I think not so ugly as to attract passers-by'[1]), and neatly but shabbily dressed, with a down-to-earth turn of phrase that sometimes shocked her more proper acquaintances. She suffered from spots and indigestion, was sensitive, easily hurt, frequently uneasy, and always – even after her marriage; especially then – alone. When she felt particularly miserable she liked to console herself by walking. These were long walks, twenty miles or more a day, through Wales, the Isle of Man and, on one never-to-be-forgotten visit, London. In the village where she grew up her mother considered most of the children too common for her to play with, while because of her shyness, girls of the right standing intimidated her. This meant that, apart from the local minister's family, the Braithwaites, who remained her staunch friends, she was socially almost entirely reliant on her family. Yet her brother, aunt, uncle and cousin, one and all, betrayed her. And her mother, whom she loved and who loved her, nevertheless did her daughter the greatest disservice of all, by ensuring that Nelly did not receive the education she might have had and so clearly merited.

Only one trusty friend never let her down: her pen. Nelly maintained her sanity by writing an endless stream of letters and an intermittent journal, the composition and copying of which constituted her chief pleasure. In a life notable for its otherwise almost total lack of fulfilment, this freedom to indulge her way with words, and to express otherwise inadmissible thoughts, was a cherished safety valve, 'a great amusement during many a solitary hour when ... I should only have been engaged in some fine, tedious piece of needlework or other ... I do not intend them to be seen whilst I live, for there is not one intimate acquaintance I have I could show them to ... I have spoken too freely of most of them, or their near connections.'[2]

Nelly Weeton's dealings were not with the aristocrats and intellectuals whose literacy generally mediates our view of past times, but with the lower middle classes – petty tradespeople, small businessmen and their wives and daughters. She gives us nineteenth-century provincial life as we rarely see it: acutely recorded from below. These were her friends and relatives, and also, on occasion, her employers; for although her two spells of work as a governess were with wealthy businessmen (one a banker, the other a clothier) their families did not live grandly.

Nelly's world reads for the most part like a terrible dream. To all appearances so chokingly staid, it was in reality a realm of drunkenness, semi-starvation, sadism and domestic slavery that throws a wholly new light on the melodramas of Mrs Radcliffe and Sheridan Le Fanu. They may seem exaggerated, with their kidnappings, imprisonments, festering evils and all-rescuing legacies, but, if we are to believe Nelly Weeton, they were little more than the merest transcriptions.

Nelly's working career was ended, at the age of thirty-seven, by a marriage so hideous that to label it 'disastrous' is barely to scratch the surface of its horror. From the Pooterish tedium of a companion's stultifying lot: 'I lead a very dull life here . . . Miss Chorley is extremely ill-tempered with me. She has treated me with a degree of insolence which I can scarcely forbear to resent. Indeed, I have sometimes resented it, though not one hundredth part of what I have been made to endure'[3] – and the malicious enjoyment of a hated sister-in-law's humiliation: 'Mrs Bird, Mrs Weeton's sister, has got to such a pitch of drunkenness, that she is the talk of the country. The other day, she was carried home almost senseless; and in her way up Holland streets, was followed by a mob, hooting and hissing,'[4] – her diaries move on to agonized recountings of a life as extreme as any Gothick imagining.

Nelly need not have married Aaron Stock or, indeed, anyone. Although she had known great poverty, by the time she met him she was quite well off and in fact had even considered buying a small estate on which to run a dairy farm. Why, then, after less than two weeks' acquaintance, did this competent businesswoman agree to tie herself irrevocably to an unknown brute, who from the moment the ceremony ended became the lawful owner of everything that had hitherto been hers? It is the central mystery of Nelly Weeton's life; and it leads us to the heart of that male-dominated culture in whose propagation women's education – or rather, its absence – played so vital a part.

*

Nelly's drama begins with a stolen legacy. In 1782, when she was six and her brother Tom two, their father, Thomas Weeton, died. Like his wife, he was connected to an old and well-established family, but had inherited nothing but a name. He spent his life at sea and worked his way up to captain, commanding ships in the slave trade and later in the American war of independence. Having successfully accumulated a fortune of between £10,000 and £11,000 in prize money, he informed his employers – shipowning relatives of his wife by the name of Rawlinson – that he wished to retire. They persuaded him to undertake just one more voyage; on that voyage, he was killed.

Now that Captain Weeton was dead, the Rawlinsons denied that they owed him anything. They were prominent and powerful; they refused to open their books; and, as they doubtless calculated, his widow dared not sue them for fear of losing what little money she had. She was left with about £30 or £40 a year – enough for subsistence, but not enough to keep a family in any comfort. So she moved from expensive Lancaster to cheap Up Holland, where her mother came from, and like many another woman in her position, started a school.

Mrs Weeton was not an educated woman; before her marriage she had been a lady's maid. But she was literate, and expectations of village schools were not high. John Ruskin's mother, who attended a country dame-school at about this period, 'there learned severely right principles of truth, charity, and housewifery'[5] – all of which, along with reading and writing, Mrs Weeton was no doubt as well qualified as anyone to pass on. That would be enough for Nelly. Tom, however, who would need a good education in order to enter a profession, was sent to a nearby, and superior, boys' establishment, one of whose teachers also gave daily lessons at Mrs Weeton's.

This man, a Mr Saul, taught Nelly 'Writing, Arithmetic, a little Grammar, and a little Geography'.[6] She eagerly took it all in, showing 'so strong a predilection for reading and scribbling rhymes'[7] that her mother became seriously alarmed.

My mother, who had for some time been delighted with what she considered my striking talents, and encouraged me with unbounded praises, began to think that I should be entirely ruined for any useful purpose in life if my inclinations for literature were indulged, and treated all my efforts this way with a decided discouragement; so much so as to dampen my spirits for ever. Oh! how I have burned to learn Latin, French, the Arts, the Sciences, anything rather than the dog trot way of sewing, teaching, writing copies, and washing dishes every day. Of my Arithmetic I was very fond, and advanced rapidly. Mensuration was quite delightful, Fractions, Decimals, &c., Book keeping. So would Geography and Grammar have been, but my master was sparing of his Instructions, and I could not get on as my mother would not help me.[8]

For Nelly, as for thousands of other girls, knowledge would always be an unknown country, unattainably glittering just over the horizon. Tom might cross the frontier at will – but for Tom it held little interest. Learning was just something he had to do in order, eventually, to earn a living. Later she observed, in a phrase whose two-edged nature it is unlikely she recognized: 'I could not have received an education more suited to the kind of life I had to lead than that my excellent mother gave me.'[9]

Nelly's self-confidence never recovered from her mother's dampening attitude. A friend, struck by the quality of her letters, once suggested that she should write for publication, a notion that she dismissed out of hand.

'If we were together,' say you, 'we could plan; or if you would write, I could present it with confidence.' If I did write, I must be merely your amanuensis; for my own genius has been so strongly repressed, has so long lain dormant, that now I fear it could produce nothing ... Such pains were taken by my mother to repress my too great ardour for literature, that any talents I then possessed as a child, have been nearly extinguished ... When I read the Biography of celebrated characters, my heart will yet burn within me, and I could exclaim, 'Oh, why have I been so chained down in obscurity? Why have I been secluded from every species of mental improvement? Living entirely amongst the illiterate, and unable to procure books, a dark cloud has invariably hung over me – I know little more than this – that I am very ignorant.'[10]

Rarely could one hope to find a more clear and depressing account of the effects of parental discouragement.

That Mrs Weeton had the best of intentions cannot be doubted. She simply reflected her times. A publishing phenomenon of this period was the plethora of books purporting to offer advice on the education of girls, but whose real topic was in fact the vexed question of how to prevent them from learning too much.

The authors of these books made no bones about this. Dr John Gregory, whose *A Father's Legacy to his Daughters* was one of the most popular of the genre, assured his readers that he did not see women as 'domestic drudges, or the slaves of our [i.e. men's] pleasure, but as our companions and equals'.[11] Nevertheless, he warned that 'Men ... generally look with a jealous and malignant eye on a woman of great parts, and a cultivated understanding.'[12] And since, in a culture of dependence, catching your meal-ticket was supremely important, girls' education must take account of this. Wit, Gregory advised, was to be avoided; it was the most dangerous talent a girl could possess, and he devoted large portions of his book to recommendations on how to suppress it. Indeed, the fact that even such unquenchable talents as the Brontës or George Eliot had to hide behind male pseudonyms says everything we need to know about the nineteenth-century view of intellectual women. Crabb Robinson, for one, found his enjoyment of *Adam Bede* much diminished after he found out that the author was in fact a woman.

Of recommended wit-suppressants, everyone agreed that the most efficacious was religion. Patriotism, after 1793, could be defined as everything that was not radical, not egalitarian, above all not questioning or unsettling: in a word, the established Church. Anglicanism favoured tradition over change, inculcated respect for authority and (unlike Dissent) discouraged all questioning of the status quo. For the next half-century it would set the tone for relations between the sexes.

The sternly evangelical Hannah More – a prolific contributor to the education debate and one of the most influential of the 'quisling women'[13] (in William St Clair's phrase) who played along with the men in their deadening enterprise – set out the anti-education case in her *Strictures on the Modern System of Female Education*. 'In this moment of alarm and peril,' (she was writing in 1799), 'I would call on [women] to come forward and contribute ... towards the saving of their country ... to raise the depressed tone of public morals and awaken the drowsy spirit of religious principle ... Who suspects the destruction which lurks under the harmless or instructive names of General History, Travels, Voyages, Lives, Encyclopedias, Criticism and Romance?'[14] In the 1950s, Betty Friedan made her great discovery: educated women pined when they were kept from the 'real world' and restricted to housewifery. Hannah More, and the legions she represented, pre-empted this depression not by expanding women's horizons but by suppressing their education. 'Why are not females permitted to study physic, divinity, astronomy, &c., &c., with their attendants – chemistry, botany, logic, mathematics, &c.,' Nelly wondered, then answered her own question: 'To be sure the mere study is not prohibited, but the practise is in a great measure. Who would employ a female physician? who would listen to a female divine, except to ridicule? I could myself almost laugh at the idea.'[15]

I could myself almost laugh. Even while she resented the artificial restrictions that held her back, she was still half hypnotized by the overpowering spirit of the age. Men disposed, and women accepted: that was the way it was, and the way it had to be. So effective was the brainwashing that speaking, some years later, to one of her pupils – the young, uneducated but intelligent wife of a drunken and despotic husband – and despite knowing that 'the more we submit, the worse he grows', she advised not resistance but submission: 'I say it is a disgrace to the dignity of the female character for any woman to strive to become master in her husband's house, or to make her husband afraid of her. It is an equal disgrace to a man, so to submit.'[16] Hannah More could not have put it better.

In 1797, Mrs Weeton died. Tom, articled to a lawyer, still had four years of his clerkship to run; as his fees and living expenses used up most of the family's small income, Mrs Weeton requested Nelly, on her deathbed, to give him sole use of it until two years after he came of age. Until then, she must support herself by continuing with the school; after that, Tom should be able to earn his own living, and the income should revert to her.

Nelly's circumstances now became truly desperate. 'I would rather be a teacher at a school (and I can think of nothing worse) than marry a man I did not like,' says Jane Austen's Emma Watson, to which her sister, who has actually experienced it, retorts, 'I would rather be anything than a teacher at a school.'[17] Even while her mother was alive Nelly's word for the life they led between teaching and keeping house, plus some sewing to order, was *slavery*. They subsisted mainly on the poor people's diet of bread and potatoes. Nelly could not bring herself to eat the dearer and more varied food that her mother urged on her but would not share.

Her mother's death may well have decreased the physical burden of Nelly's days: Mrs Weeton had been asthmatic and had needed constant nursing. But that was far less important than her now almost complete isolation. Mr Saul from the boys' school no longer visited; he 'was not', Nelly concluded, 'the best instructor for a female', being too concerned with mathematics and not enough with geography or grammar;[18] this meant that she now had to do all the teaching as well as everything else, which meant working even when she was ill.

Despite this unending workload, there was never enough money. On the face of it, this is hard to understand: the income from their mother's money went, as she had requested, to Tom, but there was still the school to bring in an income. The funeral expenses, added to existing debts, left her owing £49. Her chief creditor seems to have been her mother's sister – rich, mean Aunt Barton – who now pressed and pressed for repayment.

The day you were paid was indeed a day of rejoicing to me, though left without a halfpenny. For a fortnight after that, I went daily without a dinner, and sometimes without my supper too; as to tea, I seldom or never drank any when alone. I had not wherewith to have purchased a pennyworth of potatoes ... One day one of my pupils paid me a penny for some thread. It was a treasure to me! I bought some potatoes, boiled and mashed them with milk (which I paid for half-yearly). 'Well, *I shall* have a dinner today!' thought I. I was *too* sure, and accordingly, punished for the presumption. When they were ready for eating, I placed them on top of the oven, whilst I fried some bacon and eggs for some of my pupils, who generally brought their dinner. One of them in passing the oven hastily, threw down the dish of potatoes on the floor amongst some ashes, so that they were utterly unfit to eat. I can *never* forget what I felt at that moment. I hastily placed the frying pan on the floor, and without speaking, ran upstairs into the parlour where, shutting myself up, I gave vent to my disappointment in a violent fit of crying. I had borne patiently till then, but the loss, though only of a pennyworth of potatoes, was too much for me.[19]

Nelly consoled herself with the thought that she was doing this to help her beloved brother, and that although he gaily spent shillings on pleasure when she had not even pence for food, he at least appreciated her and returned her love. So he did, at first. But this affectionate relationship was undermined by his sudden marriage to Jane Scott, which took place when he was twenty-one.

Jane's family disapproved of the match, so the wedding was unannounced, and after the ceremony the young couple made for Up Holland. Neither of them had any money, and since they had no house of their own to go to they took over Nelly's, kindly allowing her to stay and help with the housework. Soon, however, they were reconciled with Jane's family and left. After that, Tom would call by on a Saturday, hoping to pick up a little business in Up Holland; on one of these Saturdays, he told Nelly that he was short of money. She explained to him that far from giving him any, it was now her turn to benefit from their mother's income. She had kept him for five years, washed his clothes, mended his linen, bought him handkerchiefs, waistcoats, stockings, cambric for ruffles ... 'He stood almost aghast ... He thought I had given him all these without hope of return.' For was he not a man? And was not Nelly a mere woman? 'We were but *female* relatives, and had only done our duty.'[20] Unfortunately, however, their mother had not left a written will; in its absence, there was no chance that Tom would relinquish the whole of the income. An agreement was reached that they would divide it between them, '£100 excepted, of which I was to have the interest, promising him to restore it if I married'.[21]

Like Mary Wollstonecraft, Nelly Weeton clung to the old-fashioned view of family ties and responsibilities. She had assumed that she would eventually keep house for her brother – she had even turned down an offer of marriage because she did not wish to disappoint him – and, after his own marriage, had thought she would live with him and his wife. The new Mrs Weeton, however, did not care for this arrangement. She doubtless resented Nelly's appropriation of what she and Tom had considered their rightful funds, while her family did not like being constantly reminded that the sister of this up-and-coming young lawyer was only a humble village schoolmistress. 'I cannot bear puff. Mrs W. admires it much.'[22]

Jane eventually agreed to receive Nelly, though requiring in exchange virtually her whole income – thirty guineas a year – for board. But she quickly decided even that was not worth her sister-in-law's constant company and instead invited her own sister to live in her house. From that moment on, the sisters-in-law were sworn enemies.

Tom, torn between his wife and his sister, inevitably joined his wife's camp. Quite apart from anything else, he was in love with her: Nelly records that every evening, after dinner, they kissed and cuddled. But she could never bring herself to believe that her relationship with her beloved brother – the one constant friend of her childhood – had really changed. She continued to write to him as trustingly as though they were still on the old terms, roundly criticizing Jane and expecting him to keep from her such details as that good investments had almost doubled Nelly's income . . . For the next ten years she would bombard him with relentless affection, while each affectionate word, reminding him of sacrifices he would have preferred to forget, sharpened Tom's – and especially Jane's – antipathy.

Still, Nelly now had an income and could at last close the school. It was only £36 10s but, with her plain habits, it should be enough to live on. How, though, would she occupy the time? Her Uncle and Aunt Barton assumed that it would be by looking after them, but as they offered no reward for this privilege – 'no, not even a cup of tea occasionally'[23] – Nelly declined.

However, she did not enjoy her new, leisured life. All alone – there could be no question of living with Tom – the solitary, unoccupied days hung heavy. Yet when she sought out company, 'from being so little accustomed to it, I cannot enjoy it.'[24] The sight of other people's happy family lives was almost too much to bear, so far was it from her own experience. One such evening, with old friends, reduced her to floods of sudden and embarrassing tears. A local tradesman hinted that he might like to marry her, but she dismissed the prospect, reasoning that it was her money he wanted; he had never been interested in her before, 'and to feel the conviction that one is merely addressed for the sake of the money one is worth, is an idea too degrading to dwell on'.[25] She was not – yet – desperate enough for that.

The obvious solution was to look for a job, but the possibilities remained as limited as ever: companion, schoolmistress, governess. Although there was talk of a situation at Miss Mangnall's school, Crofton Hall, where an assistant was needed and she might have picked up some teaching hints, it did not come to anything. Her brother urged her to open a school in Liverpool; Nelly, however, had had enough of that lone and desperate life.

When one of her friends, a Miss Chorley, a maiden lady of fifty who lived with her parents in Liverpool, proposed that Nelly come and join them as a companion, the idea seemed a good one. She would not be paid, but would have her board and lodging. The Chorleys were rather staid and stuffy, the back parlour where the family always sat 'so dark one might almost as well be in a prison',[26] with its windows fastened and draughts stopped with sandbags even in August. But at least there would be company.

It was a step in the right direction, away from her bullying family, towards a life of her own. But what Nelly had not appreciated – perhaps neither of them had – was that the fact of being employed at once altered the terms of her friendship with Miss Chorley. In becoming a companion, albeit unpaid, she crossed the invisible threshold separating the world of equals from the indeterminate netherworld of dependants, who although not servants could no longer be classed as friends. 'They give me board and lodging, but they pay themselves again in the spleen they vent upon me ... Miss C. in particular treats me in a manner scarcely to be endured ... Oh, Miss Chorley! You are to this house what Buonaparte is to Europe – a scourge.'[27]

Nelly was in the act of writing this in her journal when the door of her room opened and Miss Chorley entered. Consumed with curiosity regarding Nelly's interminable writing, and with the antennae of the underemployed (or perhaps because she had sneaked a secret look), she had divined that therein lay the innermost secrets of her companion's soul. And *that*, now, belonged by right to Miss Chorley. She insisted on reading the journal; Nelly indignantly refused. The bathetic upshot came very near to a physical fight.

'Only read me one line,' said she, angrily. 'You shall either read me one line, or tell me what it is about, or I shall not stir out of this room.' 'I shall do neither,' I drily answered ... Let me be cool, thought I, I *won't* give way to anger. 'So, Ma'am, if you please,' said I laughingly, 'please to walk out of my room.' 'I'll see what it is you have written first,' she said, attempting to take the book. 'Indeed you shan't,' I replied, taking hold of her hands ... We struggled, and I had almost got her out of the room, when, recollecting that I too was using force, I let her go, and seizing the book, ran out of the room and hid it.[28]

After that there could be no more pretence of politeness. Mr and Mrs Chorley looked on astonished as their daughter took every opportunity to abuse her one-time friend. Nelly had arrived at the Chorleys' in November 1808, intending to stay six months; but, by the new year she had left these tensions behind and was installed in pleasant sea-side lodgings just outside Liverpool, where she helped with the vegetable garden, enjoyed the sea views and got on well with the landlady.

For the next year, she lived a life of leisure. She was better off now; Mr Chorley had looked out an excellent property investment which raised her income to £60 a year. Tom noticed an improvement in her social manner: he attributed it to his wife's example, but Nelly assured him it was purely on account of 'an increase of chearfulness'.[29] Perhaps this was not unconnected with a possibility of marriage that seems to have cropped up at this time, although the flirtation came to nothing. Some younger friends, the Winkleys, invited her to stay, but it was awkward – not because they were intrusive but because, on the contrary, she felt excluded from their girlish lives. And since the only alternative to these unsatisfactory arrangements was a return to her old loneliness, she decided to look for another post. She told herself that it was all for Tom, that 'the friends I make for myself may eventually prove valuable ones to him',[30] but in fact she had reached a dead end and this was the only way forward.

Towards the end of 1809, Mrs Winkley happened to mention an advertisement that she had seen for a governess. Nelly answered it, and an elderly gentleman came to appraise her suitability on behalf of the advertiser, a Mr Pedder who lived in the Lake District. He had recently married for the second time and had a ten-year-old daughter by his first marriage. The gentleman 'related several circumstances respecting the family he wished to engage me for; said I should be treated as an equal by them, more as a companion to Mrs Pedder than as governess to Miss P., to assist her in regulating the management of a family such as Mr P. wished his to be. He enquired what salary I should expect. I answered, thirty guineas. He engaged me, and – I am going.'[31] It was a good wage; a year later, holidaying on the Isle of Man, she met a woman who paid her governess only £12 a year.

Nelly kept her plans secret, in case they should not work out. When she finally left to take up the situation, her nasty Aunt Barton took the opportunity to do her a parting disservice, originating (and her brother gleefully spreading) the tale that she had gone off with a man. It was years before Nelly found out who had started the rumour; her aunt, the obvious suspect, denied knowing anything about it. It was Tom's collusion, however, that rankled. For the next two years both he and her aunt cut off all communication with Nelly – shocked, perhaps, by the outrageous nature of their own behaviour.

Ironically, given the job's miserable reputation, the years she spent governessing were probably the happiest – or least unhappy – of Nelly's life. Not that her expectations were high. Actual happiness does not seem to have been a feature of any of the lives that Nelly describes. But her world was particularly unsympathetic to lone women. Living on her own was unbearably lonely. At her brother's house there was always the awful knowledge that Jane hated her and was persuading Tom to hate her too; if she stayed with friends there was a constant danger that (as with Miss Chorley) the friendship might not survive such close proximity.

Governessing was not perfect: Nelly suffered, as most governesses did, from the lack of any social possibilities and resented being at the mercy of her employers' unreasonable temper. Nevertheless, it was a way of participating in some aspects of family life. She liked children and enjoyed playing with them; she was also used to teaching and long hours. *In extremis* there was always her journal, to let off steam and say what she really thought. And because unlike most governesses Nelly already had an income, she was freed from the enforced sub-mission and barely masked resentment that overlay the desperate calculations of a Claire, an Everina, an Eliza – even, from time to time, an Agnes Porter – for whom unemployment always held the threat of destitution. Unlike them, Nelly was working because she chose to, not because she had to.

This independence must inevitably have affected her relations with her employers. For most governesses, one of the worst aspects of the profession was the constant necessity to bite one's tongue; a sad contrast, in most cases, to the relaxation and warmth of family life at home. In Nelly's case, quite the opposite applied. With her own family she had always to be on guard lest they round on her and persecute her. On the other hand, if her employers bullied her she could (and did) simply leave. Meanwhile there must have been a satisfying sense of her savings mounting up as her income continued unspent, while she was not only boarded and lodged at someone else's expense, but paid a salary as well.

The Pedders lived near Ambleside in a pretty house called Dove's Nest. It was situated at the head of Lake Windermere, with a hill at its back, lawns sloping down to the water and a spectacular view that took in almost all the lake. Nelly arrived at four on a December afternoon to find Mr and Mrs Pedder 'seated at their wine after dinner, Mrs P. dressed in a pink muslin, with a very becoming head dress of the same'. There were two liveried servants, and the table gleamed with silver plate, silver nutcrackers 'and some things of which poor ignorant I knew not the use'.[32]

However, despite their wealth – Mr Pedder's family kept a bank in Preston, and his income was between £1,500 and £2,000 a year – the Pedders were in no way intimidating. Families such as theirs had never been accustomed to such aristocratic perquisites as a private governess; they had hired one because that was what people of their standing did at that time. When she actually arrived, they treated her with so much deference that it almost unsettled her.[33]

This reaction was rather unusual. As more and more families of middling means employed governesses whose original social status was virtually indistinguishable from their own, the necessity of maintaining a proper distinction between employer and employee more usually (as with Miss Chorley) led to stiffness, embarrassment and an exaggerated emphasis on almost imperceptible niceties of status. But what Mrs Pedder needed, above all, was an ally. Still not eighteen, she had been a dairymaid at Mr Pedder's Preston house when he fell in love with her. Her father, afraid that she would be seduced, ordered her home, but her lover followed and whisked her off to Gretna Green. Now she found herself mistress of a wealthy establishment, without the slightest idea of how to run it. For that she would rely on Nelly, and for that friendship and confidence Nelly was duly grateful. Mrs Pedder's many virtues, she assured Mrs Chorley, 'make her more than equal to the rank to which she is raised – *in my opinion*. Miss Chorley perhaps will smile at this,' she added snippily, 'for she thinks no qualities of mind, no dignity of character, can compensate for want of high birth.'[34] As for the house's other inmates, Mr Pedder, though very small, seemed amiable enough, while the little girl suffered from fits – sometimes as many as five a day – and at first seemed 'not a pleasing child'.[35] But as she got to know her better and became more accustomed to dealing with the fits, Nelly grew fond of her.

Nelly's duties were numerous. She had 'to attend to the direction of the House, the table, &c., as well as literary studies; to assist in entertaining company in the parlour; and give directions to the servants'[36] – a truly terrifying responsibility, considering her utter lack of housekeeping experience at any but the most basic level. Still, however minute that experience, it was more than Mrs Pedder's. She had also to hold Miss Pedder when she fitted, which was less distressing than she originally feared.

Nelly's time at Dove's Nest was marked by a series of disquieting events, which built up to a horrific climax worthy of Poe himself.

They began in a small way. Several of the house's guard dogs began worrying sheep, so that all but one had to be put down. And shortly after that, inexplicable sounds began to be heard – the unquiet spirit, it was said, of the house's former owner.

One night, around two in the morning, Nelly awoke to the sound of opening and shutting windows and shifting furniture in the next room. Tremulous but determined, she rose and investigated; all appeared normal. She looked for Mr Pedder – for no one could have slept through the din – but there was no sign of him; the next morning he confessed (to her scorn) that he had clung onto his wife from midnight till five in the morning, his head under the blankets. Nelly was convinced the 'ghost' was rats, a suggestion that was greeted with general mockery. But, when she looked, the attic was full of their traces, and it seemed clear that the noise came from their running over its bare boards, which were not nailed down.

Following this prelude, the crescendo approached its climax. Large fires were kept going in all the rooms, so that the house was always pleasantly warm; one day the epileptic girl fell into one. Her screams brought help running; she was pulled out and the flames extinguished. But her face, arms and legs were terribly burnt – 'the skin hung from her poor trembling limbs like shreds of paper'[37] – and despite the efforts of several doctors and the entire household, she died soon after. No sooner was the poor little corpse laid out than the rats, scenting the dead meat, came swarming into the room where the body lay and began to attack it, so that while it remained in the house it could not be left alone.

All this quite literally drove Mr Pedder to distraction.

> Before the corpse was taken away, thinking perhaps he should be accused of want of feeling, he went, completely drunk, into the room where the body lay, and worked himself up into an almost complete frenzy; lying down by the side of the coffin, getting astride of it, pulling and mawling the body, till the servants attending durst stay no longer in the room, expecting every moment he would have it out of the coffin . . . He opened the mouth repeatedly, kissing it and declaring she was not dead; calling her to speak to him.[38]

Nelly was deeply shocked by these antics. 'He felt a little, I will allow, but real grief acts not like this,' she observed severely. She had become fond of the child, whom she had found 'peculiarly affectionate' with 'understanding beyond her years'; they had spent many hours talking together. Mr Pedder had shown scant interest in the girl then; now that she was dead, his main concern was to disclaim guilt, which he did by apportioning it elsewhere, telling anyone who would listen that 'Had it not been for Miss Weeton and Mrs Pedder, the child would have been living now.'[39]

Nelly was naturally indignant, but she forgave him: 'His repentance is oft as great as his fault.'[40] Far worse to her eyes was Pedder's hypocrisy. Despite the shows of excessive grief, his main concern, it seemed, was to keep down the funeral costs. Everyone in the house would be required to wear mourning, and those who did not already possess the necessary black clothes would be expected to acquire them in time for the funeral. Since this meant dressmakers working day and night, mourning was expensive, and it was customary for the master to buy it for the servants. But Pedder, who could easily have afforded it, refused to do this, even for the nurse who had burned her own hands in an effort to save his daughter from the flames. As for Nelly, '"Miss Weeton said she would pay for her mourning herself; he wished she would." – You need be on no fear on that head, Mr Pedder,' Nelly riposted. 'I do not grudge it, if you do.'[41]

Although her main charge was now dead, Mr Pedder asked Nelly to stay on as companion to his young wife. She was undecided, so revolted was she by her now constantly drunk employer. Mrs Pedder, however, desperate not to lose her one sane friend in this madhouse, begged her not to leave and she relented.

The young wife's plight was indeed unenviable. At first nothing had been too good for her, but Pedder's attention span was very short and had moved on to boats, of which he had four. But although his wife now bored him, she was unfortunately less easily discarded than a holed boat. His impatience manifested itself in miserliness. He would not let her keep house, would himself order goods wildly, then refuse to pay the tradesmen; he refused her money for the washerwoman's bill; he grudged her a decent gown; and all the while squandered money on his latest hobbyhorse. To save face and salve his conscience, the day after a violent quarrel he would suggest that he and his wife go out in the carriage, so that the world might see them together, apparently happy and united. Nelly had no more time for him in his good humours than when he lost his temper. When he was angry he was unbearable, when in a good mood, 'little more than a fool'.[42]

With Mrs Pedder at her wits' end, Nelly pondered whether to advise defiance or submission. Every sane instinct pointed to the first, all her upbringing to the second. In her journal, she debated the unanswerable question.

> It would almost seem as if Mr P. ill-used those most whom he most regarded. Mrs P. suffers much more than I do. What a tyrant he is to her! He seems to think that by lording it over two or three women, he increases his own consequence; and the more we submit, the worse he grows. Mrs P. has often told me that she has been strongly advised never to let him abuse her without making

resistance. I have often advised submission. She says she is told by those who have known him long, that the more a person submits to him, or seems afraid of him, the oftener he exerts the power he finds he has over them; and that when a strong resistance is made ... he in turn will become afraid of those he would oppress. Still, I advise *her* from pursuing such a conduct. I say it is a disgrace to the dignity of the female character for any woman to strive to become master in her husband's house, or to make her husband afraid of her ... I shall almost be a convert to Mrs P.'s advisers and their opinions – that it will be more for the comfort of the whole household not to submit to all his humours – and yet I am very, very unwilling to either give, or take, such advice.'[43]

At a time when upbringing, society and the law stood so bitterly at odds with both common sense and natural justice, it was a dilemma that must have faced many a woman. Nelly would confront it again, at closer quarters, when she married Aaron Stock. Yet so ingrained was the principle of submission that only a sustained campaign of violence would finally drive her to defiance.

Nelly left Dove's Nest in February 1811, just over a year after her arrival. She, too, had been a passing fancy; Mr Pedder had tired of her and by the end there was no pleasing him. He threw tantrums if she disagreed with him on any subject and took offence if she listened to him in silence; his ill-humour might last for a week or more. But although Dove's Nest was no longer tolerable, she stayed several more months in the Lake District, which she had grown to love. For a while she thought of selling her houses and buying a small dairy farm there – 'for I am sure I could manage a milk-farm and be fond of it'.[44] But that, which might have been her salvation, came to nothing. Then she stayed in Liverpool for a few months, again with the Winkleys. However, the sister she most liked, Ann, had left to become a governess in Ireland, and time hung heavy. So she resolved to take another post and in March 1812 told Ann Winkley that she was 'on the point of engaging to instruct the children of a lady in Yorkshire'.[45]

Her new employer, Joseph Armitage of High Royd, near Huddersfield, was a wool manufacturer, a trade that his family had followed in the same place since the fourteenth century. He and his wife were young – 'not 30 yet I dare say, either of them,' Nelly observed[46] – and rich, but they lived very unpretentiously, keeping no carriage and with no indoor manservant. Armitage ran his house 'with tradesman-like regularity and bustle; no sitting after breakfast as we used to do at Mr Pedder's. I generally rise from table with some of the meal in my mouth. Yet I like the family far better than Mr P's; no quarrelling, rioting or drunkenness here, that used, when I was at Dove's Nest, to terrify me so. Here, I know what I have to do; there, I never did.'[47]

The Armitages, like the Pedders, had not employed a governess before. Unlike the Pedders, however, their discomfort manifested itself in an awkward coolness. When Nelly first arrived,

> I could plainly see that my *master* and my *mistress* did not know how to treat me, nor *what to do with me*; and their distant manner froze me so, that for the life of me, I could not tell what to do with myself when they were by. My arms and my legs were unusual encumbrances; ... and my bottom! ... Lord help it! When I walked out of the room, it felt three times as big as it ever did before, and I thought it shaked most uncommonly![48]

However, the Armitages soon found out what one did with a governess and made sure they got their money's worth out of this new investment.

> My time is totally taken up with the children; from 7 o'clock in the morning, till half past 7, or 8 at night. I cannot lie any longer than 6 o'clock in the morning; and if I have anything to do for myself, in sewing, writing &c., I must rise sooner. At 7 I go to the nursery, to hear the children their prayers, and remain with them till after they have breakfasted, when I go out with them whilst they play; and am often so cold that I join in their sports, to warm myself. About half past 8, I break fast with Mr & Mrs Armitage, and then return again to the children till 9, when we go into the school-room till 12. We then bustle on our bonnets, &c., for play, or a short walk. At One, we bustle them off again, to dress for dinner, to which we sit down at a quarter past; the children always dine with their parents. By the time dinner is well over, it is 2 o'clock, when we go into school, and remain till 5. Whilst I am at tea in the parlour, the children eat their suppers in the nursery. I then go to

them, and remain with them till 7, either walking out of doors, or playing within, as the weather may permit. I then hear their prayers, and see them washed; at half past 7, they are generally in bed.[49]

Nelly did not mind the hard work – it was part of the job – but what she did find dispiriting was her employers' lack of interest in what she was doing with their offspring. They never enquired about the children's lessons, nor asked how they were getting on; they were clearly bored by the weekly reports that Nelly insisted on giving them. But despite the long hours and her employers' coolness, life at High Royd on the whole pleased her. 'I am too comfortable here, my dear Catharine, to have any thought of leaving,' she informed her old friend Miss Braithwaite six months into her engagement. ' . . . I love my little pupils, and receive many an affectionate embrace from them; it must be an advantageous offer indeed, that would now induce me to leave them.'[50] The only drawback to this pleasant situation was Mrs Armitage's uncertain temper when she was pregnant. Unfortunately, she was pregnant more often than not. However, in the intervals there was peace.

Things pottered on, more or less contentedly, for a year and a half. A baby arrived, followed by six months of tranquillity. But by the spring of 1814, Mrs Armitage was expecting once more. And Nelly, who had heard nothing from her family since her arrival at High Royd, was once again being persecuted by them.

Her rich Aunt Barton had died, leaving long-awaited legacies: three sealed purses, one for Tom, one for Nelly, one for their cousin Miss Latham. Tom's and Miss Latham's purses had each contained forty guineas in gold and £10 in notes; but when Nelly arrived in Up Holland to collect hers, she found the seal broken and the contents mysteriously comprising only a ring and five £1 notes. Her uncle told her he had been intending to send her the purse, had broken the seal to check its contents in case the carrier was robbed – and this was what he had found. Nelly challenged him; the old man rose up in a rage. Was she accusing him of theft? She should be careful, or he might cut her out of his will.

Nelly was no fool, and the pretence insultingly transparent. Clearly the money had been stolen. Was the thief her uncle, taking his revenge for her past refusal to be browbeaten into unpaid housekeeping? Was he in conspiracy with her cousin (whose uncharacteristically fawning conduct seemed to imply a guilty conscience) or her brother? All her old fears redoubled. She was alone in the world: her family was set on destroying her. It sounded paranoid, but it was the simple truth. To cap her misery, her uncle took this opportunity to enlighten her as to who had been behind the malicious rumours five years earlier.

> He said that it was indeed my aunt who reported that I had *gone off with a gentleman!!* and that she did it, because she knew not what was to become of me, and was *afraid* it was so! My brother, out of *delicacy* to my *aunt,* had not confessed to me who it really was that told *him* so; but now that my aunt was dead, he did not doubt but that Thomas . . . would tell me all about it . . . I was astonished and filled with horror! that . . . my aunt could *so positively* tell me, in the presence of my cousin, that she had never said any such thing, nor had ever any such report been circulated, either by her or my cousin; and that *no one had ever told my brother so.*[51]

Shortly after her bewildered return to High Royd following this disgraceful episode, the insult was compounded. Tom – who for two years had ceased all communication – wrote brusquely saying that, now their uncle was all alone, Nelly must give up her post in order to take care of him. Nelly, submitting meekly as always to his wishes, agreed, on the sole condition that she should not have to pay for her board and lodging. She even began casting around to find someone who would take her place at High Royd. However, it seemed that Tom – clearly less concerned with his uncle's health than to make sure that their branch of the family was in evidence when the old man came to make his will – had not consulted his uncle before writing to Nelly. Old Barton once again refused to provide her even with meals, leaving Nelly in the embarrassing position of having to renege on all her arrangements.

Even so, with ill-temper once more the order of the day, her time at High Royd was clearly coming to an end (perhaps this was why she made so little objection to Tom's outrageous demand). Abandoning the children, whom she had come to love, the garden glade that she had cut out of some woodland (and where Mrs Armitage, without thanking her, had that spring erected a latticework arbour), the attentions of an old farmer with £30 a year who had conceived an embarrassing fancy for her hand, and the interesting but goggle-eyed new curate whose acquaintance she had not yet had the chance of making, in July 1814, Nelly returned to Up Holland.

Nelly quit High Royd a respectable woman of adequate means. She had made some excellent investments in cottage property, she had capital of £100 (as well as the £100 due to Tom under the terms of their mother's will if she married) and her income from all sources was a healthy £75 a year. Two months later she was married to Aaron Stock, a man she had never previously mentioned in any of her letters or her journal, and no longer had a penny to call her own. Her life's third act had begun.

How Nelly met Stock we do not know. Since he lived in Wigan, the nearest town to Up Holland, they may have had acquaintances in common. Perhaps the connection was Jane Weeton's mother, from whom he rented a factory. (Jane, snobbish as ever, spitefully urged Stock, after his marriage, to forbid his wife the company of her old friends the Braithwaites, whom Jane did not think suitable. 'A high piece of meddling,' Nelly furiously commented. 'What had she to do with it? ... Who likes her?')[52] Nelly asked Tom to look into Stock's character and situation: a wholly pointless move, since her welfare was by now a matter of complete indifference to her brother, while he stood to gain £100 if the wedding went through. In fact Stock was on the edge of bankruptcy, and his violent nature had already led to some brushes with the law. But Tom said nothing of this, and Nelly duly became Mrs Stock. (Tom did not, however, get his money, as he doubtless hoped, in cash. Instead Nelly transferred an outstanding £50 loan to his name, along with a cottage whose tenant was constantly behind with his rent. Tom and Jane showed their appreciation by circulating another malicious rumour: that Nelly had only married because she was pregnant. In fact, as she indignantly reminded him, her daughter Mary was born exactly nine months and nine days after the wedding.)

At Dove's Nest, Nelly had seen, at close quarters, what a bad marriage might be, and how helpless was the lot of the trapped wife. She must also have known that the law was unequivocal: marriage meant forfeiting not just her property but her independent legal existence. Unless a special settlement was drawn up, everything she owned – including any children she might have and anything that might come to her in the future – would henceforth belong to her husband. She knew, too, what it was to be attracted to a man; for lack of that feeling she had turned down three offers of marriage, while at Dove's Nest she had lamented the unattainability of a visiting cler-gyman whom she thought so agreeeable that he should 'either marry, or be confined'.[53] Can Aaron Stock, threadbare and overbearing, have been any more alluring than those discarded suitors?

The most convincing explanation for this otherwise inexplicable about-turn is Nelly's age. She was now thirty-seven; this might well be her last chance of marriage. Always bitterly self-conscious, she was keenly aware – she mentions it more than once – that 'an old maid is a stock for everyone to laugh at'.[54] More importantly, she loved children and her childbearing years would soon be over. Unlike the rejected farmer, Stock, a widower of thirty-eight with two grown daughters, was excellent father-material. And Tom had vouched for him. Why should she turn him down? What was the alternative? Only more of the same: a solitary lifetime spent in other people's houses.

Stock, for his part, evidently recognized in this yearning spinster his lucky salvation. She had enough money to get him out of trouble; indeed, from then on his business affairs prospered. To get his hands on it, he need only hold out the possibility of family life – after all these drifting years a household, and with any luck children, of her own. It was an opportunity she could not afford to miss and she jumped at it.

The gold-digging wife for whom marriage is little more than genteel prostitution was a stock figure:

> To be a mistres kept the strumpet strives,
> And all the modest virgins to be wives.
> For prudes may cant of virtues and of vices,
> But faith, we only differ in our prices.[55]

In this case, however, the position was reversed: it was the husband who played the whore.

Nelly instantly got pregnant. And motherhood, the one gift Aaron Stock ever made her, was quite as engrossing as she had imagined.

'My little Mary ... is the delight of all,' she happily informed her friend Mrs Price in 1816. 'She is just 16 months old ... Her hair is very light, and curls all over her head like a little mop; and she is all over so fat and so soft. I have many a kiss in the course of the day, and many a laugh at her little droll ways; her father would be quite lost without her, and I am sure, so should I. I wish I had another ... but hush! don't tell.'[56] The coy tone suggests that at the time this may still have seemed a real prospect. Although Nelly quickly came to the bitter realization that 'Mr Stock is a man of that kind that would like a fresh wife every three or four months', there were, during the early years of their marriage, interludes of kindness when 'to live with him all my days would be most desirable, and to leave him, my greatest grief'.[57] But these happy moments soon receded. '[Mary] is all I have, and there is no prospect of more,' she wrote two years later. 'I could have much wished for 2 or 3 more, I am so doatingly fond of children.'[58]

In all other respects, the marriage was a disaster. Stock's money-grubbing motives at once became apparent. Following the ceremony he even objected to Nelly's retaining £23 of her own hard-earned cash for pocket money, even though she spent £3 of it on presents for his daughters by his first marriage, Hannah and Jane. Despite this they quickly entered into more or less open warfare with the newcomer, as did most of the servants, who were terrified of their bullying master. When the time came, Nelly would urge her own daughter never to marry without first taking a hard look at the way her potential husband treated his family and dependants.

Nelly tried various strategies to face down her husband's tyranny. She began with the submission she had urged upon Mrs Pedder. Predictably, it failed; so abandoning her principles, she turned to defiance and for a while this led to an uneasy truce. 'I could smile at the idea ... which you hold very tenaciously ... that if *one* of a married couple gives way to the wayward humours of the other, they are sure to be tolerably comfortable,' she wrote to Mrs Price, explaining this about-turn.

I know how little success you would have, could you take my place for one year ... You have not the most distant idea of such a situation, nor can words express it; yet I am indeed much happier

171

of late than I was, entirely owing to being determined not to submit to a continuation of ill-treatment. Had I not acted with greater spirit, had I continued to take every means to please (which was taken for a principle of fear), I must have lost my senses or my life.[59]

It is hard to believe that these attempts at defiance were very convincing. Nelly was one of nature's victims; that was what made her such a target for bullies and perhaps, in a supreme irony, it was what had drawn her to Aaron Stock. But she was right in one thing: meekness was not an option. She describes scenes of attempted reconciliation that would be comic if they were not so tragic.

His saying I never was the first to be friendly, is false. I have numberless times made the attempt. I acknowledge that his repulsive manner intimidates me so, that my attempts are feeble; generally, by striving to enter into some conversation with him, or by some little delicate attention, which he has not delicacy enough to discover, but which *would win a heart like yours* directly. When I have attempted to put my arm round him, he has often pushed it away from him so rudely, that his hard gripe has hurt me exceedingly; the few times that I tried that way, I never recollect that it succeeded.[60]

Stock's behaviour became ever more abusive. He denied Nelly money — her own money – for months on end, while giving it freely to his daughters and the servants. His violence constantly forced her to take refuge from his house, once in Liverpool with a cousin, once with the unsympathetic Tom in Leigh, once with her old friend Mrs Braithwaite in Up Holland. Each time she took Mary with her; each time they were forced back by lack of funds. In a long letter of bitter complaint written to her brother when all illusion had been finally stripped away, she describes a marriage so hellish as to be barely imaginable.

Repeatedly turned out destitute; twice imprisoned – the first time for a first offence of [assault]; the 2[n]d., *perfectly innocent*, having myself been beaten almost to death; several times obliged to flee for my life; the time when I broke the windows, if I had not by that means forced my way in, I must have been out all night, on the cold and wet pavement of a dark November night. I had then been turned out only for complaining ... I was threatened with being sent to a Lunatic Asylum, only for asking for food. Cloaths I could not procure until I got them on credit ... With my bruises thick upon me – bruises such as the Doctor said would have mortified had I not been so extremely thin – was I imprisoned for two days, and you would not bail me out! Oh, oh, you unnatural being ... Oh! This was a climax of misery! 'Tis strange I did not lose my senses, to think that I should have such a husband and such a brother!

I soon returned to my miserable home, for I dared not stay long away, now expecting nightly or daily to be murdered – or worse, sent to a Lunatic Asylum in my right mind; for so I was threatened; and I had no help to expect from you (for so you had assured Mr Stock)! ... I expected to be again turned out, although Mr Stock lived in another house, and to be driven out destitute as I had often been, so that I kept myself locked up day and night in my bedroom, going out only by stealth in the evening, to fetch provisions, and let Dr Hawarden's see that I was in Wigan, and alive. On returning one night, I found my room on fire, and my bed burnt! I most solemnly declare that I was not in the house when the fire commenced. In my opinion, it was done to procure my transportation, or perhaps even hanging; for I had no help from you ...

I had now no bed! As I was reduced lower and lower in affliction, I often exclaimed – what next? After lying some nights on a Sofa rolled in blankets, I again found shelter at the kind Mrs Braithwaite's of Holland.[61]

Inevitably, little Mary became a weapon in the marital war. Nelly speaks of Stock's attachment to his youngest daughter, but it cannot have run excessively deep; at any rate, he was willing to deprive himself of her company and to sacrifice her well-being if that was the only way to deny her to her mother. In 1819, at the tender age of four, Mary was sent to boarding school – a miserable establishment called Parr Hall at nearby St Helens, kept by a warring, drunken couple by the name of Grundy. There she would be removed from Nelly's influence; since Grundy did not wish to alienate Stock, who paid his fees, communication between mother and child would be strictly controlled. Having achieved this, Stock could turn to the real business of the day: driving his wife out of the house.

> Mr Stock wants me either to remain at home pennyless, as an underling to his own daughter, or to be kept by anyone that will take me. I cannot agree to such a reconciliation, or such a separation, whilst he has plenty of money. I am obliged totally to withdraw myself from any domestic affairs ... to live in an apartment alone, not to sit at table with the family, but to have my meat sent to me ... when, and how will this end?[62]

It ended in 1821, in a deed of separation, negotiated on the harshest of terms. Although Nelly was unwilling to agree them, Tom persuaded her there was no alternative. She signed the paper without being allowed to read it for herself – it was read to her by a clerk – and regretted it ever after. She was never to come within a two-mile radius of Wigan. Her contact with Mary was limited to three visits a year at her school, always in the presence of one of the school's proprietors. She was to be paid an allowance of £70 a year, in arrears; about what her income had been before she married and far less than her now-wealthy husband was able to afford. And in all this, Tom not only failed to argue her side, but, she later found, advised her enemy.

At first Nelly refused to visit her daughter under Stock's intolerable conditions, but that meant she did not see her at all for fourteen months, and when they did eventually meet, 'Mary knew not her mother! and her mother hardly recognized her child, her only one!'[63] She wrote to Mary, naturally; but her correspondence was monitored, both by the Grundys and the Wigan postmaster, so that most of her letters never arrived, nor the toys and clothes she sometimes sent.

In the end Nelly was reduced to lying in wait furtively on Sundays, when the school crocodile passed en route for chapel. Having walked all the way from Up Holland, she would hide in a neighbouring cottage until the line had drawn abreast, then insinuated herself among the girls and walked beside Mary. The two would chat as well as they could, but of course the whole proceeding was exceedingly awkward, not least since there were members of staff present. 'I fell into the rank and walked to St Helen's. Miss Hammond seemed agitated, but what cared I? She appeared inclined to be insolent when I apologized for coming in such a manner; but I avoided altercation.'[64]

It was far from satisfactory, and Nelly made constant efforts to prevail upon Stock to lift his restrictions. But he refused to do so. After two months of snatched Sunday conversations, it became clear that they would no longer be tolerated. If Nelly persisted, she was told, Mary would be removed from the school.

We then left the Chapel, and continued talking as we walked down the street; my little darling held my hand and we gave each other many an affectionate squeeze. Tears were in Mary's eyes; bless the tender-hearted child. Miss Jackson continued to represent to me the *dreadful* and *tremendous*, the *deplorable* and *terrible* consequences of my coming to see my Mary ... All of a sudden Miss Jackson popped into Dr Gaskell's shop without saying a word, and left Mary and me quite alone; this was an unexpected delight, so we walked on above a mile, and got a great deal said. I assured her most solemnly that I would never desert her ... At last Mr Grundy overtook us. I took not the least notice of him; at length he opened his mouth, and he spoke, but only on indifferent subjects, to which I replied civilly. Not a word did he say upon the subject of his instructions to Miss Jackson – a mean fellow, to load a blunderbuss for her to fire, and dare not produce a pop-gun himself ... I then took leave, an affectionate leave of my Mary, possibly for the last time! When she found that I stood in the road looking after her, she continued turning her dear face to the last moment, and she walked on to the house. When the hedge intervened, she continued jumping up to look again at me, and again. At last, she disappeared. Oh, what hearts of stone are those that can separate mother and child. I got home, weary and depressed. 12 miles.[65]

To combat her depression, Nelly took herself off to Wales, where she hoped vigorous walking and sightseeing might distract her. Climbing Snowdon, she felt as if she might fall off a precipice. But no, she was not so easily destroyed. She strode on, and soothed by the beauty and the grandeur prepared herself for the solitary life to come.

At this point, despite all Stock had done to her, she actually tried to effect a reconciliation. The gist of the letter she wrote him was to request a more generous settlement – the £200 a year he could easily afford, that would allow her to live in a respectable small house of her own, with a maid to help with the housework. Still she proclaimed her friendship for him – and 'it would be very consoling, could I be permitted to use a term warmer than friendship; let me at least ask for yours in return; be my friend, and be no longer my enemy.' She was even ready to attribute his behaviour to 'mischief makers' without whose malicious whisperings 'we might still be as happy a couple as most in our own rank'.[66] However, nothing came of this, nor had she really expected it would.

Such miserable treatment of wives, if by no means unusual, was generally unacknowledged; the legal position of married women was so hopeless, and earning a living so problematic, that – like Nelly – most would try anything rather than actually leave the marital home. But occasionally something so terrible happened that the scales were tipped and the victim left. One of the last letters we have of Nelly's congratulates a friend who has recently offered refuge to another unfortunate wife – 'poor Mrs Littler', whose treatment had evidently passed the bounds of the bearable.

> I feel deeply concerned for her. I had long suspected that she was a sufferer like myself; hers is a situation most miserable! None can have even a distant idea of it, but they who have suffered likewise. I hope she will have friends more willing to exert themselves for her than any I ever had, that she may not fall a sacrifice, as I have done, to brutality, depravity, hypocrisy, falsehood, and an unfeeling world ... And what is painful to the last degree in situations like Mrs Littler's and mine, when our husbands use us cruelly, the whole world are open-mouthed against us too, instead of pitying, soothing and comforting us. A wife, though her conduct be as corrrect as a mortal's can be, yet if her husband unnaturally drives her from his roof, from the ferocity of his own disposition, she is avoided as if she were infamous.[67]

Nelly must often have asked herself how it was possible that the world, knowing both Aaron Stock and his wife, could seriously have taken his part, believing his tales and ostracizing her? The answer surely is that most probably they did not believe Stock. But in holding all the money he held all the cards; and whatever people really thought, they were more concerned to conciliate him than to make life tolerable for his unfortunate wife. The grossest example of this was the local church, where she had for years taught at the Sunday School. Now, at the moment when Nelly's fortunes stood at their lowest, when she was regularly beaten, humiliated and locked out of the marital home, these Christians took her torturer's side and declared her, at a solemn meeting, unfit to join their congregation. Stock, it seemed, had an excellent Calvinistic library and the minister was afraid that, if he admitted Nelly, he would no longer be able to borrow from it.

Nelly's forebodings of permanent separation from Mary were wide of the mark. Her journals end shortly after her sad and (as both thought) final parting from Mary. Two years later, however, she was recorded as resident in Wigan; and that same year, Aaron Stock moved away, retiring from cotton spinning to take up an interest in coal mining at Ashton-in-Makerfield, a few miles to the south. And since, two years after that, Mary joined her mother's Wigan chapel, we may presume that mother and daughter were then living together. Perhaps that was why Stock moved away from Wigan; after all his man-oeuvrings, to see Nelly and Mary reunited may have been more than he could bear.

That men's absolute power over their wives and sisters poisoned the relations between the sexes is evident, both from Nelly's own story and from those of Mrs Pedder and Mrs Littler. Even Tom Weeton, who at the outset seems genuinely to have loved his sister, was unable to resist its venomous pleasures, effectively selling her into servitude and then, when it came to arranging the terms of the separation, pretending to advise her while really acting on behalf of Stock and urging upon her the cruel terms her husband was determined to enforce. And as Stock well knew, in the marital or quasi-marital power struggle, there exists no more potent weapon than a child.

Nelly's story, though less tragic in its outcome, recalls Claire Clairmont's. Both were chilling reminders that as desperation grows, so does both the power of the weapon and the fury of its holder. Byron's dealings with Claire quite obviously had as much to do with a cruel and not unpleasurable determination to show her who was master, and how far she had overstepped the mark, as with any real concern for Allegra. And

Byron was, generally speaking, a humane and liberal man. Aaron Stock, crude and vindictive to begin with, naturally seized with delight upon such a perfect means of tormenting his unfortunate wife.

Given that two in our small and random selection of women suffered this treatment, we can only conclude that perhaps it was not so very uncommon. We do not know whether Mrs Pedder went on to have children, but if she did and (as seems all too probable) subsequently found married life unbearable, it is easy to imagine Pedder – weak, spoiled, alcoholic – using them against her in this way. This is what happens in Anne Brontë's *The Tenant of Wildfell Hall*, published in 1848 but set twenty years earlier, in 1827. The terrible marriage portrayed in that book, whose brutality so shocked reviewers, was, she said, based on what she had observed during her five years working as a governess for the Robinson family at Thorp Hall, where she recorded having undergone 'unpleasant and undreamt-of experiences of human nature'.[68]

Perhaps one reason she set the novel when she did was that, by the time she wrote it, the balance of power regarding children (on which much of her plot hinges) had shifted. For when this same ill-usage was meted out to Caroline Norton, the granddaughter of the Whig politician and playwright Richard Brinsley Sheridan, the men found that they had met their match. Trelawny admired Mrs Norton tremendously. Fearless, articulate, and ferociously well connected, she was his sort of woman: the kind Claire might once have been but had ceased to be.

In its essentials, Caroline Norton's story is little different from Nelly's. In 1827, aged nineteen, she married the Tory MP George Norton, who had long been in love with her. She did not like him and they disagreed on almost everything. But the match pleased her widowed mother and promised financial security, so she went through with it and dutifully bore three sons.

Caroline's dislike of her husband increased with the years. She did not bother to hide it; he, infuriated, beat her up so savagely that she had several times to be rescued by the servants. Although she twice tried to leave him, the fact that this also meant leaving the children always drew her back.

She had meanwhile become suspiciously friendly with Lord Melbourne, who in 1830 was appointed Home Secretary in the Whig administration. In 1831, when he became prime minister, Norton resolved to force him from office, while definitively disgracing Caroline, by suing him for adultery. Despite losing the case resoundingly, he still kept the children, and – as was his legal right – still denied Caroline all access.

In a comparable situation, Nelly eventually despaired. Caroline, however, with her contacts in the ruling party, was in a position to get the law changed. She wrote a pamphlet, 'The Natural Claim of a Mother to the custody of her Children as affected by the Common Law Rights of the Father', and got Thomas Talfourd MP to introduce a bill into Parliament that would allow mothers against whom adultery had not been proved to have custody of children under seven, as well as rights of access to older children. It failed, but in 1839 was reintroduced and this time passed, to become the Custody of Children Act.

Norton vindictively refused to submit. He sent the children to school in Scotland, outside the jurisdiction of English law, where, in 1842, William Norton, then aged eight, fell off his pony while out riding with his brother. His only injury was a cut to his arm, but the cut became infected and the child died of blood poisoning, joining the hecatombs of children for whom hurts that to us seem trivial yet proved fatal. After that Norton allowed the two remaining children, Fletcher and Brinsley, to live with their mother. But he still played his power games, over divorce (which he refused) and money, claiming not just his wife's earnings, but her legacies both from Melbourne and from her mother, all of which by law belonged to him. That situation would not be wholly rectified until the Marriage and Divorce Act of 1857 and the Married Women's Property Act of 1882.* But at least after 1839 it was no longer legal to debar a mother access to her children, as Aaron Stock debarred Nelly.

Anne Brontë was of course not the most famous chronicler of

---

* Under the terms of this Act, married women had the same rights over their property as unmarried women. It therefore allowed a married woman to retain ownership of property that she might have received as a gift from a parent. Before the Married Women's Property Act was passed in 1882, this property would automatically have become the property of the husband. The passing of the 1893 Married Women's Property Act completed this process. After that, married women had full legal control of all the property of every kind which they owned at marriage or which they acquired after marriage, either by inheritance or by their own earnings.

downtrodden governesses. That was her sister Charlotte: and it so happened that there was a direct connection between her and Nelly's old employers, the Joseph Armitages.

Nelly's stay at High Royd coincided with the Luddite disturbances – she records a 'dreadful execution'[69] at York during her stay there in which seventeen men were hanged for involvement with the riots. And in this connection the Armitage family had been involved in some dramatic incidents that, to Brontë enthusiasts, will sound oddly familiar. Just before Nelly's arrival at High Royd, a local mill owner called Cartwright had introduced shearing frames, which did away with many local jobs and attracted the attentions of Luddite rioters. A hundred and fifty men, from various locations, assembled in a nearby field one night, from which they set off to attack the mill and destroy the frames. But Cartwright was ready for them. For the past six weeks he had been sleeping at the mill, along with a garrison of ten soldiers. The attackers were fired on and dispersed; some were wounded, apprehended and brutally interrogated until they died.

Sir George Armitage, Joseph Armitage's father, was a local Justice of the Peace and firmly on the side of law and order. A week after the attack, Cartwright was shot at as he rode back from the court-martial of a soldier who had refused to fire on the rioters; that same night, stones were thrown at the windows of the house then belonging to the hated JP's son Joseph Armitage, situated near the mill, followed by shots as he and his wife lay in bed. That was the real reason Joseph and his wife had moved to High Royd, which was some distance from these happenings and which had been recently vacated by Sir George. One can hardly blame him, though he seems to have been rather ashamed of his cowardice; he told Nelly he had been forced to move there, even though he did not much like High Royd's out-of-the way situation, because his father had threatened 'to leave the estate out of the family if he did not come to it now'.[70] The riots were also the reason why the Armitages, despite their wealth, kept no indoor manservant. They had done so before, but since the attack on their previous house had 'not ventured to keep a man in the house, as many gentlemen have been betrayed by their servants, who have been discovered to be of the Luddite party'.[71]

This incident – both the riot at the mill and the subsequent shooting – provided the plot for Charlotte Brontë's novel *Shirley*. But *Shirley* is not solely – or even mainly – about Luddism and its causes. That is just the setting for its real subject, which as always with Charlotte Brontë is love and, eventually, marriage between unequals: the penniless governess, and the wealthy employer who recognizes her true worth. If Jane Eyre's 'Reader, I married him'[72] instantly became one of the most famous phrases in English literature, that is surely because of its direct line to the core of its writer's soul.

For Charlotte Brontë, marriage – and, specifically, marriage for love – was the only real and possible goal. Yet, as *Jane Eyre* also shows, her view of marriage was highly ambivalent. What is the first Mrs Rochester – the madwoman in the attic who eventually sets the house ablaze and blinds her husband as she kills herself – but an expression, whether conscious or unconscious, of terminal frustration? In the eighteenth century, marriage had involved not just the individuals concerned but had been a public contract in which two clans, as well as two people, were joined together. But by the time *Jane Eyre* was written it had become a private emotional bond between two individuals based on the promise (and premise) of personal fulfilment, with no outside interference and no redress when things went wrong. Under the doctrine of *feme covert*, as expounded by William Blackstone in the late eighteenth century, a woman, once married, had no independent legal existence but was reduced to a wholly owned subsidiary of her husband. When Mr Rochester tired of his wife's behaviour, he was perfectly within his rights to shut her away in the attic. If she, on the other hand, wanted to escape, setting the house on fire was her only option.[73]

And yet – another reason why, as a single woman in a comparatively comfortable position, Nelly Weeton was nevertheless ready to take a chance on Aaron Stock rather than continue unmarried – the alternative was even less alluring.

Part of the answer must surely lie in the desperate nature of the lone woman's life. It was true that Nelly had enough to eat and could keep a roof over her head. But what could she *do*? More than once she gives us glimpses into her unbearable boredom and isolation. Thus, when she had finally achieved sufficient income to give up the drudgery of her school, she writes:

With being so long alone, I was completely moped. I tried to amuse myself with reading, but it only stupified me. I took a walk, but could not enjoy it, and returned home quite melancholy. Like a spoiled baby, I was not to be pleased with anything but that which I could not obtain – society. I could not work, drawing was insipid, and music had lost its usual charm. I took up my Flageolet [a small woodwind instrument] and put it to my lips, but my throat was full, and I could not blow.[74]

What Nelly needed was work – proper work, the kind of thing for which her brother Tom had been educated. But of course, even had she had Tom's education, such work would not have been forthcoming. And this absence of possibilities was no accident. If single life had been more desirable, no independent woman would have tied herself to a man on the terms available. But it was not desirable. The sum of £76 a year, Nelly's income when she married, might be more than most lone women could count on, but it would support only the plainest and most solitary existence. 'I should weep till I died for the want of you,' Nelly told Mary in 1825, when she was living on a similar sum – the £70 a year that Stock paid her,

if I did not strive all I could to amuse myself by going from home sometimes. I would travel much if I had money enough, but ... coach hire is too expensive, and I have not strength enough to walk to every place I should wish to go. If I stay at home I become low spirited for want of your entertaining company; for I cannot afford to invite my acquaintances often. And besides, as I cannot keep a servant, it is so much trouble to wait upon them myself, that it prevents all the pleasure of their society, and I do not choose to visit where it is inconvenient to invite them again. If I were rich enough to buy furniture, and to take a house and keep a servant, I could have as much society – highly respectable – as I could wish.[75]

For this – the kind of life any decently married woman might expect – she reckoned she would need £200 a year: the sum she had requested, and that he refused to pay her.

That is why, although it must have been obvious almost instantly that she had made a terrible mistake in marrying Stock, Nelly still, two years into this singularly imperfect marriage, thought herself right, on balance, to have taken the step she had – or, at the very least, could still see why she had done so. Compared to the alternatives, almost any marriage – even hers – seemed preferable.

I could smile at your thinking that I had been so long my own mistress, because I had remained so long unmarried. I never was uncontrolled more than 2 years of my life. No one, used to live in another person's house, can be said to have much of their own way. You don't know what it is, nor how great a trial and breaking of the temper it is, to keep a school, or to be a private teacher; married to one of so peculiar a temper as I am, it is scarcely worse.[76]

However, if you took the view that marriage – any marriage, even under the conditions obtaining in early nineteenth-century England – was better than remaining single, then important psychological adjustments had to be made. In particular, women had truly to believe that they could never be men's equal. Even that doughty political operator Caroline Norton, whose suffering at the hands of her vindictive husband was known to all the world, nevertheless proclaimed that 'The wild and stupid theories advanced by a few women of "equal rights" and "equal intelligence", are not the opinions of their sex. I for one (I, with millions more), believe in the natural superiority of man as I do in the existence of God.'[77]

One of the most forceful of Charlotte Brontë's independent young women – those plain-spoken girls 'whom we should not care for as an acquaintance, whom we should not seek as a friend, whom we should not desire for a relation, and whom we should scrupulously avoid for a governess'[78] – is *Shirley*'s eponymous heroine, Shirley Keeldar. Shirley is rich, well educated, forceful, indifferent to society's opinions and disinclined to marry. In the end, however, she succumbs and, in an inversion of the usual scenario (where the penniless governess falls in love with her rich master), is captivated by a penniless tutor, Louis Moore. And how does Charlotte Brontë picture their union? As a forfeiture, by Shirley, of all the mannish forcefulness that, until this moment, has seemed so strongly to characterize her.

There she was at last, fettered to a fixed day: there she lay, conquered by love, and bound with a vow.

Thus vanquished and restricted, she pined like any other chained denizen of deserts. Her captor alone could cheer her; his society only could make amends for the lost privilege of liberty: in his absence, she sat or wandered alone; spoke little, and ate less.[79]

At one point Shirley even addresses her husband-to-be as 'My master'.

If even the formidable Miss Brontë had so absolutely internalized this view of marriage, it is scarcely surprising that Nelly Weeton should have done the same. Though a habitual victim, she was no weakling – the mere fact of her surviving Aaron Stock's brutality shows, on the contrary, an exceptional inner strength and stubbornness. But the long training that had conditioned her always to place her own interests below those of any man was too much even for her.

Anna and the King:
the unbreakable bonds of class

In 1956, the world was presented with a new avatar of governesshood: ladylike Deborah Kerr, crinoline awhirl, teaching King Yul Brynner (those cheekbones! those masterful arms!) to polka in that year's runaway movie success, *The King and I*. In novels the governess marries her metaphorical prince, but in Hollywood nothing less than a genuine king will do.

The King and I is adapted from Margaret Landon's best-selling *Anna and the King of Siam*, published in 1943, and in its turn based upon two almost forgotten memoirs. In *The English Governess at the Siamese Court*, and its sequel *Siamese Harem Life*, Anna Leonowens recounted the five years that she spent in Bangkok, between 1862 and 1867, as governess to the wives and children of King Mongkut – to be precise, his thirty-nine sons and forty-three daughters by twenty-seven royal princesses, thirty-four concubines and seventy-four daughters of noblemen.[1] Landon described her adaptation as 'seventy five percent fact, twenty five percent fiction':[2] as it turned out a distinctly over-optimistic estimate.

Landon's retelling reawakened interest in her exotic heroine. *Siamese Harem Life* was reissued in 1952 with an introduction by Freya Stark, doyenne of intrepid female travellers, who concluded that 'few people can have wielded a stronger influence in that corner of Asia' than Anna Leonowens'.[3]

That, though undoubtedly hyperbolic, was perhaps less far-fetched than it sounds. Soon after Anna's arrival, the King, who needed an English-language amanuensis, requested her to act for him in this capacity, over and above the teaching for which she had originally been hired. Since his dealings with England and America were important and highly political, this gave her a good deal of de facto power, as well as much more frequent and intimate access to the king than would otherwise have been the case. Being an exceptionally intelligent and energetic woman, she made the most of this rare opportunity to participate in high-level politics, offering advice as well as correcting the king's idiosyncratic grammar and spelling. She appears to have had no qualms about this. She might be a mere governess, but in the days of Empire, any Briton was *ipso facto* superior to any native. (This was of course the culture in which Freya Stark herself had grown up.)

In the second half of the twentieth century, however, such assumptions seemed increasingly anachronistic. And there are passages in Anna's books that fatally undermine our confidence in the author. In particular, although she frequently acknowledges Mongkut's modernizing ideas and profound culture, other parts of her account are liberally sprinkled with highly coloured tales of the cruelty supposedly meted out by this 'pagan' to the slaves and concubines of his harem: '"You may lash me with a million thongs," I told them, "but you shall not expose my person." My silk vest was torn off, my scarf was flung aside, my slippers were taken from my feet. My arms were stretched and tied to a post, and thus I was lashed ... My flesh was laid open in fine thin stripes, but I do not remember flinching. My feet were then bastinadoed, and I still preserved, I know not how, my secret.'[4]

In 1970 these purple passages provoked the Scottish historian, Ian Grimble, to dismiss Anna as 'one of those awful little English governesses, a sex-starved widow' whose books were 'pornographic ... rubbish ... the sort of books that Calvinists read beneath bedcovers'.[5] And a few years later, in 1976, much of her account was circumstantially dismantled – including the whiteness and Britishness upon which she based her claim to automatic superiority.

William Bristowe became interested in Anna when he set out to research a book about the friendship between her son Louis Leonowens and King Mongkut's successor, King Chulalongkorn. This friendship was established when Louis, then a little boy, accompanied his mother to the palace where Chulalongkorn was one of her pupils. Louis' happy childhood accounts of life in the harem sat very oddly with his mother's melodramatic claims of regular beatings, torture and imprisonment. 'I like the King,' Louis wrote to his sister Avis in London, 'he gave me some gold leaf for you which I send.' 'I have got a gun and a sword, and a beautiful boat the King gave mama and a paddle too with which I row Mama to the Palace,' said another letter, and a third, 'I am very happy. All the people loves [sic] me and Mama . . . All the little princes love and play with me.'[6] This does not sound like a man 'envious, revengeful, subtle and cruel'[7] – the words Anna used to describe the king's personal life.

This was far from the only flaw in Anna's allegedly 'true' tales. Bristowe pointed out that the subterranean dungeons in which she described errant wives supposedly mouldering could not possibly have existed in waterlogged Bangkok. A description of the sacrificial murder of an innocent woman and the subsequent disposal of her body beneath some gateposts, was culled from a French missionary's account, whose phrases were faithfully reproduced. An account of the burning of an adulterous woman and her lover was entirely made up. These were just a few of many examples.[8]

These anomalies induced Bristowe to look more closely at Anna's version of her own origins. What he found was both pathetic and highly revealing.

Anna's account is as follows. She was born in Caernarvon on 5 November 1834, the only child of Captain Thomas Maxwell Crawford and Selina Edwards, who belonged to an ancient Welsh family. When Anna was six she was left with an aunt in Wales while her parents went to India, where in 1841 her father, then acting ADC to the commander of British troops in Lahore, was killed in a Sikh uprising. Anna stayed in Wales until her education was finished, then went out to India, where her mother had remarried. She fell in love with Thomas Leonowens, a young army officer, but her stepfather, whom she hated, wanted her to marry a rich merchant more than twice her age. The dispute was settled by sending her, in 1850, on a long educational tour to the Middle East with the Revd George Percy Badger and his wife. On her return to India she married Leonowens and lived with him in the fashionable Malabar Hill area of Bombay. In 1852 their first baby died, as did Anna's mother, so they set out for England on a voyage of recuperation. However, their vessel was wrecked near the Cape of Good Hope, and the ship that picked them up was bound for Australia, where another child died. By the time they arrived in London, it was 1854. There they settled in St James's and two more children were born: a daughter and son, Avis and Louis. In 1857, Leonowens was ordered to rejoin his regiment in Singapore. That same year, when the Agra Bank collapsed during the Indian Mutiny, Anna lost all her little fortune. In 1858, when Leonowens died of sunstroke after a tiger shoot, she found herself alone with two children and was forced to earn her own living. She started a small school for officers' children, but money was scarce. So when the King of Siam's offer of employment came along, she gratefully accepted it.

Although a touching tale, it was unfortunately not true. The facts, as Bristowe winkled them out, were these. Anna was born on 6 November 1831, not 5 November 1834, and in India, not Wales. Her father was Sergeant, not Captain, Thomas Edwards; her mother, Mary-Anne, née Glasscock, was probably half Indian. She had an elder sister, Eliza, whom she never mentions and from whom she seems to have cut herself off (which was essential, presumably, if her fabrications were not to be exposed).

Thomas Edwards died, penniless, in 1831; his widow was awarded a small pension, but that stopped in 1832 when she remarried. Anna's stepfather, Patrick Donoughey, was a corporal, later demoted to private. Their home life in the cramped married men's quarters, where whole families were squeezed into a single room, was probably fairly unbearable; to escape it, Eliza (not Anna) married, at the age of barely fifteen, a sergeant-major of thirty-eight. (One of her grandchildren was the actor Boris Karloff.) Anna took a different route out of the parental home: the Egyptian trip in the company of the Revd George Percy Badger. There was, however, no Mrs Badger; as Bristowe puts it, 'we must draw the conclusion that everything was paid for by Mr Badger'[9] – and that Anna's repayment was probably in kind.

On Christmas Day 1849, back in India, Anna married Mr Thomas Leon Owens, an assistant in the Military Pay Office in Bombay. Between then and his death (of apoplexy, in Penang in 1859), they do indeed seem to have travelled to Australia and England. There had also been four children, of whom Avis and Louis survived.[10]

It is not far from Penang to Singapore; the widowed Anna was indeed keeping a school there when in 1862 King Mongkut, finding himself with twenty-seven children of an age to start learning, commissioned his agent in Singapore, Tan Kim Ching, the local manager of the Borneo Company, to find him an 'English school mastress'[11] [sic] at a salary of $100 a month, plus a free house in or near the palace.

It is impossible to know for certain how much of what Anna wrote was true and how much embroidered or invented. But of course invention is quite as interesting as truth – often more so. Few of even the most authentic descriptions are as fascinating and revealing as pretence – or, rather, as what lies behind it. In this context, talk of 'awful little English governesses' and 'sex-starved widows' may be more germane than Ian Grimble supposed. For Anna's story is all about prejudice – and those phrases tell us plenty about the prejudices of a certain class of Englishman (or Scotsman). The kind of lady traveller represented by Freya Stark – that is to say, upper or middle class, well heeled, the kind of woman who, had she been a man, would have been an accredited explorer, funded by the Royal Geographical Society or *The Times* – attracted no such obloquy; and many respected travellers, male and female, wrote highly coloured tales. But a governess! What else could one expect?

In fact by the mid-nineteenth century, English governesses were in demand worldwide, and a good many published memoirs of their travels in far-flung places. At least two (though not Claire Clairmont, who never intended her letters and journals for publication) described their experiences in Russia;[12] Miss Emmeline Lott's account of *Harem Life in Egypt and Constantinople*, published in 1866, described her experiences as governess to the Grand Pacha, heir to the viceroy of Egypt; Maria Graham wrote of her experience as a valued household member of the emperor of Brazil ... Not only could teaching provide a respectable single lady with a ticket to see hidden parts of the world, but there might also be useful extra income in the form of a book once the actual posting had come to an end.

Anna Leonowens, however, is interesting because she was different. Unlike the other memoirists she was not an English lady, as English ladies understood the term. Paradoxically, this meant that she cast a particularly revealing light on the nuances of class. Because she was an outsider, she revealed (although she did not see) more of the game.

When Anna accepted his offer of employment, King Mongkut sent her the following letter:

> *English Era, 1862, 26th February.*
> *Grand Royal Palace, Bangkok.*
>
> *To Mrs A.H. Leonowens: –*
> *Madam: We are in good pleasure, and satisfaction in heart, that you are in willingness to undertake the education of our beloved royal children. And we hope that in doing your education on us and on our children (whom English call inhabitants of benighted land) you will do your best endeavor for knowledge of English language, science, and literature, and not for conversion to Christianity; as the followers of Buddha are mostly aware of the powerfulness of truth and virtue, as well as the followers of Christ, and are desirous to have facility of English language and literature, more than new religions.*
> *We beg to invite you to our royal palace to do your best endeavorment upon us and our children. We shall expect to see you here on return of Siamese steamer Chow Phya.*
> *We have written to Mr William Adamson, and to our consul at Singapore, to authorize to do best arrangement for you and ourselves.*
> *Believe me*
> *Your faithfully,*
> *S.S.P.P. Maha Mongkut.*[13]

Anna's story – and much more than that – lies in the gap between what he hoped for and what he got.

When Mongkut's invitation arrived, Anna had first to make arrangements for her own children. She evidently concluded that a Siamese harem was no place for a small girl and despatched her daughter Avis to England in care of a Mr and Mrs Heritage, to be educated at the Miss Kings' school in Fulham – a highly respectable establishment whose pupils included the bishop of London's children, who lived down the road in Fulham Palace. That left Anna, her son Louis, then six or seven, their Newfoundland dog Bessy, her Persian teacher and general retainer Moonshee, and Moonshee's wife Beebe. These all embarked, as instructed, on the *Chow P'hya* and on 15 March 1862 arrived at the mouth of the river Meinam, upon which Bangkok is situated, with its 'narrow serpentine canals and creeks ... conical roofs thatched with attaps [nipa palms], and ... the pyramids and spires and fantastic turrets of the more important buildings'.[14]

Since Anna had spent most of her life in south Asia, spoke some Malay and was used to confronting new faces and places, all this was perhaps not as intimidating as it might have been to some fresh green import direct from England. But she spoke no Thai and knew no one in Bangkok, while her little boy, Moonshee, Beebe and the dog, all looked to her for guidance. Her first contact with the Siamese court (one of her more believable accounts) was not encouraging.

Before long a showy gondola, fashioned like a dragon, with flashing torches and many paddles, approached; and a Siamese official mounted the side, swaying himself with an absolute air. The red *langoutee*, or skirt, loosely folded about his person, did not reach his ankles; and to cover his audacious chest and shoulders he had only his own brown polished skin. He was followed by a dozen attendants, who, the moment they stepped from the gangway, sprawled on the deck like huge toads, doubling their arms and legs under them, and pressing their noses against the boards, as if intent on making themselves small by degrees and hideously less. Every Asiatic on deck, coolies and all, prostrates himself, except my two servants, who are bewildered. Moonshee covertly mumbles his five prayers ... and Beebe shrinks, and draws her veil of spotted muslin jealously over her charms.

The captain stepped forward and introduced us. 'His Excellency Chow P'hya Sri Sury Wongse, Prime Minister of the Kingdom of Siam!'

Half naked as he was, and without an emblem to denote his rank, there was yet something remarkable about this native chief, by virtue of which he compelled our respect from the first glance – a sensibly magnetic quality of tone or look. With an air of command oddly at variance with his almost indecent attire, of which he seemed superbly unconscious, he beckoned to a young attendant, who crawled to him as a dog crawls to an angry master. This was an interpreter, who at a word from his lord began to question me in English.

'Are you the lady who is to teach in the royal family?'

On my replying in the affirmative, he asked, 'Have you friends in Bangkok?'

Finding I had none, he was silent for a minute or two; then demanded: 'What will you do? Where will you sleep tonight?'

'Indeed I cannot tell,' I said. 'I am a stranger here. But I understood from His Majesty's letter that a residence would be provided for us on our arrival; and he has been duly informed that we were to arrive at this time.'

'His Majesty cannot remember everything,' said his Excellency; the interpreter added, 'You can go where you like.'[15]

Anna settled Louis down in a makeshift bed, and prepared to spend the night on deck. However, in the nick of time the harbourmaster, an Englishman called Captain Bush, came to the rescue and offered to put her up at his house until she should find somewhere of her own to live – an offer that she gratefully accepted.

Writing in the enlightened 1970s, William Bristowe, who was familiar with Thai society, was shocked and dismayed by Anna's ignorant dismissal of the proud and powerful prime minister as a half-naked, barely civilized native chief. Even though the message he conveyed was both dismaying and insulting, she should have behaved better: 'Shyness, anxiety or even fear might have been natural.'[16] But Anna was not just the protector of her brood; she was also, in her own mind, and as far as these natives were concerned, a British lady. And Prince though Sri Sury Wongse might be, he was undoubtedly a native. His dress told the whole story. No jacket, no shirt, *no breeches*.

However, Britishness, as she now found out, did not necessarily count for much when dealing with the British themselves. There were British and British, and middle-class Britons were not about to welcome a governess into their midst just because they happened to be living in Bangkok. Captain Bush the harbourmaster is the only member of the Bangkok British colony whose name Anna mentions as a friend. Of the consul, Sir Robert Schomburgk, we hear nothing; though his deputy, Thomas Knox (later to become Louis' father-in-law), is occasionally invoked as a threat when the king reneges on some promise, there is no mention of Henry Alabaster and Dr James Campbell, the other members of the consulate. They did not offer her hospitality, nor ease her passage with the king. As far as they were concerned, she was on her own.

The same was true of the merchants. The search for an English governess for the royal children had been sponsored by the Borneo Company, which dealt in teak and of which Louis, when he grew up, would become a director. This, however, was no selfless act of educational beneficence. Siam was situated at the confluence of empires, between British Singapore and French Indochina; during Anna's time in Bangkok, and to the king's alarm, France advanced into Cambodia, which had until then been under the Siamese sphere of influence, and which had acted as a buffer between Siam and Indochina. The king was deeply aware of his powerlessness when confronted by such French manoeuvres – 'like a mouse before an elephant', as he put it.[17] But from the empire-builders' standpoint, the French move only increased Siam's strategic importance. As far as London was concerned, it clearly made sense to to try to tilt the court – and, in particular, the young heir to the throne – towards Britishness. In this endeavour his education would obviously play a vital role. In the same way, Emmeline Lott, engaged specifically to tutor the viceroy of Egypt's young heir, noted: 'Well did I know that the Greeks and Germans in the Harem were emissaries of parties who were then doing their utmost to surround H.H. the Viceroy with creatures of their own.'[18]

The policy succeeded, at least in Siam. Under Anna's tuition Mongkut's heir, Chulalongkorn, became both an Anglophile and a particular friend of Louis Leonowens. This would, in the fullness of time, be good news for the Borneo Company. In the meantime, notwithstanding the new governess's diplomatic and mercantile importance, the Borneo Company merchants were no more disposed than the diplomats to receive her socially.[19]

It is possible that Anna may have anticipated this reception. We do not know when or why she concocted her false, and falsely respectable, personal history. Perhaps it was in Singapore, when she opened her school for officers' children. Avis, too, would need a convincing family history if she was to survive in the alien environment of the Miss Kings' school. It is through her that we know it: it appears only in Margaret Landon's book, and Avis's granddaughter was one of her informants. But whatever the story's origins, Anna must have hoped it would act as an entry card to British society in Bangkok. Although they would never receive the Eurasian daughter of a non-commissioned officer, the daughter of a captain and the widow of a lieutenant was (or should have been) another matter.

If she did have this in mind, however, it only reveals her deep unfamiliarity with the infinite gradations of social acceptability within the British middle classes. Given the circumstances of her life, this is not surprising: the divisions involved were subtle and unspoken, and would not have arisen in any society that Anna was likely to have encountered. Her unfamiliarity with them can be gauged from her books' comparatively straightforward approach to society, quite unmarked by the touchy defensiveness so characteristic of Emmeline Lott's account of her life in Egypt. The uncertainty of the governess's social position was perhaps most poignantly embodied in the vehemence with which she distanced herself from the servants; one of Miss Lott's great trials was that the harem authorities failed to recognize this vital difference. For them, all Europeans shared the same strange preferences and practices, and all, regardless of what they did, were lumped together. 'Looking at the German maid Clara,' she recounts, 'I found that she had seated herself at the table, and was prepared to *hobnob* it with me. This was treatment I had never expected to receive.'[20] Worse, it was assumed that Miss Lott would clean her own room and wash her own linen, 'both of which I resolutely refused to do'. The difficulty, it transpired, was that the harem slaves refused to wash the linen of an unbeliever; in the end, a Greek laundress had to be found in Cairo.[21] It was only with considerable effort that Miss Lott managed to carve out a suitably dignified position for herself.

The Egyptians' failure to recognize these social distinctions was understandable. To anyone not brought up in Britain, they must have seemed wholly mysterious. If the governess was a lady, why did she not live like a lady and mingle with ladies? And if she was not a lady, she must be a servant. What else could she be?

This betwixt-and-between situation, which plagued every governess, was summed up, insofar as that was possible, in Lady Eastlake's article on *Jane Eyre* and *Vanity Fair* written for the *Quarterly Review:*

> The line which severs the governess from her employers is not one which will take care of itself, as in the case of a servant. If she sits at

table she does not shock you – if she opens her mouth she does not distress you – her appearance and manners are likely to be as good as your own – her education rather better; there is nothing upon the face of the thing to stamp her as having been called to a different state of life from that in which it has pleased God to place you; and therefore the distinction has to be kept up by a fictitious barrier which presses with cruel weight upon the mental strength or constitutional vanity of a woman.[22]

It was, of course, precisely because the governess might so easily be mistaken for a lady – because she *was*, in all non-pecuniary respects, a lady – that the line had so urgently to be drawn. The result was often hurtful and insulting. *Fraser's Magazine* recorded an incident in a fashionable household where one of the daughters remarked on the absence of the governess's tallow candle, which was taller than the wax ones reserved for the family and their guests.[23] Harriet Martineau discovered 'a suburb of London where the rules of the book-club contain, or did recently contain, a provision that no person engaged in education shall be admitted as a subscriber'.[24] Anne Brontë's alter ego Agnes Grey always has to ride to church with her back to the horses, even though it makes her ill; she makes a note of the people who do not speak to her after the service – including the clergyman; and (like Anne's sister Charlotte) she has orders always to walk a little way behind her charges, so that they may talk together without being constrained by her presence. Nevertheless the English governess, herself brought up to maintain these minute social distinctions, would (Lady Eastlake assured her readers) have it no other way. 'That familiarity which should level all distinction a right-thinking governess would scorn to accept.'[25]

The tenuous nature of these differentiations meant that employers, as well as governesses, were beset by paranoid social dreads regarding the overstepping of invisible marks. For example, a then-current urban myth was that lower-class girls took posts as governesses to better themselves in life, 'adventuresses', as Harriet Martineau described them, 'who hope to catch a husband and an establishment of one or other degree of value; fawning liars, who try to obtain a maintenance and more or less luxury by flattery and subservience'.[26]

Anna's post was indeed a step up to a better life. Even if her social stratagems did not succeed, the experience of living in such an exotic setting as the Siamese harem provided the basis for a successful future career on the American lecture circuit. But that could happen only because she operated in non-British arenas. For the ordinary English governess, social advancement through her job was an improbable scenario. Although mammas supposedly lived in constant terror that their sons (not to say their husbands) would fall prey to the temptress in the schoolroom, this rarely occurred – or not in any way that led to a meaningful change for the governess. As Lady Eastlake sternly pointed out, 'She is a bore to almost any gentleman, as a tabooed woman, to whom he is interdicted from granting the usual privileges of the sex, and yet who is perpetually crossing his path.'[27]

The effect of taboo is, of course, not straightforward. One of its results is to make the tabooed subject mysteriously and threateningly desirable. So the governess whose adjective – 'governessy' – encapsulates all that is dingy, petty and prim, today ranks alongside the nun as a sexual fetish: the most powerless of women transmogrified, by an ironic twist of fate, into the dominatrix. And this aura of sexuality is by no means a modern introduction. Governesses were disliked because according to rumour some had been 'the first to lead and to initiate into sin' by seducing the father or sons of the house, or their visitors.[28] Indeed, one of the more intractable contradictions of governess life was that while nobody wanted to share their house with an ugly or frowsty woman, prettiness was no recommendation either – was indeed, as the author of *Governess Life, its Trials, Duties and Encouragements* asserted, 'conclusive against her'.[29] 'Miss Tuffin, who is a daughter of the late Reverend Thomas Tuffin (Fellow of Corpus College, Cambridge), can instruct in the Syriac language, and the elements of Constitutional law,' writes Thackeray's Miss Pinkerton, headmistress of Miss Pinkerton's school in *Vanity Fair*. 'But as she is only eighteen years of age, and of exceedingly pleasing personal appearance, perhaps this young lady may be objectionable in Sir Huddleston Fuddleston's family.'[30]

Inevitably, these fears were sometimes justified: T.E. Lawrence was the product of one such liaison. However, affairs of this kind rarely ended in marriage. Although such marriages are a staple of governess fiction, whether because (as with Charlotte Brontë) this was an abiding authorial fantasy, or because the mere fact of such a union constituted a plot in itself, in real life they were the exception. 'Give up all thought of love or matrimony while in the position of governess,' advised one manual. 'Any attention you may receive is merely, to begin with, condescending kindness, or admiration that is little better than an insult.'[31]

One of the few real-life instances of a son who actually did marry the governess was John Ruskin's father. Ruskin's mother was a poor orphan from Surrey who had come to live with grand Edinburgh relatives. One of her duties was to help look after their son, and with the inimitable passionlessness that seems to have characterized the Ruskin family so far as personal relations were concerned, her charge 'made up his mind that Margaret, though not in the least an ideal heroine to him, was quite the best sort of person he could have for a wife', choosing her 'with the same kind of serenity and decision with which afterwards he chose his clerks'.[32] The engagement lasted nine years, until the (by then not so young) man had paid all his debts. Only then did the marriage take place – and in secret: the servants of the house had no suspicion of it until the couple drove away together. Ruskin *fils* never enquired as to the reasons for this secrecy, though it surprised him; he thought the marriage something the couple's delighted friends and families had always expected and had been long awaiting. But the obvious explanation was surely that it was just what they did *not* expect, and would not have approved.

The union, though happy in itself, proved as socially disabling as any respectable mamma might have feared. Despite her personal happiness, Margaret Ruskin (like Mrs Pedder at Dove's Nest, who had made a comparable jump in status, from dairymaid to banker's wife) never felt easy in her new, elevated station. 'My mother always felt in cultivated society, – and was too proud to feel with patience – the defects of her own early education; and therefore (which was the true and fatal sign of such defect) never familiarly visited any one whom she did not feel to be, in some sort, her social inferior.'[33] The household that she kept reflected this defensiveness. She would use only tallow candles and plated candlesticks, and would keep 'neither horse nor carriage'.[34] As a result, the wealthy Ruskins rarely entertained or visited. 'My father was too proud to join entertainments for which he could give no like return, and my mother did not care to leave her card on foot at the doors of ladies who dashed up to hers in a barouche.'[35]

It is probably no coincidence that in the one famous instance of an acknowledged grand passion between an English governess and her employer, the lover was a Frenchman: Gustave Flaubert. The governess in question, Juliet Herbert, had been engaged to teach Flaubert's niece Caroline; and although their correspondence is lost, it is generally accepted that the two conducted a long liaison. Flaubert, at least, made no secret of it, asking Caroline at least once to write to him in London care of Juliet. Circumstantial evidence suggests that he several times visited London with the sole purpose of seeing her.[36] That was possible because Rouen was geographically not far from London. But in matters of this sort it was infinitely more distant than Bangkok.

So Anna was shut out of the British colony, with the result that she failed to abide by one of Mongkut's most heartfelt instructions: to keep Christianity out of it.

The reader of Anna's books cannot fail to notice that they seem to be written by two quite different people. One of these is a knowledgeable and tolerant observer of Asian culture and religion. This Anna – the one who grew up in India, who was herself part Indian – holds her Muslim servants Moonshee and Beebe in great affection and is well informed regarding Hinduism. She also seems deeply sympathetic to Buddhism and understands what it is about. For instance, she refers to a treatise written by Mongkut during the twenty years he spent as a Buddhist monk before his accession 'in which he essays to prove that it was the single aim of the great reformer to deliver man from all selfish and carnal passions, and in which he uses these words: "These are the only obstacles in the search for Truth. The most solid wisdom is to know this, and to apply one's self to the conquest of one's self. This it is to become the *enlightened* – the Buddha!"'[37] She also quotes a Christian missionary's remark that 'In almost every respect [Buddhism] seems to be the best religion which man has ever invented', noting only: 'Mark the "invented" of the wary Christian!'[38]

Turn the page, however, and a quite different voice makes itself heard. Shrill, sensationalizing, wholly unconvincing, it proclaims in gory evangelistic detail the misery of the pagan hell that is Bangkok and (in particular) the harem:

I had never beheld misery till I found it here; I had never looked upon the sickening hideousness of slavery till I encountered its features here; nor, above all, had I comprehended the perfection of the life, light, blessedness and beauty, the all-sufficing fulness of the love of God as it is in Jesus, until I felt the contrast here – pain, deformity, darkness, death, and eternal emptiness ... The misery which checks the pulse that thrills the heart with pity in one's common walks about the great cities of Europe is hardly so sad-dening as the nameless, mocking wretchedness of these women, to whom poverty were a luxury, and houselessness as a draught of pure, free air.[39]

These passages are crudely grafted on to the more factual descriptions of Anna's life in Siam. And in the same way their sternly Christian author seems to have been grafted on to that other, relaxed and tolerant Anna. As indeed she was: for when the Bangkok British colony refused to receive her, even though she was stranded in the midst of this alien city, speaking no Thai, Anna naturally sought out other possible friends – preferably English-speaking and with white skins. And those friends were American Protestant missionaries.

The American Presbyterian Mission in Bangkok was long estab-lished and, like many such missions, deeply versed in the indigenous culture. The missionaries' aim was after all to reach out to as many of the heathen as possible – and that meant being able to communicate. The mission's remarkable head, Dr Dan Beach Bradley, had for years been compiling a Siamese–English dictionary; his colleagues the Mat-toons had prepared lessons in the Siamese language and a Siamese Gospel of St Matthew. It was Mrs Mattoon who had prompted the king's outburst against attempts to convert his wives and children to Christianity. Ten years before Anna's arrival, she, together with two other mission women, had been employed to teach English in the harem – a post for which, in many ways, they were ideally qualified. But of course they were not merely teachers. They were also – or, as they saw it, primarily – missionaries, in Bangkok to spread the Chris-tian word. Their teaching had inevitably, to the king's indignant fury, been laced with evangelism. He ended the arrangement and – as his letter to Anna indicated – wanted no repetition of the attempts at conversion that had so displeased him.

Now Dr Bradley and the Mattoons became Anna's close friends.

And the two personalities on display in her books surely represent the two Annas that henceforth coexisted every time she set foot in the harem. One was the person she had been since birth – essentially a south Asian, familiar and comfortable with the cultures and religions of the region, practical, intelligent, not herself particularly religious, the woman who gaily set off to Egypt with the Reverend Badger and travelled the world in the company of her rolling-stone husband. The other was the person she was trying, at the behest of her missionary friends, to become: a hellfire-breathing Christian, intent on converting the heathen, and on showing their uncivilized customs in the most lurid possible light. The first Anna calmly and approvingly describes Buddhist doctrine, priests and worship, movingly recounts the cremation of a dead little daughter the king had much loved, and remarks on the 'spirit of moderation and humanity'[40] that governs public festivals in Siam. The second seeks to portray these same people and events as godforsaken pagans, to whom torture and vile enslavement were everyday and commonplace.

And alongside these two, as she lurched from one mode to the other, was a third self of Anna's own invention, respectable and respected, who hobnobbed confidentially with kings and advised prime ministers: Anna as she would have wished to be.

One of the many ways in which Anna's engagement in Siam differed from most governess posts was her independence. The king's letter setting out the wages and conditions on offer had specified a separate house, but when she first arrived none had been set aside, and the prime minister suggested that she and Louis lodge in the harem. This was what Emmeline Lott had to do in Egypt at this same period, locked in every night by the eunuchs together with the wives and concubines, and condemned to share their life of gossip and backbiting, of slovenly habits and the competitive amassing of jewels, of Turkish cigarettes laced with hashish and unending, hawk-eyed jealousy. Who was the current favourite? Who had been dismissed from the Presence?

This Anna refused, stipulating that she would not start work until a suitable house had been found, as promised. The finding of it took several weeks and in the meantime she, Louis, Moonshee, Beebe and their dog Bessy lodged in two rooms at the palace of the prime minister who had first received her. Eventually a place was found – dirty, but possible.

> Where to begin? – that was the question. It was such filthy filth, so monstrous in quantity and kind – dirt to be stared at, defied, savagely assaulted with rage and havoc. Suddenly I arose, shook my head dangerously at the prime minister's brother – who, fascinated, had advanced into the room – marched through a broken door, hung my hat and mantle on a rusty nail, doffed my neat half-mourning, slipped on an old wrapper, dashed at the vile matting that in ulcerous patches afflicted the floor, and began fiercely tearing it up.
>
> In good time Moonshee . . . returned with half a dozen buckets but no coolies; in place of the latter came a neat and pleasant Siamese lady, Mrs Hunter, wife of the premier's secretary, bringing her slaves to help, and some rolls of fresh, sweet China matting for the floor . . . The floors, that had been buried under immemorial dust, arose again under the excavating labours of the sweepers; and the walls, that had been gory with expectorations of betel, hid their 'damned spots' under innocent veils of whitewash. . . . [41]

That is the voice of the real Anna, unselfconsciously rolling up her sleeves and getting on with the cleaning in a way that no English lady would ever dream of doing. And this, too, is the voice that describes the school she now began to establish in the harem. It was situated in a pavilion, or temple, dedicated to the wives and daughters of Siam, a tranquil place set among orange trees and palms and an old sacred Bho tree with a carved trunk, where 'the goddess of Mind presided'. Here she and Louis were 'most kindly' received by the king, who introduced her to her future pupils with the simple words, 'The English teacher.' He went on: 'Dear children, as this is to be an English school, you will have to learn and observe the English modes of salutation, address, conversation, and etiquette; and each and every one of you shall be at liberty to sit in my presence [something etiquette normally forbade] unless it be your own pleasure not to do so.' [42]

School proper began the following week.

> We advanced through the noiseless oval door, and entered the dim, cool pavilion, in the centre of which the tables were arranged for

school. Away flew several venerable dames who had awaited our arrival, and in about an hour returned, bringing with them twenty-one scions of Siamese royalty, to be initiated into the mysteries of reading, writing, and arithmetic, after the European, and especially the English manner.

It was not long before my scholars were ranged in chairs around the long table, with Webster's far-famed spelling-books before them, repeating audibly after me the letters of the alphabet. While I stood at one end of the table, my little Louis at the other, mounted on a chair, the better to command his division, mimicked me with a fidelity of tone and manner very quaint and charming ... About noon, a number of young women were brought to me, to be taught like the rest. I received them sympathetically, at the same time making a memorandum of their names in a book of my own. This created a general and lively alarm, which it was not in my power to allay, my knowledge of their language being confined to a few simple sentences; but when at last their courage and confidence were restored, they began to take observations and an inventory of me that were by no means agreeable. They fingered my hair and dress, my collar, belt, and rings. One donned my hat and cloak, and made a promenade of the pavilion; another pounced upon my gloves and veil, and disguised herself in them, to the great delight of the little ones, who laughed boisterously. A grim duenna, who had heard the noise, bustled wrathfully into the pavilion. Instantly hat, cloak, veil, gloves, were flung right and left, and the young women dropped on the floor, repeating shrilly, like truant urchins caught in the act, 'ba, be, bi, bo.'[43]

Full Victorian regalia in the heat of Bangkok – no wonder Anna's pupils were astonished.

Emmeline Lott, too, in her Egyptian harem, retained her crinoline – a thoroughly impractical garment that made it hard for her to move about in her small room without knocking the furniture askew; as in Bangkok, her clothes aroused deep curiosity. The Mother of the Harem, an important figure who acted as midwife, doctor, friend and counsellor, visited her and, after some preliminary questions (Had she been married? How long? Where had she lived? What did her parents do? etc.), asked to see her wardrobe.

Conducting her into my room, into which I was followed by a whole bevy of white and black slaves, I placed in her hands several articles of wearing apparel, such as dresses, bonnets, hats, &c. She passed them over to the slaves and coolly walked off with them into the Reception Hall, and there exhibited them to H.H. the Princess Epouse [the viceroy's mother, widow of the famous Ibrahim Pasha] who admired them, and seemed particularly pleased with the hats and bonnets, all of which she requested me to put on, so that Her Highness might see how they became me.

After she had amused herself in that manner, the Princess retired to her chamber to take her *siesta*. I then went down into the Stone Hall, where I partook of what was to me my luncheon, and was again subjected to the mortification of having the German laundrymaid as my companion, notwithstanding that I had already complained to Her Highness of such treatment.[44]

It is clear that neither Anna nor Emmeline ever for a moment considered abandoning their stays and crinolines, gloves and bonnets. This was their uniform – part of the culture they were there to purvey. The frontispiece of Emmeline's book *Harem Life in Egypt and Constantinople* shows her coyly got up in a sort of halfway house, with a veil covering all but her eyes *à la musulmane*. But even here, her elaborate mantle and voluminous robe look distinctly crinoline-like. To wear anything Eastern would be a kind of capitulation, a victory for the forces of paganism against which they daily battled.

This marks an important difference between the Annas and Emmelines – who judged the world from the standpoint of the imperial power they represented – and proto-anthropologists like Freya Stark. Where the upper-class lady travellers were concerned to observe and absorb the customs and language of the peoples among whom they found themselves, Anna, like Emmeline, saw herself as representing a higher civilization whose ways English governesses were employed to impart. Far from adapting to native habits, they steadfastly refused to do so, even when this unbending stance involved considerable inconvenience – even hunger. When refreshments were brought in to Anna and her pupils, the absence of cutlery meant that 'Boy and I were fain to content ourselves with oranges'.[45] In a similar situation, Miss Lott found herself obliged to borrow a knife and fork from a

German servant-maid, the very person from whom she otherwise went to such lengths to dissociate herself. However, since the alternative was starvation, she gritted her teeth and took the implements. In neither case was there any question of doing as everyone else did and eating with the fingers. Miss Lott, indeed, hated all Arab and Turkish food, and would not even eat the delicious Arab bread, which she found too salty, grumbling that the slaves stole all the European bread. Evidently used to a reviving glass in the evening, she was also much put out by Muslim abstinence from alcohol, frequently bewailing the absence of wines and spirits, 'to which I had always been accustomed, and of which it is absolutely necessary that Europeans should partake in warm countries, to counteract the hostile, debilitating effects of the climate'.[46] She recounts proudly how the inmates of her harem 'did their best, poor ignorant, deluded and neglected creatures, to abandon any habits which I explained to them were repugnant to delicacy'. Otherwise 'it would have been utterly impossible for me to remain within the walls of the Harem.'[47] She did not, however, succeed in imposing knives and forks for all.

Of course, working in a foreign country was unlikely to replicate conditions in Kensington or Bath. And from the governess's standpoint, this might well be a good thing. In Lady Eastlake's opinion, 'foreign life is far more favourable to a governess's happiness [than life in England]. In its less stringent domestic habits, the company of a *teacher*, for she is nothing more abroad, is no interruption – often an acquisition.'[48]

In Europe, that was probably true; it certainly seems to have been Claire Clairmont's experience. Whatever the drawbacks of Vienna, Russia and Italy, there was never (unless she was working for an English family) the terrible, icy reserve that walled up the governess in a social limbo. With the Bojtis she had been part of the family, while for the Russians, at least in rural areas, any cultured person was a treasure to be drawn into the life of the household. In countries like Egypt and Siam, on the other hand, where the status of women in society was so very different, the situation was more complicated. Working as they did inside the harem – which, of course, was where the children lived – the position of women like Anna and Emmeline was deeply ambivalent. Although they taught 'reading, writing and arithmetic ... after the English manner'[49] they were not just – or perhaps even primarily – teachers, but talismans of Britishness, symbols that their employer was up with everything modern.

However, although welcome status symbols, they simultaneously threatened, by their very presence, everything the courts and their cultures represented. They were, after all, independent women, travelling under their own steam; they embodied possibilities that the harem ladies could never contemplate. Victorian women may have been – indeed, *were* – unfree in a myriad ways. But in the end – and particularly if they remained unmarried – their lives were their own, to dispose of as they wished. As we have seen, this was unwelcome enough to Victorian men. To potentates like the Siamese prime minister or the Egyptian viceroy, it must have been incomprehensible. King Mongkut's wives were certainly not enslaved; they were free to leave the harem if they wished. But should they do so, there was little better on offer. They had not even the narrow range of options open to such as Anna and Emmeline. Houselessness 'a draught of pure, free air'? Perhaps Anna had never herself been homeless.

Both Anna and Emmeline were at one time or another invited to join the harem; both declined, in Anna's case with shrieks of religiose horror, in Emmeline's, more cold-bloodedly.

The Viceroy was sitting on the sofa smoking a cigar ... I curtseyed and was on the point of leaving the apartment, when His Highness exclaimed, '*Approchez! Approchez! Madame.*'

I did so, took my station in the centre of the room, and there remained, leaving the hangings of the door drawn aside, which gave the officials in attendance an opportunity to overhear all that transpired; and luckily I did so, for I soon found on my return to the Harem that the inmates had already begun to make 'mountains out of mole-hills' ... As soon as I reached the Prince's apartment I was surrounded by a whole host of ladies of the Harem, *Ikbals*, and slaves exclaiming, 'Oh, madame! Oh, madame! You have been in the *Baba's* bedchamber. Now you must ask this, and this, and this, for me,' naming all their requests sim- ultaneously together ...

'No, indeed,' [said] I; 'you are mistaken, I have no desire to please the Viceroy in that manner; that is an honour I do not covet; so I cannot and will not ask any favours either for myself or for any of you' . . .

Their hitherto restless fiery orbs resumed their habitual calmness. The crisis had passed. I had been tried and found to be faithful and trustworthy.[50]

It might have been a good story, but the telling inevitably reflects the teller. Where a Freya Stark would have turned those harem years to good account, Miss Lott, determined from the start to cut herself off from all that surrounded her, had as a result nothing of interest to say. For her, eyes were never anything other than 'fiery orbs'. Used to chairs and tables, she found it impossible, in her crinoline, to adapt to the Turkish habit of low tables and ottomans. They gave her backache: but for her, it was always 'spinal injury'.

Miss Lott was recruited in London by the viceroy's agent, who doubtless set some store by the usual credentials. And what he got was a typical agency governess: a victim of circumstance, snobbish, set in her ways, all juice and curiosity long since replaced by indignation. Of her background we know only what can be deduced from her book. Internal evidence – a mention of meeting the royal family when she was a girl on holiday near Frogmore, a familiarity with life in India, a question as to how long (rather than whether) she had been married – indicates that she came from a respectable family, had travelled to India and was left a widow, to fend for herself. But all this is guesswork. When she leaves the harem she fades from view.

By contrast, King Mongkut's selection process seems to have been more or less haphazard. Although it seems unlikely Anna would ever, in England, have been employed as a governess, for the king one English-speaking woman was much the same as another. So long as she was not a missionary, what her father did was neither here nor there. And the energy and lively intelligence, and most importantly the empathy that make the non-evangelical parts of her book so interesting, enabled her, later, to take advantage of what America could offer: a country where those qualities counted for more than any ancestry.

Anna left Siam in 1866 following a breakdown in her health. King Mongkut granted her six months' leave of absence, but once reunited with Avis in London, she was reluctant to return, and in any case,

could not pay her passage. Neither could Mongkut; he too was chron-
ically short of money. Margaret Landon quotes a letter he wrote her
at this time (February 1868):

> *I beg to say briefly that I am very desirous of complying with your desire,*
> *but fear lesst you by any cause would not be able to return to Siam*
> *soon, and many foreigners may rumour more and more that I am a*
> *shallow-minded man and rich of money &c. &c. as usual general*
> *rumour, many and many trouble me in various ways. – You had better*
> *be indebted to anyone in London yourself, when you was [sic] arrived*
> *here I can give you the required Loan at once and moreover if you please*
> *to – I can allow the Loan of $200 to you freely but it may be not.*
> *I beg to remain your faithful*
> *S.P.P.M. Mongkut R.S.*
>
> *In 6115 day of reign.*[51]

In the event, Anna never went back. And six months later, King
Mongkut died.

Anna's first book, *An English Governess at the Siamese Court*, was
published in 1870, her second, the lurid *Siamese Harem Life*, three
years later. By then, however, she had left London for America, where
dynamic women could more easily make a living. She was soon booked
on lecture tours and warmly welcomed in literary circles managing by
writing and speaking to parlay her Siamese experiences into a respectable if not always an easy living. Anna and Avis remained in America
until Avis married, when they both went to live in Halifax, Nova
Scotia. And there, in 1915, Anna died, her active and independent life
appropriately crowned by fervent work in the suffragette cause.

7

Anna Jameson:
the pursuit of independence

⟨◦⟩

In 1846, Mrs Anna Jameson, a well-known writer on art and literature, published two unusually political essays, 'Woman's "Mission" and Woman's Position', and 'On the Relative Social Position of Mothers and Governesses'. For the first time since Mary Wollstonecraft's *Vindication of the Rights of Woman*, a respected public figure unambiguously set out the current reality of women's lives. In the mid-nineteenth century, Mrs Jameson declared, marriage and homemaking, the supposedly pre-eminent female vocations and occupations, were for vast numbers an unattainable dream. Tens of thousands of women, far from being provided for by their 'protector *Man*', had to work for a living. But because they were not supposed to exist, such women laboured under terrible disabilities. 'And what is the source of this wrong?' Mrs Jameson demanded.

> It lies in the singular, unaccountable, and as it should seem, irreconcileable antagonism between the moral law and the law of opinion ... It appears ... that all attempts to legislate or interpose in favour of women interfere with masculine privileges, with rights of husbands or of fathers, and are fraught with difficulties and dangers; – no one ventures to state openly of what particular nature, or even to give them a definite shape in his own fancy; but every one feels them, and every one shrinks from them.[1]

The impact of these papers did not lie in the facts: as she said, everyone more or less knew those. Where Mrs Jameson differed from other commentators was in her standpoint. For one thing she was a woman; for another, one of the employed, rather than the employing classes. While Harriet Martineau and Lady Eastlake certainly sympathized with the governess's lot, they did not empathize with it: for them governesses were always *them*. Their fate was unfortunate but inevitable, and their misfortunes did not stop them being tiresome. Anna Jameson, however, had actually been a governess and saw no reason to justify the way they and other working women were mistreated. 'As usual,' she wrote of the reaction to the government's commission of inquiry into female and child labour,

> there was a large outlay of pity, of indignation – but as usual, there was no real sympathy, no perception of justice or injustice on the broad scale. In the midst of all the discussions, lamentations and expostulations with which the press teemed . . . it was curious to see how completely custom had blinded, hardened the otherwise acute mind and feeling heart . . . Man's legislation for woman has hitherto been like English legislation for Ireland: it has been without sympathy.[2]

The real problem, however, was that these benighted attitudes were not confined to men. Women themselves had internalized their inferiority. And in this respect the reactionary Anglicanism purveyed by such as Hannah More and Dr John Gregory remained pivotal. It influenced, for example, Lady Eastlake's criticisms of *Jane Eyre* – ironically, a book whose plot turns upon a stern Anglican morality. 'I will keep the law given by God; sanctioned by man,' says Jane, justifying her decision to leave Mr Rochester who loves her and whom she loves, but who is still married to the fatal madwoman. 'Laws and principles are not for times when there is no temptation; they are for such moments as this.'[3] That, however, was not enough for Lady Eastlake, who found Jane 'not precisely the mouthpiece one would select to plead the cause of governesses'. Why not? Because (among other evils including 'vulgarity of mind' and 'total ignorance of the habits of society') Jane lacked the Christian spirit of resignation upon which the whole edifice of governessing was founded.[4]

Jane Eyre is throughout the personification of an unregenerate and undisciplined spirit ... It is true Jane does right, and exerts great moral strength, but it is the strength of a mere heathen mind which is a law unto itself. No Christian grace is perceptible upon her ... It pleased God to make her an orphan, friendless and penniless – yet she thanks nobody, and least of all Him, for the food and raiment, the friends, companions and instructors of her helpless youth – for the care and education vouchsafed to her till she was capable in mind as fitted in years to provide for herself.[5]

Arguably, Eliza Bishop and Everina Wollstonecraft led lives quite as depressing as Jane Eyre's. But at least the England in which they grew up pre-dated the war on France and the hypocritical and reactionary climate that followed it, and did not require them to thank God for the miserable lot He had seen fit to allocate them. By the mid-nineteenth century, however, mere resignation to misfortune was not enough; women were required actively to embrace it. 'It must be granted that there are certain things connected with [the governess's lot] which cannot fail to be trying, even in the best circumstances,' writes the author of *My Governess Life*, one of the many governess advice books. These feelings, however, should be overcome 'by habituating ourselves to look upon the circumstances in which we are placed as God's appointment'.[6]

Religious resignation thus played two important roles: it presented the unbearable as a sort of divine providence, and thus defused any rebellious instincts. It was no coincidence that almost all the nineteenth-century feminist activists were either Unitarian, irreligious, or (like Harriet Martineau, who was born a Unitarian but who in 1851 published a book, *Letters on the Laws of Men's Nature and Development*, which completely rejected religion) both. In those cases where they did later turn to religion, their activism ceased.

Lady Eastlake's extraordinary view of *Jane Eyre* shows how hard it was for even the most intelligent women to distance themselves from the received ideas that underpinned the misery of so many governesses' lives. Despite the fact that she was herself a career-woman – a distinguished art historian used to working as an equal alongside the director of the National Gallery (who happened to be her husband) – the established Church's tenets of religious resignation and the God-given superiority of men were so fundamental to her world-view that she could not step outside them. For the same reason, the devoutly Anglican novelist Charlotte M. Yonge could never support the campaign to open university education to women. 'Nothing would induce me to be associated with such a project,' she replied when Emily Davies invited her to become a member of Girton College's Executive Committee. 'A college would mean the loss of the tender home bloom of womanliness which is a more precious thing than any proficiency in knowledge.'[7] A close friend of the Oxford Movement divine, John Keble, who for many years was her local vicar, she thought female minds should be shaped (as hers had been) by 'sensible fathers', not women's colleges.[8] Fortunately for Miss Yonge, her own considerable abilities lay in the socially sanctioned sphere of writing: she described herself as an 'Authoress living on her own means'.[9] Had she been less conveniently gifted, she might have felt rather differently.

Anna Jameson, too, was an 'authoress living on her own means'. Like Miss Yonge and Lady Eastlake, she was both successful and childless; all three were living refutations of the touted female role-model. As with Mary Wollstonecraft, the question arises: why were her views on woman's mission and woman's position so very different from theirs? And as with Mary, the answer seems to lie in a quirk of background. Because Mary's father was a drunk who took no part in proper society, she grew up in a sort of social limbo, denied the advantages that should have been hers but at the same time unhampered by the usual prohibitions. Similarly, though for quite different reasons, Anna Jameson's father was crucial to her later independence.

Denis Brownell Murphy was a miniature painter, at a time when artists constituted a very special group in classbound British society. Talent excused certain social laxities (regarding, for example, churchgoing) while at the same time opening social doors that would always remain firmly closed to mere tradesmen. Clients were necessarily well-to-do and often well connected, and those clients often became friends. The most famous example was the great nineteenth-century painter J.M.W. Turner, who between 1809 and 1830 spent much of his time living and working at Petworth House, the stately home of his patron George Wyndham, the 3rd Earl of Egremont. Denis Murphy, too, had a number of aristocratic friends with whom he and Anna spent time socially and with whom they even went on holiday. So doors were open to her; and for the rest, the fame that she achieved, and her considerable influence, testify to her exceptional talent, energy and magnetism.

The Murphys were not well off (in fact, Anna never really achieved financial comfort, dying in 1860 of what one friend described as 'underpay and overwork'[10]). That much was clear from the fact of her having been a governess: as she later remarked, 'I have never in my life heard of a governess who was such by choice.'[11] Nor was she beautiful. Although red-haired, white-skinned and plumply pretty when young – 'her hands and arms might have been those of Madame de Warens,' commented her friend Fanny Kemble, referring to Rousseau's famous 'Maman' and muse[12] – by the time she reached middle age any physical charms had evaporated. 'Last Sunday coming out of church I observed [a] redhaired, ugly, red faced woman staring at me . . . and was presently informed it was – Mrs Jameson! . . . Who would ever have supposed from her writings which are everything that is elegant and lady-like that she was red haired and fat!'[13] She was then forty-one.

Nevertheless, everyone agreed that she was captivating. Her American writer friend Catherine Sedgwick described her as 'the best talker I ever heard, and I have heard many gifted unknown and many known and celebrated'.[14] Her charm and intelligence were apparent in every word she wrote and beguiled all who met her: and that, by 1846, included almost everybody who was anybody. Her intimate friends were Lady Byron, Ottilie von Goethe (the great man's beloved daughter-in-law) and the actress Fanny Kemble; she toured Venice with Ruskin and accompanied the eloping Elizabeth Barrett and Robert Browning on their journey from Paris to Pisa. Her books were not only successful in her own country – with many reprintings – but were widely translated. When Mrs Jameson spoke, people listened: proof, as with Mary Wollstonecraft, that over and above vision there must also be personal brilliance if politics are not merely to be deplored, but moved on.

Anna Jameson was born Anna Murphy in Dublin in 1794. As those were turbulent times in Ireland, in 1798 her father took his wife and eldest daughter to England, settling in Whitehaven. In 1802 they made another move, to Newcastle-upon-Tyne, where Murphy's prospects

I am not superstitious enough to put any faith in dreams; but, such a repetition of them affected my spirits greatly, and I was hurt at myself for being so childishly weak!

This last letter has relieved me a little in regard to himself, and family; but, has increased the load at my heart — it is heavily oppressed. — A little time will raise my sunken spirits. — If my brother does but live, and be happy, I can be happy too, notwithstanding the unjust severity I have met with.

I have faults, not small in number; but, levity, or giddiness, are not I think amongst them; if they were, my aunt and cousin, might have some shadow of reason, for speaking as they have. My brother ought to sift the matter to the utmost, and find out the authors of such a report, that a sister's fame may be cleared; if he does not, I shall not urge him to it, he knows who they are perhaps as well as I do, and is afraid of offend-ing my aunt.

I shall be glad to hear from you soon my dear Winkley; and I hope when next I write to you, to treat on more agreeable subjects.

Remember me affectionately to your sister and mother.

Say nothing of the subject of this letter to M.r Chorley's, should you happen to see them, unless they first mention it to you. Remember me respectfully to M.r and M.rs C. when you happen to see them.

I have written a little unconnectedly, but at such a time I know you have candour enough to make allowances for,

Your affectionate
suffering friend
E. Weeton

Letter from Miss Weeton to her friend Miss Winkley, written while she was at Dove's Nest, 1810.

Dove's Nest, near Ambleside.

Mrs Weeton's school-house.

Anna Leonowens, 1862

King Mongkut with one of his
favourite wives, c. 1862.

Emmeline Lott outfitted à
l'orientale.

Anna Jameson in her prime.

Barbara Bodichon, self portrait, c.1850. © The Mistress and Fellows, Girton College

Bessie Rayner-Parkes, (Madame Belloc), after a daguerreotype, c.1850. © The Mistress and Fellows, Girton College

Girton students, the first and second years, 1870. © The Mistress and Fellows, Girton College

Emily Davies, 1901. © The Mistress and Fellows, Girton College

improved enough for him to send for Anna's two little sisters, who had been left in Ireland, and who were soon joined by yet another baby, Charlotte.

Given the run of her indulgent father's house, Anna was familiar from childhood with the pictures and artistic discourse that would become her writer's stock-in-trade. She read every book that came her way, from Shakespeare (whose appeal was enhanced by his position on the Forbidden shelf) to Hannah More's pious tracts, which wholly failed in their desired effect.

It is most certain that more moral mischief was done to me by some of those than by all Shakespeare's plays together. These so-called pious tracts first introduced me to a knowledge of the vices of vulgar life, and the excitements of a vulgar religion, – the fear of being hanged and the fear of jail became co-existent in my mind; and the teaching resolved itself into this – that it was not by being naughty, but by being found out, that I was to incur the risk of both ... Although no pains were spared to *indoctrinate* me, and all my pastors and masters took it for granted that my ideas were quite satisfactory, nothing could be more confused and heterodox.[15]

Clearly, and crucially in that pious age, this was not, despite the 'pastors and masters', a household in which piety ruled; with the result that Anna was for ever freed from the disabling bonds of Christian resignation. In later life friends such as Lady Byron and Catherine Sedgwick would scold her for her lack of religion, so shocking and unusual in a respectable lady. 'You think I am not religious enough,' she wrote to Miss Sedgwick. 'I fear you are right; for if I were, God would be to me all I want, replace all I regret thus selfishly and weakly ... but ... I am afraid it is thus and not what it ought to be.'[16]

Like most children, Anna was pragmatic. Perhaps ironically, perhaps significantly, she hated the governess whom for a few years Mr Murphy was able to afford. Miss Yokeley, the daughter of a Frenchwoman, later married Mr Murphy's brother; Anna thought her 'one of the cleverest women I have ever met with'[17] but disliked being under her authority. However, the characteristics fostered by this dislike proved useful later in life, when she took up the cause of downtrodden women such as governesses. She acquired habits of leadership by organizing her little sisters in acts of rebellion, discovered an aptitude for lying when that seemed necessary and especially enjoyed the thought that the governess could not know what was going on inside the privacy of her head. This habit of silent rebellion she would retain for the rest of her life. 'My ... nature is so reserved,' she told her beloved (and wholly unconstrained) friend Ottilie von Goethe, 'that discretion is in me scarce a virtue, for my mind and heart – though always full, too full – seldom overflow.'[18]

In 1803, Denis Murphy took his family to London. They settled first in Hanwell, near Ealing, then three years later moved to the fashionable and expensive neighbourhood of Pall Mall. Perhaps he hoped to run into potential clients in those well-bred streets. But despite the good address, the family fortunes did not prosper. Anna proposed, when she was twelve, that the four sisters should make their way to Brussels to learn lacemaking. It was perfectly simple, she assured them: one travelled along the Paddington canal to the sea, and so onwards. The girls dressed in their best to bid their parents a fond farewell; Louisa, the second sister, was even allowed a little wine – 'For there's no telling when we may be together again, my darling,' pronounced their father. It was too much: Louisa threw her arms round his neck and promised never to leave him. Thus the expedition foundered.[19]

When Anna became sixteen, however, it was time to earn a living in reality, which inevitably meant becoming a governess. Many of the fifteen years between 1810, when she reached this age, and 1825, when she married, were spent in various schoolrooms.

Her first post was looking after the four small sons (evidently not yet old enough to merit a tutor) of the Marquess of Winchester. Lady Winchester was highly pleased with her; in 1812 a mutual acquaintance told Mr Murphy, who passed it on to his 'dear and very dear Anna', that 'Lady W. has a *treasure* in you and ... is sensible of it.'[20] The boys, however, were evidently a handful, and at the end of four years Anna was glad to leave. 'My mind is not well,' she told her mother. 'I feel as if it were stretched beyond its strength, as if a little repose would save me, my head at least.'[21] There is at least one passage in her essay 'On the comparative social position of mothers and governesses' that sounds highly autobiographical:

I recollect an instance of a young girl of twenty, with the best will and intentions, and some qualities admirably suited to her task, who, within two years, became languid, nervous, hysterical, and at length utterly broken down. She was obliged to give up her situation. Here, though great and lasting injury was inflicted, no unkindness was intended – I should say, on the contrary, all *kindness* was intended; and the services of the young lady were well paid and highly valued. The mother was full of lamentations at her own loss, and her friends condoled with her. The whole scene, which I witnessed, reminded me of an anecdote told by Horace Walpole: how my lord Castlecomer's tutor broke his leg, and how every one exclaimed, 'What an exceeding inconvenience to my Lady Castlecomer!'[22]

Anna left the Winchesters in 1814 and, her father then experiencing a spell of relative comfort, probably spent the next five years living at home. Then in 1819, when Mr Murphy's fortunes waned, she took another 'situation', this time with the wealthy Rowles family of Bradbourne Park, Kent. They had two children, a daughter, Laura, and a son, Henry; Anna was happy with them and got on particularly well with Mrs Rowles.

The following year, however, it seemed her governess days would soon end, for in 1820 she met and agreed to marry an up-and-coming young lawyer from the Lake District: Robert Jameson, a talented painter and a particular friend of Hartley Coleridge, son of the poet. In 1821, however, the engagement was broken off. Anna's niece Gerardine hinted that there were deep incompatibilities: on his side, temperamental oddities that made him very difficult to live with, on hers, perhaps, an unacknowledged preference for women, who always seem to have aroused her emotionally far more than men.

Nonetheless, it is possible that Anna, always ruthless in pursuit of what she wanted, simply preferred the other choice on offer: to accompany the Rowleses on the Grand Tour through France, Switzerland and Italy. This would also enable her to perform the same sisterly service for her sister Louisa as Mary Wollstonecraft had for Everina: of sending her to Paris for a year to improve her French and make her more employable. Charlotte Brontë had taken a similar course, spending a year in Brussels and paying for *her* younger sister Emily to accompany her, so it seems that this was quite an accepted form of training and an accepted way of obtaining it.

The Rowles family were extremely wealthy and travelled in style. Anna sent frequent reports back to her family. 'Today Mrs Rowles dines out; she has left me the carriage and I shall take all the children to St Cloud immediately after an early dinner. We shall spend the rest of the day there, sup in the gardens upon coffee, cream and fruit (a la francaise [sic]) and return at bedtime. I shall make the little elfs as happy as I can. How you would enjoy such a day! All of you!'[23]

Not every day was as ideal as this. Mr Rowles, she reported, was 'a wet blanket', and her dependent situation as governess 'cuts one out quite of society, and I have felt it more abroad than anywhere'.[24] Nevertheless it was an unparalleled opportunity and she made the most of it.

> I think I shall be able to amuse you all, dear girls and Mamma and Papa, with some of my *scribbles*. I have always a notebook and a journal; in the first I merely put down dates and occupations of the day; the other, which is secured by lock and key contains all my remarks on the characters scenes and incidents I meet with and this I never trust out of my hands to any human being ... I have collected material which, if I live and Heaven grants me health and that peace to which I have long been a stranger, I will turn to good account.

Meanwhile she urged them to write and 'mention all friends – Mr Jameson and everybody'.[25] For Jameson continued to press his suit – 'very unhappy and persevering and vehement', Anna reported in 1822.[26]

On her return to England she thought of trying for independence in the usual way, by starting a school with her sisters, but there was not enough money. She therefore took another governessing job, with Mr Littleton, later Lord Hatherton, of Teddesley Park in Staffordshire. Anna grew particularly fond of the Littletons' eldest daughter, Hyacinthe, and was soon established as part of the family. They would remain friends for the rest of her life, and Teddesley became a frequent retreat.

There are obvious parallels between Anna Jameson's governessing career and that of Mary Wollstonecraft. Both worked for wealthy families and so were spared the discomfort of too close quarters. And in both cases the magnetism and intelligence that marked them out for future success obviated many of the social discontents that afflicted most governesses. Anna, who always enjoyed the grand life, welcomed her inclusion in her families' social round; Mary did not. But in neither case did their personal good fortune convince them that governessing was anything but a second-class job for unwilling middle-class women who had no alternative. 'After all,' wrote Anna in her essay on mothers and governesses, 'the best preparation is to look upon the occupation to which you are devoted (I was going to say *doomed*) as what it really is, – a state of endurance, dependence, daily thankless toil; to accept it as such courageously and meekly, because you must, – cheerfully, if you can; – and so make the best of it.'[27] Like Mary, she hoped governessing might one day be 'done away with'.[28]

Inevitably, the times had left their mark on her. Anna thought women 'not born in the servile classes' should not have to work, their 'proper sphere' being the home; her proposal for 'a systematic and generally accessible education for women of all classes'[29] fell some way short of the *Vindication*'s radical proposal of universal co-education. Despite this – or perhaps because a less drastic remedy is more easily assimilated – this was the seed that would eventually lead to the foundation of Girton College and the end of governessing as an educational system.

In 1825, Anna finally agreed to marry Jameson. She was thirty-one, he twenty-seven. She had summed up the situation shortly beforehand: 'I have the firm conviction that there exists a disparity between our minds and characters which will render it impossible for me to be *quite* happy with him … yet I think that he will have me simply because I shall not, in the long run, be able to stand out against my own heart and his devoted affection, which is continually excited by the obstacles and the *coldness* which I throw in his way.'[30]

This was not exactly a ringing endorsement, but at thirty-one Anna had reached an age when single women might expect to remain for ever unwed. And as with Nelly Weeton, the alternative – a lifetime alone, or in the schoolroom – must have seemed even less attractive than a passionless marriage. Now, after so many years of other people's children, she might be able to look forward to babies of her own. Furthermore, Mr Jameson was doing well: the parish of Marylebone had recently chosen him to execute some business for them at a fee of 250 guineas.

The fatal flaw in Robert Jameson was that he was two quite different people. In writing he was fluent, persuasive, affectionate and charming: in person, tongue-tied, awkward – almost autistically incapable, it seemed, of normal human relations. This became clear the Sunday after the wedding, when he set out, as he did every Sunday, to dine with friends. Anna protested; she did not know them and they might not want to know her. Should Robert not wait at least until she had been introduced? However, he shrugged her off, saying that she might do as she wished; *he* was going to see his friends. After they set out together it began to rain; she took the opportunity to declare they would have to turn back, as the rain would spoil her white gown. ' "Very well," once more said the bridegroom; "you have an umbrella. Go back by all means, but I shall go on." He was as good as his word and, though received, as his astonished hosts afterwards related, with exclamations of bewilderment and consternation, he calmly ate his dinner with them, remaining for the rest of the evening until his usual hour with perfect equanimity and unconcern.'[31]

It was hardly a perfect start to life together, but there were compensations. In particular, Robert encouraged his wife's literary aspirations. Through his friend Hartley Coleridge he had some access to literary London: he knew Charles Lamb and also Basil Montagu, the natural son of the Earl of Sandwich, whose salon was an artistic meeting place. Montagu, a successful lawyer, took Robert into his chambers and frequently invited the young couple to his home. His wife, their daughter Mrs Procter and son-in-law Bryan Waller Procter, better known as the poet Barry Cornwall, and, later, *their* daughter Adelaide, at this time a charming baby known as 'Poppet', would all become Anna's close and faithful friends.

It was through Robert that Anna's first book was published. He had a friend called Thomas, who had begun as a cobbler but whose enthusiasm for old books and engravings had led him through collecting to dealing, and finally to publishing. Thomas wished to become a lawyer, and Jameson, who had undertaken to advise him, brought him home to meet his wife. Thomas, on his side, volunteered to teach Mrs Jameson the guitar. One evening Robert mentioned Anna's diary of her Grand Tour; she read out some extracts and Thomas offered to publish it. Anna agreed, adding jokingly, 'If it sells for anything more than will pay the expenses, you shall give me a Spanish guitar for my share of the profits.'[32] Thomas agreed; the book was printed as *Diary of an Ennuyée*. Real life was slightly emended in that the authoress presented herself as wanly consumptive, than which nothing could have been further from the reality. However, the lively observation remained and the book was an immediate success, quickly running into further editions. In the event, Anna's guitar hardly represented a fair royalty. But she had broken into print and (what was more important) into public consciousness. Her next publications bore the announcement: 'By Mrs Jameson, author of the "Diary of an Ennuyée".'

Despite its promising start, Robert Jameson's career, hindered by his hopeless inability to present a case in person, did not go well. He therefore took an easy way out, and in 1829 abandoned London's keen competition for a judgeship in the colonies, on the island of Dominica. Anna did not accompany him. They would never live together again.

Jameson did not like sulphurous Dominica, which he compared 'morally and physically' to Hell.[33] But he could have made his wife no better present than his departure. Unencumbered by a husband she did not much like, she was now able to pursue an independent life while still enjoying the freedoms available to a married woman. The Procters and the Montagus smoothed over any social awkwardness by welcoming her into their drawing rooms, where she enjoyed a pleasant buzz of interest as the author of a successful book.

Not all were charmed. Henry Crabb Robinson justified his lack of enthusiasm for Anna by recalling another woman he did not much like: 'She ha[d] the voice, as well as the fair complexion, of Mrs Godwin, whom Lamb always called the Liar.'[34] Thomas Carlyle was equally unenthusiastic. 'Ach Gott! A little, hard, brown, redhaired, freckled, fierce-eyed, square-mouthed woman; shrewd, harsh, cockney-irrational: it was from the first moment apparent that without mutual loss, we might "adieu and wave our lily hands".'[35] Anna, however, was unconcerned. From now on her chief emotional engagements would be with women: Fanny Kemble, Ottilie von Goethe, Lady Byron, Catherine Sedgwick. 'Need I tell you, dearest, *dearest* Ottilie, how I have thought of you ever since those bitter hours in which we parted?'[36] began a letter written six weeks after their first meeting; and two months later, 'Leaving Germany was leaving *you*, you, round whom some of the deepest feelings of which my nature is capable, had imperceptibly twined themselves.'[37] To Lady Byron: 'Think of me as being literally *yours to* command besides being your grateful and affectionate Anna.'[38] To Miss Sedgwick: 'You have this instinct of benevolence and affection in a degree that no other possesses, no other that I have ever known; how can I but love you dearly? ... *you* are on the other side of the Atlantic, and I have known you only to feel how hard it is to be without you.'[39]

These letters do not necessarily denote physical relationships. Ottilie von Goethe was almost frenziedly heterosexual, although of course she may well have been bisexual. Lady Byron was taken up with good works; Catherine Sedgwick's attraction was kindness and intelligence. Yet the depth of emotion in these letters is greater than anything Anna ever wrote to any man – certainly not her husband.* So that to her freedoms from conventional religiosity and the confines of class was added another that would prove equally important: a freedom from any need to please or placate men, and from the least notion that they were in any way her natural superiors. Emotionally they had no hold over her; intellectually she was their equal; financially, as the years went on and her reputation grew, she was – albeit shakily, and with help from the husband whose main function this proved to be – her own woman.

As the years passed, the books multiplied. In 1829 she published a volume entitled *Loves of the Poets*; in 1831, *Celebrated Female Sovereigns*; and in 1832 a highly successful two-volume study of Shakespeare's female characters, *Characteristics of Women*, that went into many editions and languages, propelling her into literary celebrity.

In 1833 this pleasant life was briefly interrupted when Jameson returned from Dominica, but after a few months he left again, this time for Canada, where he had been appointed Attorney-General for Upper Canada – the last non-Canadian to take this position. He would receive £1,200 a year, out of which he agreed to send Anna £150 every six months until she should join him in Toronto.

---

* The one exception is the sculptor Henry Behnes Burlowe, whose death of cholera in 1837 was evidently a heavy blow. However, since none of their letters to each other survives, it is impossible to know the exact nature of their relationship.

For the next three years the ghastly prospect of Canada hung over her, threatening everything that made her life worth living. At this time she was mostly in Germany with Ottilie and her circle, petted and made much of; if not freed from money worries, then at least to some extent distanced from them – only to be faced with leaving all this behind for a husband with whom she had nothing in common and whom she had thought safely stowed at the far ends of the earth.

Robert's occasional letters were, as always, charming and affectionate. In Octobers 1834, he wrote:

Dearest Anna, let me look forward to our meeting with hope. Let me not lose the privilege of loving you, and the hope of being loved by you. Let me come to my solitary home with the prospect that my daily labours shall, before any very lengthened day of trial, be rewarded by your presence and your most precious endearments. I have no single hope that cannot depend on this one. Do not school your heart against me, and I will compel you to love me. I have been fencing in a nice little piece of ground on the banks of the lake, where I am promising myself the happiness of building you a pretty little villa after your own taste.[40]

But since these letters were very occasional indeed, Anna persuaded herself that the protestations of affection they contained were not serious. 'My Dear Robert,' she wrote two years later from Weimar,

The feelings of perplexity and uncertainty into which I have been thrown by the whole course of our correspondence almost discourage me from writing to you ... From October 1834 down to this present February 1836, I have received from you *two letters* ... and these two letters contained no syllable which could give me the slightest idea of your social position in Canada; and though you expressed in the last letter a general wish that I should join you, very slightly and vaguely expressed (a *hope* rather than an intention or an expectation), there was not a word which I could interpret into any decision on the subject, no instructions as to my voyage, and no answer to the questions and enquiries with which my letters were filled. Between October 1834 and October 1835 I wrote you *eleven* letters. ... A union such as ours is, and has been ever, is a real mockery of the laws of God and man. You have the power to dispose of our fate as far as it depends on each other. I placed that power in your hands in my letter written from England, and had you used that power in a decided manly spirit, whether to unite or part us, I had respected you the more, and would have arranged my life accordingly. But what an existence is this to which you have reduced us both! If . . . it is your purpose to remain in Canada, to settle there under any political change, and your real wish to have me with you and make another trial for happiness, tell me so *distinctly* and *decidedly* – tell me at what time to leave England – tell me what things I ought to take with me, what furniture, books, &c., will be necessary or agreeable, what kind of life I shall live . . . I shall await your next letter, and according to its contents I shall regulate my future plans. Farewell! I expect your answer in July next.[41]

To her surprise and chagrin, the answer duly arrived. Early in August she wrote to a friend, 'I am going to Canada – that is, my husband has sent over his very peremptory request that I should join him, giving some cogent reasons.'[42] She was still not quite certain, 'such is Jameson's very peculiar character',[43] that he really meant it, but for the moment she would take him at his word. It remained to be seen how permanent her stay would be.

I consider, dear Ottilie, that I am placed this moment between two *duties* [she wrote the following month, September 1836]. If I could make you happier and soothe your wounded and weary spirit I should think it as much my *duty* to go to you as to go to Canada, and God knows *far* more my inclination – far, far more!, to go to you for three days only, to see you once more has often been a wish like a *thirst* in my heart. I can only compare it to that feeling; but I could not . . . Dearest Ottilie, believe that I love you more entirely than perhaps you would think.[44]

The truth was that a sense of wifely duty was less of a spur than shortage of money. Her literary efforts were making her a name, but not a living; her sister and brother-in-law, with whom she lodged, wanted £150 a year for her room and board; she was in debt to her bookseller . . . Jameson had sent some money, but not enough to pay her debts; and what he had sent to buy tickets and make other preparations for her voyage, she could not with a good conscience divert to her own uses. Meanwhile, 'They tell me that at New York my name is so popular, that I shall probably obtain a good sum for another edition of the *Characteristics* printed under my own eye and with my own corrections.'[45]

She reached New York in November to find that Jameson had not come to meet her, as he had promised, nor sent anyone in his place. By December winter was setting in hard; it became clear she must make her own way north. The plan had been to travel by water, but by the time she set out the Hudson was already frozen thirty miles below Albany. From there to Queenstown overland took six days and nights of weary voyaging, the roads being so bad that at one point it took six hours to cover eleven miles. At Lake Ontario, by a fortunate chance, the last steamer of the season had not yet left. The travellers hastened aboard and Anna fell into a deep sleep; when she awoke, they had arrived.

> The wharf was utterly deserted, the arrival of the steamboat being accidental and unexpected; and as I stepped out of the boat I sank ankle-deep into mud and ice. The day was intensely cold and damp ... Half-blinded by the sleet driven into my face, and the tears which filled my eyes, I walked about a mile through a quarter of the town mean in appearance ... and through dreary miry ways, never much thronged, and now, by reason of the impending snow-storm, nearly solitary ... And these were the impressions, the feelings, with which I entered the house which was to be called my home.[46]

The weather did not break until May, and the cold was such as she had never known. All that winter, despite the roaring fire that burned continuously in her room, the glass of water left overnight beside her bed was frozen solid by morning. Toronto she found mean and provincial; she missed her old friends and made no new ones. When the Canadian Parliament discussed education, on which she considered herself something of an expert, she was shocked by the 'strange, crude, vague, ignorant opinions'[47] that she heard in conversation and read in the debates. No one, however, was interested in what she had to say on the subject. By the time spring came, she had made her plans.

> Jameson is appointed Chancellor *at last* [she wrote to her sister Charlotte]. He is now at the top of the tree . . . No-one loves him, it is true, but every one approves him . . . The organisation of the new Court of Equity and the moving into his new residence, will occupy Mr Jameson and me for a month or two . . . The place itself, the society, are so detestable to me, my own domestic position so painful and without remedy or hope, that to remain here would be death to me. My plan is to help Jameson in arranging his house, and when the spring is sufficiently advanced, to make a tour through the western districts up to Lake Huron. Towards the end of the year I hope by God's mercy to be in England.[48]

In all but law, the marriage was over.

As poor, awkward Jameson was keenly aware, a better marriage – any marriage, even one that existed only in form – might have transformed his life. Had it been possible to divorce, he confided to a friend, he would have married again instantly. He was good-looking, he held a highly prestigious job: surely some girl would have been happy to become the attorney-general's wife. Anna assured him she 'wished it only depended on me'.[49] But since their difficulties resulted from incompatibility rather than misconduct, and incompatibility did not constitute grounds for divorce, the question remained hypothetical. One cannot help wondering whether she would have been so categorical had this not been the case, for in reality the formal separation that effectively hamstrung her husband could not have suited her more admirably. Jameson no longer weighed on her conscience nor cramped her style; the threat of an uncongenial life in Canada was for ever removed; and to cap her felicities, he had agreed to pay her £300 a year to continue her full and lively European life, unencumbered. When she died, Anna's friend Bessie Rayner Parkes observed, with slight surprise, that 'her views on marriage were extremely rigid – [she felt] the best interests of women were served by the marriage tie'.[50] It certainly served hers.

Jameson, by contrast, led a sad and lonely existence: by day discharging his distinguished duties – vice-chancellor, the post he eventually held, was only one step below governor-general – by night spending his time in solitary drinking. When Anna left, he sent a characteristically charming note, assuring her that 'My affection you will never cease to retain.'[51] But when he died, in 1854, she was outraged to find that he had cut her out of his will. He had ceased payment of her allowance on his retirement in 1849, explaining that he wanted to use the money to buy land, and that she would inherit his property. To her indignation, however, he left it all to what the will termed his kindest – possibly his only – friends, a clergyman called Maynard and his family. Knowing the facts, it is hard to blame him.

It was no coincidence that Anna's entry onto the political stage took place following her return from Canada. *Winter Studies and Summer Rambles in Canada*, the book she published about her journeys amid the native Americans of the Canadian interior, established her as something of a literary celebrity, but it was Jameson's £300 a year that counted. Her literary earnings had always been uncertain, but now that they could be seen as welcome additions to a steady income, she was free to give time to what interested her, regardless of whether or not it would sell. And what interested her was women's lack of power in society.

Her newly uncompromising and politically charged path was presaged in *Winter Studies*. As one reviewer remarked,

> No one reading these 'Winter Studies and Summer Rambles' can possibly disentangle the outbreakings of the journalist's disappointed hopes and wounded feelings ... from the enthusiast's constant resolution to represent any arrangement of the position and duties of her sex whatsoever – even that where the Squaw is the Red Man's drudge in field and wigwam ... as more equitable and to be desired than that existing according to the present system of European civilisation.[52]

Anna was unabashed. In 'Woman's "Mission" and Woman's Position', which first appeared in the *Athenaeum* in 1843, she reiterated her view that women leading primitive lives 'individually ... never appeared to me so pitiable as the women of civilised life'.[53] In an England that prided itself on its colonial mission to enlighten the native, no remark could have been more calculated to enrage.

'Woman's "Mission" and Woman's Position' was a response to the commissions of inquiry and government reports that would eventually lead to a Ten Hour Act, limiting the working day. The essay that followed, 'On the Relative Social Position of Mothers and Governesses', was similarly prompted – this time by the publication, in 1844, of the first report of a newly established charity: the Governesses' Benevolent Institution.

'There are so many ways in which Governesses might help each other if there were but a way of bringing them together,' mused one writer in an article entitled 'Isolation and combination'.[54] Unfortunately, such a thing was almost unimaginable. Isolation was built into governesses' lives, and with employers effectively controlling their free time, combination was virtually unattainable. The resulting destitution was by the mid-century becoming a public scandal, the subject of innumerable novels and newspaper articles; and since by this time almost every middle-class family could count at least one governess among its relatives or acquaintances, a body of opinion finally built up behind the agreement that something must be done.

The Governesses' Benevolent Institution, launched on 7 May 1841, was that thing. It had two aims: to help the indigent by raising a Governesses' Benevolent Fund from individual bequests, donations and subscriptions; and to administer a Governesses' Provident Fund, which would advantageously invest governesses' own savings. A committee was formed, a bank account opened, and a secretary hired – Miss Jane Tucker, an ex-governess, at £4 3s 4d a month: the GBI's first and last female employee. Miss Tucker claimed to have originated the idea of the GBI and had spent 'years of unrewarding toil ... devoting all of my time (always valuable, but at my period of life, particularly so) in this arduous undertaking'.[55] However, she was caught fiddling her expenses, including in them not only a number of suspiciously vague items of stationery but also the cost of her own lodgings, at 10s a week for a year. Accordingly, in November, six months after being engaged, she was given a month's notice, with £10 over and above her salary. Over the next two years more than one subscriber confided money – in the case of Miss Burdett Coutts, ten guineas – to 'a lady calling herself Secretary and Treasurer of the Institution'[56] – money that was never seen again.

Disgraceful, no doubt; but perhaps we should think of Miss Tucker as the first of the institution's beneficiaries. Impoverished governesses, once they had discovered some alternative form of support, were notoriously hard to dislodge. In 1853, the year before her departure for the Crimea, Florence Nightingale became Superintendent of the Institute for the Care of Sick Gentlewomen in Distressed Circumstances, most of whom were broken-down governesses. Her most unpleasant task, she told her father, was having to discharge patients from hospital, since it constituted 'the cheapest lodgings they can find, with the added luxury of taking medicine and sympathy'.[57]

The GBI was soon overwhelmed with applications for help from 'those who, standing on the brink of destitution, shrinking from seeking *private* benevolence, and without any claim on any one who could help them, hailed the establishment of the Institution as a message from Providence to save them from despair'. Out of 102 applicants in its first year, fifty-six were given money. Some of those rejected wanted loans, which the institution did not provide; a few did not give satisfactory references; but 'many MANY more were reluctantly declined for want of sufficient funds'. An investment of £500 was made to provide an annuity of £15 per annum, whose applicants had to have attained the age of fifty and 'who from pressure of domestic claims, or from ill health, have been unable to make a provision for themselves ... for this annuity, small as it is, there are about 30 candidates, *many of them entirely destitute*'.[58]

The Revd Mr Laing, the GBI's indefatigable secretary, itemized the various situations that had driven these ladies to throw themselves upon his charity. The list made almost unbearable reading.

A governess 22 years and laid by a small sum of money; part of which she lost by placing it in the hands of one of her employers, and the rest has been expended for maintence and medical treatment for cancer;

sight affected from over-exertion, never giving herself a rest, having a mother dependent on her;

incapable of taking another situation from extreme nervous excitement, caused by over-exertion and anxiety.

Saved nothing during twenty-six years of exertion, having supported her mother, three younger sisters, and a brother, and educated the four.

Many were victims of improvident menfolk:

Entirely supported her father till his death, and largely assisted three brothers, who all married badly.

Lost her whole property by the failure of a brother.

Lost the greater part of her savings by advancing the money to benefit a brother, since dead.

Lost all her property by the misconduct of a trustee of her father's property.

Lost the whole of her property, £6000, by the failure of a brother, and in consequence became a governess.

Advanced the whole of her property to assist her brother in the purchase of a vessel, which foundered at sea.

And so the list went on.

The GBI's shocking revelations opened both eyes and pockets. By 1859, over £177,000 had been invested in the annuities fund.[59] Even so, it remained desperately oversubscribed. It was clear that charitable help, however generous, could never solve the problem.

Many thought that if governesses were better prepared for the job – and could show proof of that preparation – they might command more respect and better terms. Doctors, engineers and other professionals were all organizing themselves into colleges and institutes whose imprimatur guaranteed standards and was a necessary condition of practice; why not governesses? To this end, Queen's College, in Harley Street, opened its doors in 1849, under the auspices of a distinguished group of Christian Socialists led by Charles Kingsley and F.D. Maurice. Maurice himself taught theology and mental and moral philosophy; Dr Sterndale Bennett, harmony and musical composition; Dr Whewell, Plato; the impressive timetable included lessons in reading, history, arithmetic, singing, drawing, French, Italian, German and natural philosophy. If the emphasis on theology – three periods a week with three different tutors – seemed a little excessive, it doubtless reflected the chief interest of the kind enthusiasts who so generously donated their time to the new foundation.

Obviously an education of this standard was desirable in itself. But Anna Jameson, for one, did not think diplomas necessarily made good governesses. 'For myself,' she proclaimed, 'I should not like to take into my family a woman educated expressly for a teacher. I should expect to meet with something of a machine.'[60]   Indeed, given that women's subordinate position was maintained by specifically *not* exposing them to 'unnecessary' knowledge, and bearing in mind the half-ignorant governess's vital role in perpetuating this system of demi-education, a Queen's College diploma might seem, to many families, the very reverse of a recommendation.

It was hard to believe that Mrs Jameson really underwrote this view of things. Yet 'To instruct is one thing, and to educate another,' she insisted. 'It requires a training of quite a different kind from any that could be given in a college for governesses.'[61]

This, however, raised some uncomfortable questions. If governessing was not about instruction, what was it about? A clue was perhaps given by the lady who advised prospective governesses that 'your father's profession and where he lived is always the first question I put to a governess'.[62] The implication of that was unequivocal: the governess's duties were indeed not primarily educational. Her task was to turn little girls into marriageable young ladies, something only a lady could be trusted to do.[63]

In her famous article 'The girl of the period', Eliza Lynn Linton scolds the eponymous maiden for her greed and frivolity and compares her, in so many words, to a whore.

> The legal barter of herself for so much money, representing so much dash, so much luxury and pleasure – that is her idea of marriage ... [But] after all her efforts, she is only a poor copy of the real thing; and the real thing is far more amusing than the copy, because it is real ... If we must have only one kind of thing, let us have it genuine; and the queens of St John's Wood in their unblushing honesty, rather than their imitators and make-believes in Bayswater and Belgravia.[64]

Mrs Lynn Linton looked back nostalgically to 'the simple and genuine girl of the past, with her tender little ways and pretty bashful modesties'.[65] But such a girl (if she had ever existed) stood little chance in the capitalist market place that marriage had become. Given the imbalance recorded by the 1851 census, with 30 per cent of females over twenty still single, mid-century girls needed to sell themselves or risk being left on the shelf – and becoming governesses.

What Mrs Lynn Linton did not point out was the central paradox of the situation: that without the spinsters, the whole edifice of nineteenth-century middle-class marriage would crumble. It was a symbiosis in which single women were unable to live without the employment married women offered, while middle-class marriage could not function without its pool of needy singles.

Many of these lone women provided the most unambiguous of commodities: their labour as servants. In 1851 single female servants numbered 905,165, of whom 582,261 were twenty years of age or older. Servants, declared W.R. Greg, did not 'constitute any part ... of the problem we are endeavouring to solve'. For unlike governesses, those emblems of failure and disquiet,

> They are in no sense redundant. We have not to cudgel our brains to find a niche or occupation for *them;* they are fully and usefully employed; they discharge a most important and indispensable function in social life; they do not follow an obligatorily independent, and therefore for their sex an unnatural career: – on the contrary, they are attached to others and are connected with other existences, which they embellish, facilitate, and serve. In a word they fulfil both essentials of woman's being: *they are supported by, and they minister to, men.*[66]

The governess's contribution was more ambivalent, but it was no less essential to this man-centred universe. Many an independent-minded woman must have thought twice before irrevocably surrendering her identity as a *feme covert* marriage required. However, as the century wore on, and the pool of unmarried women grew, almost any marriage may have seemed preferable to being driven in half-educated desperation to search for an unpleasant, underpaid job, offering neither security nor prospects, in an oversupplied market. Behind every bored and discontented wife loomed the shadowy spectre of the governess. Her downtrodden situation might wring middle-class heartstrings. But it was in fact an essential element of the middle-class ecology.

Anna Jameson, of course, knew only too well that a bad marriage, even if it represented a way out of the schoolroom, was no escape from anything. Indeed, one might well say that she had turned on its head the notion of marriage as a career; for almost uniquely, the balance of the Jameson marriage had been weighted in such a way that the man was imprisoned, the woman freed. Nevertheless, half a century of subjection had left its mark even on such a woman as Mrs Jameson. What was required was a vision of a world in which women might take important decisions entirely independently of men. But that was beyond her. And that ability, as it turned out, would be crucial.

8

The Reform Firm:
what do women want?

◦⟨⟨◉⟩⟩◦

Anna Jameson's forthright pronouncements on women's dis-advantaged position in the world of work made her something of a heroine to radicals. Edward Trelawny, drawn as ever to obstreperous women, welcomed her to the progressive fold, which he alone of the Lerici survivors still stoutly inhabited. 'We are living in a Cockney Villa a sort of cockney life – occasionally coming into town,' he announced to Anna from his current perch in Putney. 'Why do you not hoist your flag of independence and come to us? you will be received triumphantly and will find nothing but good men and true. We are earnestly at work on a work whose theme is divine, the '*Wrongs of Women*' which we have the audacity to imagine we can lighten, if not aid in setting to rights.'[1]

Trelawny's reference was to Mary Wollstonecraft's posthumously published novel *Maria, or, The Wrongs of Woman*, and this full-hearted enthusiasm for Wollstonecraft marked him out as one of a select band. Even those whose educational views coincided with hers were wary of expressing too much enthusiasm for one whose name, at a time when progress was indivisibly allied to respectability, represented all that was dangerous and undesirable. William Thompson's *Appeal of One-Half of the Human Race, Women, against the Pretensions of the other Half, Men, to retain them in political and thence in Civil and Domestic Slavery*, published in 1825, deprecated the 'narrow views which too often marred Mary Wollstonecraft's pages and narrowed their usefulness',[2] though his sympathies are apparent from the title of his book and it is clear he assumed those pages would be known to his readers. Although Harriet Martineau in 1822, aged twenty, had caused a stir with an article 'On Female Education', advocating equal educational opportunities for boys and girls, she observed, dismissively, that 'I never could reconcile my mind to Mary Wollstonecraft's writings, or to whatever I heard of her ... [She] was, with all her powers, a poor victim of passion, with no control over her own peace, and no calmness or content except when the needs of her individual nature were satisfied.'[3] For Miss Martineau's generation, convinced that 'Women who would improve the condition and chances of their sex must ... be not only affectionate and devoted, but rational and dispassionate',[4] Mary's personal excesses ruled her out of consideration.

This view of the *Vindication* as the undisciplined product of an over-emotional mind originated, surprisingly, with Godwin. His *Memoirs* extolled Mary as a woman of feeling, a 'female Werther'[5] whose greatest writing was to be found in her early novel, *Mary*, and her passionate letters to Imlay. The *Vindication*, though a considerable achievement, 'contain[ed] sentiments of a rather masculine description and it must be confessed, occasional passages of a stern and rugged character'.[6] When Godwin declared approvingly that 'a mind more candid in perceiving and retracting error when it was pointed out to her perhaps never existed',[7] it was clear who had done the pointing out. And if even that enlightened husband and father of female geniuses considered reasoned argument a male rather than a female prerogative, it boded ill for Mary's vision of truly equal education for boys and girls.* Queen's College, the new governesses' academy in Harley Street, was an admirable institution, and F.D. Maurice and Charles Kingsley were remarkable men. Nevertheless, the world of which governesses formed such an integral part was too deeply founded in patriarchal Anglicanism for Anglican clergymen to do more than ameliorate its excesses,

---

* This patronizing attitude to female intellect was evidently widespread in Godwin's set. His friend Charles Lamb not only omitted to credit his sister Mary's (predominant) contribution on the title page of their *Tales from Shakespeare* (published in 1807) but explained in the preface that they were not designed for young gentlemen, 'who can read them so much better in the originals', but for their sisters, to whom the young gents were requested to explain 'such parts as are the hardest for them to understand' before, perhaps, 'carefully selecting what is proper for a young sister's ear' from the original.

whether through the GBI or Queen's College. If it was to be changed, women themselves would have to do the changing.

Bedford College was the first step in this more radical direction. Opened in 1849, the same year as Queen's, it had far more subversive intentions. Bedford College's founder was Elizabeth Reid, an old anti-slavery campaigner who had now turned her attention to the liberation of women. 'My dearest wish,' she wrote, 'is that the whole proceeding may be as an Underground Railway, differing in this from the American UR that no one shall ever know of its existence.'[8] Unlike Queen's, Bedford was non-denominational; crucially (and unlike Queen's), it was managed by women (its secretary was Harriet Martineau).

One of the first students to enrol at Bedford College was a young woman of twenty-two called Barbara Leigh Smith. She was studying art, not because it was pleasant for young ladies to draw prettily, but because she seriously intended to make her living as a painter. Barbara was well off: her wealthy father, Benjamin Smith, had settled £300 a year on her when she became twenty-one. But despite the fact that she had no need to earn money, both she and her great friend Bessie Rayner Parkes were convinced that without work (as Bessie put it) 'it is as if the sinews are taken out of life'.[9] Indeed, that had been the gist of Barbara's very first letter to her friend, written in 1847, when Barbara was twenty and Bessie eighteen, expansively scrawled with many drawings and underlinings. 'Dearest Bessie – I have a great deal to say to you about *work*, & *life*, & the necessity of *your* fixing early on a train of action – *you* I mean, what is so sad, so utterly black as a wasted life, and how common! – I believe that there are thousands and tens of thousands who like you and I intend doing, – intend working but live and die, only intending.'[10] Bessie and Barbara would never stop at mere intending. Such was the campaigning energy generated by their friendship that it would change women's prospects for ever.

Reform ran in their blood: the Unitarian reform that had been Mary Wollstonecraft's springboard, in which practical political questioning was allied to a fairly minimal form of religion. Bessie's great-grandfather had been the celebrated chemist and Unitarian divine Joseph Priestley, while her father, Joseph Parkes, the son of a Warwickshire businessman, was a lawyer who by sheer force of intellect had overcome the disadvantage of being debarred from university as a Dissenter to become Parliamentary Solicitor. Barbara's grandfather,

William Smith, a member of the Unitarian congregation led by Prie-stley's friend Theophilus Lindsey, had been a rich businessman, an MP and one of William Wilberforce's abolitionist friends. Her father, Benjamin Smith, also an MP, was a distiller so successful and wealthy that in 1816, when his sister married, he gave the couple his house in Duke Street, near St James's Park, together with all his furniture, and bought himself a new one. Barbara's aunt, Julia Smith, sat with Elizabeth Reid on the board of Bedford College.

It was a formidable lineage and, in Barbara's case, formidably careless of convention. Ben Smith had been single until he was forty, when he met Anne Longden, a milliner's apprentice and, as Barbara put it, began 'notorious cohabitation as man and wife'.[11] For some reason – perhaps, Barbara's biographer suggests, because Ben did not want to impose upon Anne the legal shackles involved in wifehood – the couple never married: a detail so scandalous that most of Ben's brothers and sisters (including the family of Barbara's cousin Florence Nightingale) refused to know them. By the time Anne died in 1834 there were five children, of whom Barbara, the eldest, was seven.

Bessie and Barbara were very different in both character and appear-ance. Barbara, tall and well built, was described by her friend, the poet and painter Dante Gabriel Rossetti, as 'blessed with large rations of tin, fat, enthusiasm and golden hair, who thinks nothing of climbing up a mountain in breeches, or wading through a stream in none in pursuit of pigment'.[12] Bessie was slender, of medium height, brown-haired, grey-eyed and dressed soberly; a tactful and dutiful daughter, and deeply romantic. She nurtured (her own daughter remembered) 'a passionate admiration, and indeed a personal reverence, for Shelley'.[13] She soon conceived an equally passionate admiration for Barbara.

At the Smith houses, by the sea in Hastings and in London at Blandford Square, Barbara and her siblings met an endless stream of visiting intellectuals, refugees and assorted subversives whose unin-hibited discussions honed her incisive mind and encouraged a blunt-ness that sometimes verged on the impolite. But at the Parkeses' Savile Row residence, Bessie lived a life of almost 'conventual exclusion'. She had received an excellent liberal education, much along the lines of that recommended by Erasmus Darwin, at the Miss Fields' Unitarian girls' school near Warwick; when she commented that it 'had its roots in opinions which the [pupils'] parents probably would have been very far from holding if directly expressed',[14] she may well have had her own parents in mind. Her feminist views made her mother nervous; her father, though interested, disapproved. 'Young English women will not believe, till older, in the natural distinctions of the two sexes, & that the Males will never allow the Females to wear their Clothes, – much less usurp their natural sexal [sic] superiority,' Joseph Parkes chided his daughter. ' ... Your GrandMother Priestley, & my Mother in Law before your birth, commenced life with the same aspirations ... but Experience told them, as I often tell you, that Society cannot be so largely or practically revolutionarized as you young inexperienced women imagine & desire.'[15] He liked clever women; when he first met the brilliant Marian Evans (better known to us as George Eliot) he took great pleasure in asking her to dinner parties and introducing her to his friends. But when she set up house with the married G.H. Lewes he would have no more to do with her and forbade Bessie to communicate with her. Bessie took no notice, but until well into her thirties the subject remained difficult. Nor, although a rich man, did he give Bessie an independence: the modest £50 a year that she enjoyed came not from him but from an uncle. Later, when she was thirty, an old friend left her an additional annuity of £150. However, she never had access to anything approaching Barbara's great wealth.

For Bessie, Barbara and her family represented dazzling freedom.

> To Hastings; mad in the train, singing, shouting, yelling, laughing. Oh how happy I was, thinking of the glorious winter to come, all the books to read, all the lovely rides, all the reading and talk with Barbara, all the acting and music, & the seaweeds & the ferns ... Then came Heaven down upon earth to my fancy, & I felt so intensely happy that I could scarcely contain myself. Oh those free wild spirits the Smiths always seem to have, how glorious to feel their rush into one's own heart.[16]

Bessie had fallen in love, and although Mr and Mrs Parkes could hardly object to this friendship, they felt distinctly uneasy. How could any potential husband compete with Barbara?

It is clear that Barbara was never caught up to quite the same degree:

'You don't understand the feelings at all nor the desire for children, which is a growing passion in me,' she admonished her friend.[17] She may well have been right: at this stage Bessie was far more interested in women than men. Barbara was not her first female passion – that had been Miss Lucy Field, one of the three sisters whose school she had attended; and for many years she evaded marriage, just as her parents had feared, by persisting in an arm's length semi-engagement to Sam Blackwell, a rather unsatisfactory ironmaster from Dudley.

Mr Parkes's worst fears were realized when, the month after recording the journal entry quoted above, Bessie turned down an offer from one Robert Fane without so much as a word to him. He considered this no way for a daughter to behave. Bessie, however, was adamant: 'A single woman is so free, so powerful; an intense love will free marriage to her but *that alone* in the present state of society.'[18] It was a statement justifying all the misgivings of those who thought it important not to make spinsterhood too inviting. In the words of W.R. Greg:

> To surround single life for [women] with so smooth an entrance, and such a pleasant, ornamented, comfortable path, that marriage shall almost come to be regarded, not as their most honourable function and especial calling, but merely as one of the many ways open to them, competing on equal terms with other ways for their cold and philosophic choice: – this would appear to be the aim and theory of many female reformers ... Few more radical or more fatal errors ... philanthropy has ever made.[19]

Fortunately for Greg, Bessie's situation was far from the norm. Her father's wealth meant she would never be forced into a job she disliked, while the schemes she hatched with Barbara filled her life with purpose in a way most women could only dream of. 'It is a rare thing to meet with a lady who does not suffer from headaches, langour [sic], hysteria or some illness showing a want of stamina. Dullness is not healthy, and the lives of ladies, it must be confessed, are exceedingly dull,'[20] observed Emily Davies, whose determination to end this state of affairs would eventually prevail.

Even should she lose all her money, of one thing Bessie was quite sure:

I will tell you what, I never *would* be a governess and give up independence, but I would if cast on my own exertions set hard to learn the higher branches of book keeping, if one may so term it, and see if like so many Frenchwomen I could not get some employment in managing a warehouse or some such thing. Such people have much better payment I think than a governess ... I should not mind losing caste at all, just all the worthless friends would be horrified ... What a Sieve such a step would be! There would be many hours in the evening and early morning to read and write you know.[21]

Barbara and Bessie were united in the conviction that women were perfectly capable of running their own affairs without male input. And this insistence on female self-reliance was an important break between their generation and the one that preceded it. When, in 1856, Barbara began to circulate a petition in support of a Married Women's Property Act, 'A Brief Summary, in Plain Language, of the Most Important Laws Concerning Women: Together with a Few Observations Thereon', Anna Jameson expressed alarm that she had not taken the advice of a man before proceeding. 'My dear Bessie, I do most cordially assent to the ... spirit of the petition – but I am afraid it will not do as to form and expression,' she wrote. 'I am afraid it must go through the hands of a man and one of legal experience and ability before it can fulfil its purpose and your hope.'[22] Mrs Jameson died convinced 'That the exclusive management of the community at large belongs to men as the natural result of their exemption from the infirmities and duties which maternity entails on the female part of the human race.'[23] Bessie and Barbara did not agree. The petition went ahead, its long list of signatures headed by the names of Mary Howitt, Elizabeth Barrett Browning – and Anna Jameson.

It was inevitable that Mrs Jameson would become friendly with this new generation of reformers. She already knew two of them: the painter Anna-Mary Howitt, daughter of her old friend the Quaker writer Mary Howitt, and Adelaide Procter, the daughter of her friends Barry Cornwall and Anne Procter, whom she had known ever since Adelaide had been a charming baby called Poppet. In 1854, Anna-Mary introduced her to Barbara – whose father she already knew through their mutual friend Robert Noel, and also to Bessie. She became their mentor and delightedly accepted their friendship. Her niece Gerardine, her sister Louisa's daughter, whom she had adopted when Louisa's husband was bankrupted, had unexpectedly married at the age of nineteen, leaving Anna hurt, disapproving and, above all, lonely. With no children of her own, she had hoped Gerardine would keep her company and look after her in old age, as she had looked after her own mother. Now these new young friends promised, at least partially, to fill the void. 'I have a *maternal* feeling about Adelaide,'[24] Anna told Bessie; and in another letter, 'You [Bessie, Anna-Mary and Barbara] are a trio of dear girls and I love you all – and am well content to accept the *maternal* honour which dear Barbara has laid upon me.'[25] She invited them to visit her, gently but firmly criticized their writings and encouraged them in their political efforts. Significantly, Barbara was particularly interested in Mrs Jameson's studies of Protestant and Catholic charitable sisterhoods – at the time the only instances of women organizing their own working environment.

Barbara and Bessie spent the 1850s in a flurry of activity. They set up an experimental school along the lines of one Barbara herself had attended: co-educational, secular and welcoming children of all classes. Bessie wrote a paper entitled 'Remarks on the Education of Girls' for Lord Brougham's National Association for Social Science, arguing that girls should not be denied the knowledge that was available to their brothers regardless of any supposed threat to their 'purity of mind': 'If women be as pure in nature as they are invariably represented, they will act on pollution like chloride of lime.'[26] They also thought about starting a magazine.

In 1856, Bessie noticed 'a stray number of a periodical, professing to be edited by ladies . . . in the window of a small shop in Edinburgh'. She found the *Waverley Journal* to be 'a paper of a very harmless, but very inefficient sort' devoted to 'the memorable, the progressive and the beautiful'. Bessie decided to try to buy it as a business, 'and then it was that I asked Mrs Jameson's advice as to the desirability of attempting to devote such a magazine to the special objects of women's work'.[27] The result transformed the *Waverley* into *The English Woman's Journal*, a 'Working Women's Journal' for 'all women who are actively engaged in any labours of brain or hand'. From 1858 it appeared monthly, with Bessie as its editor and financial support from Barbara on the basis of a notional 5 per cent return. By November 1859, there were 450 subscribers and a paid-up circulation of 700, a situation that was transformed after Bessie delivered a paper on 'The Market for Educated Female Labour' at the National Association for Social Science, meeting that year in Bradford. 'Dear, the whole kingdom is ringing with the Bradford Paper, and subscriptions pouring in at the EWJ office,' Bessie reported triumphantly to Barbara. 'We are at the flood tide, and must sail into port on it ... What a crown to our long struggle begun ten years ago: *twelve* years. Do not dream of putting all this down to the one paper read at Bradford merely,' she added hastily. 'It is the long struggle which is beginning to tell.'[28]

Barbara had by then become Madame Bodichon. She had married Eugène Bodichon, a French doctor, in Algiers, where she had been taken to distract her from her passion for the tall, handsome, permanently penniless – and, unfortunately, married – radical publisher John Chapman. A ladykiller, notorious for his string of conquests, Chapman lived with his wife and his mistress Elizabeth Tilley (who masqueraded as his daughters' governess) at 142 Strand. Marian Evans, better known to us as the novelist George Eliot, had lodged there for a while when she first arrived in London, having been invited to stay after delivering in person an article she had written for Chapman's *Westminster Review*. However, she had had to leave in a hurry, when both Mrs Chapman and Elizabeth Tilley became jealous. And everyone knew what had happened to Marian Evans: she had set up house with yet another married man, G.H. Lewes, and as a result could not be received in decent society.

Now Chapman proposed to establish a new *ménage à trois* in Blandford Square, in which Barbara would be the accredited mistress. Those who knew him suspected that the Smith fortune constituted more of an attraction than Barbara herself. But Barbara, who always remained conscious of her own mother's unmarried status, was prepared to take the step, denouncing the institution of marriage in her paper 'Women and Work' as 'tend[ing] to prostitution whether legal or on the streets'.[29] Bessie nervously supported her, though the Parkes parents, predictably, were outraged. Elizabeth Parkes, writing to Bessie about Barbara's paper, did not believe 'the sexual side of the question' was a fit matter for single women to discuss.[30] And even tolerant Ben Smith – perhaps not wishing to compound the social price his children had already had to pay for his actions, or lack of them – put his foot down. He whisked his family away to winter in Algiers, where Barbara, clearly determined to find love in some form, transferred her affections to the eccentric Dr Bodichon. The two were married in 1857; sadly for Barbara, though fortunately for her projects, the marriage proved childless. For most of their married life the Bodichons spent the winters in Algiers, the summers in England amid Barbara's old friends and interests.

Meanwhile Bessie, left alone in London, concentrated her energies on her magazine, which, simply by appearing, gave the lie to those who thought women unsuited by nature to run a business. Her life now revolved around its offices at Langham Place and the group of activists that congregated there.

The Langham Place group was an important addition to Bessie's and Barbara's existing network of interlocking feminist friendships. There was the Society of Female Artists started by Barbara and Anna-Mary Howitt; the friendship with Marian Evans, which they stead-fastly maintained in the face of general disapproval; the affectionate bond between Bessie and Adelaide Procter, whose health was poor but who was always a keen worker for the cause; the support that they all offered to Elizabeth Blackwell, a cousin of Bessie's old beau Sam Blackwell and, more importantly, the first woman in the United States to qualify as a doctor. Dr Blackwell had arrived in England in 1850 to study at St Bartholomew's Hospital in London, where Sir James Paget agreed to accept her for a year's post-graduate training, allowing her to work in every department except (she recorded) '*the department for female diseases*'.[31] It was she who memorably dubbed Bessie and Barbara 'The Reform Firm'.

And now there was the *EWJ* group. It included Matilda 'Max' Hays, whom Bessie had met in Rome where she had been living with the American actress Charlotte Cushman, and who had returned with Bessie to become the magazine's co-editor; Isa Craig, who had been associated with the *Waverley Journal* and had come to London to take part in the new enterprise; Jessie Boucherett, the youngest daughter of the High Sheriff of Lincolnshire, who arrived at Langham Place after chancing upon a copy of the *EWJ* and at once set about establishing a Society for Promoting the Employment of Women; Maria Rye, who with Isa Craig established the Female Middle Class Emigration Society, which aimed to supply single women with assisted passages to the colonies; Emily Davies, whose family had just moved to London following the death of her father, and whose project was to secure university education for women; and Emily Faithfull, the youngest daughter of a Surrey clergyman, who arrived fresh from being presented at court, learned typesetting and opened, in 1860, the Victoria Press, with an all-female staff (and an immediate client in the *EWJ*). All gathered at the *Journal's* offices, where they could enjoy the very real pleasures of professional life, so important to men but hitherto denied to women: of busy engagement in an interesting job, combined with the sense of fulfilment and mutual support that comes from working as part of a like-minded team. Once she arrived at Langham Place, Adelaide told Bessie, however trivial her original purpose in going there, she always found so much to do that she rarely went home before evening.

This club-like atmosphere was formalized with the opening of a reading room for ladies (its subscription was a guinea a year; professional ladies paid half-price) with a luncheon room attached, as well as a room where parcels might be left. A register 'for noting applications for the more intellectual and responsible departments of female labour' was also started up – and was almost immediately overrun with hopeful applicants. 'When first this Register was opened,' Bessie wrote,

> we thought ... we might occasionally find opportunities of putting the right woman into the right place; that Mrs A. might recommend an excellent matron or school teacher, and Mrs B. hear of her through our simple plan ... But when the whole question started into life, the advertisements ... appear to have aroused the attention of women in all parts of the country ... and the secretaries ... were literally deluged with applications for employment ... I remember one Friday in ... March, when twenty women applied at our counter for work whereby they could gain a livelihood – all of them more or less educated – all of them with some claim to the title of a lady ... I had to ask them what kind of work they wanted, and, indeed, a more important question, for what kind of work they were fitted ...

She ended significantly: 'The ladies did *not* want to be governesses, they wanted to be something else, and we were to advise them.'[32]

However, there was a fatal obstacle to these ladies obtaining non-governess jobs: their incompetence. Semi-educated on the assumption that they would not have to operate in the working world, when confronted with its demands they found themselves wholly at a loss.

A particular deficiency was mathematics. Arithmetic in the school-room was generally taught from a book giving the correct answers at the end: 'so mechanically', Cynthia Asquith remembered, ' ... that though as often as not my answers would be marked "R" (correct), I seldom had the faintest notion to what my calculations referred'.[33] Neither, it is fair to assume, did her governess. Jessie Boucherett quoted a gentleman who had wished to make his daughters 'good arithmeticians', but who received from several governesses in succession an answer that 'if he wished the young ladies to learn the rule of three he must employ a tutor'.

In ladies' schools a master is invariably employed to instruct the pupils in arithmetic; now why should the schoolmistress put herself to this extra expense if it were not for the fact that none of the female teachers in the house understands it? It appears from these facts that although a few women of the middle ranks might now doubtless be found capable of acting as accountants, yet that the number of them is very small. The deficiency in point of grammar is almost as great. The writer knows a person who had passed two years as teacher in a school intended to prepare girls for governesses, who yet could not be trusted to write an ordinary business letter.[34]

The fault clearly lay with governess education rather than peculiarly female incapacity. In France and Germany women were often employed as cashiers or clerks, without any problems. The American Benjamin Franklin described, in his *Autobiography*, how the widow of a man he had helped set up in business in the mid-eighteenth century, 'being born & bred in Holland, where as I have been inform'd the Knowledge of Accompts makes a Part of Female Education', continued the business with far more success than her late husband, who had not been so educated. Franklin mentioned this case 'chiefly for the sake of recommending that Branch of Education for our young Females, as likely to be more use to them & their children in Case of Widowhood than either Music or Dancing, by preserving them from the Losses by

Imposition of crafty Men'[35] – which, of course, was one of the main reasons such education was generally discouraged.* In Jessie Boucherett's view, if a governess-taught woman was employed in a normal job, 'the experiment thus tried is sure to fail: then the reaction will come, and we shall be told that attempts have been made to employ them but that they proved unequal to their duties.'[36]

Paradoxically, the standard of teaching in National Schools was far better, but because the poor girls who were taught there had such rough manners, they would never be able to work (for example) as drapers' assistants – a feminine occupation that at that time employed an estimated 30,000 men, but which was closed to polite middle-class women because they were incapable of measuring out the ribbons and laces or adding up the bills. In 'Essays on Woman's Work', Bessie suggested that 'If twenty ladies in any town would club together £5 apiece, they might open a stationery shop in which, if they gave all their own custom and tried to get that of their friends, they might secure a profit after employing a lady as manager, and if the business increased, female clerks also.'[37] But without some arithmetical and business competence, even so simple a scheme could never succeed.

Given what the 1851 census had revealed about the numbers of 'redundant women', it was clear that girls, as well as boys, urgently needed proper teaching, so that they might earn a living in the all too likely event that no one else would be available to earn one for them. That much seemed unarguable. Yet arguments there bitterly were. Previously, the restricted nature of girls' education – or non-education – had been taken for granted and was therefore little discussed except by a few advanced females. Now, however, men were forced into the uncomfortable confrontation they had avoided throughout the century and were required to justify, in so many words, the status quo.

The most solid objection – one that daunted women as well as men – was that competition from women would put men out of work. 'Many say that the professions now filled only by men should be open

---

* It is notable that the cleverest men were the likeliest to encourage women's education. Thus, in 1685, Sir William Petty, founder member of the Royal Society and a polymath genius to rival Franklin himself, observed in a letter to a friend that 'One day Arithmetick and Accountantship will adorn a young woman better than a suit of ribbands.'

to women also; but are not their present occupants and candidates more than numerous enough to answer every demand?' Charlotte Brontë wondered. 'Is there any room for female lawyers, female doctors, female engravers, for more female artists, more authoresses? One can see where the evil lies, but who can point out the remedy?'[38] When Anna Jameson, in 1850, persuaded the government to let twenty or thirty girls, as well as the extant class of 200 boys, learn wood engraving at the School of Design in Somerset House, a petition was drawn up by wood engravers 'praying that the women might not be taught, at the expense of the government, arts which would "interfere with the employment of men, and take the bread out of their mouths"'.[39]

This was easily countered. The introduction of machines had been angrily opposed for similar reasons, but their effect had been to increase commercial activity and thus employment. Nevertheless, the argument did possess a certain superficial logic, as did the *Saturday Review*'s contention that as marriage was woman's business, unmarried women, though doubtless unfortunate, must simply be considered as business failures: harsh, doubtless, but in tune with the sink-or-swim capitalist times.

However, the real argument was not logical but emotional. Thackeray, for one, recognized this: 'I don't think [women] have fair play ... I don't think they get their rights ... enslaving them as we do by law and custom ... it is for our use somehow that we have women brought up; to work for us or to shine for us, or to dance for us or what not.'[40] Nonetheless, he would have it no other way. 'I like this milk-and-water in women – perhaps too much, undervaluing your ladyship's heads, and caring only for the heart part of the business.'[41] His real opinion of powerful women is easily deduced from his treatment of Becky Sharp. Both Thackeray, in *Vanity Fair*, and Trollope, in *The Eustace Diamonds*, emphasize the outlandish nature of their anti-heroines' behaviour by making them actual criminals. And the crimes that they commit underline the enormity of their social subversion: Lizzie steals her husband's family diamonds, Becky almost certainly murders Jos Sedley. Becky and Lizzie are far more attractive and interesting in their brilliant wickedness than their more correct but infinitely less dashing counterparts, the anodyne Lucy Morris and the foolish Amelia Sedley. But their attraction – and its implications –

are altogether too dangerous for them to be granted a final-page salvation.

W.R. Greg, like Thackeray, disliked independent women, feeling that they threatened the very basis of the comfortable world in which 'the man naturally governs, the woman as naturally obeys'.[42] When faced with the problem of 'redundant women', his solution was devastatingly straightforward: wholesale export. The colonial diaspora had long been a destination of last resort for younger sons and assorted commercial failures: why should their unwanted sisters not join them? Greg calculated that 440,000 females were needed to redress the balance of the sexes in the United States, Canada and Australia – a little more than the excess disclosed by the 1851 census. If all were sent overseas, 'Such an exodus, such a natural rectification of disproportions . . . could not fail to augment the value, and the demand for, the remainder.'[43] There might be logistical problems in finding enough ships, and doubtless some ladies might not fancy the hard colonial life. Nevertheless, he was confident that these obstacles would prove relatively trivial compared with the enormous benefits – not the least of which would be an easing of the pressure to educate women for the world of work.*

Greg saw female over-education as wholly undesirable. In 'the humbler classes' it led to unnecessary celibacy, as 'the roughness and coarseness of men in their own rank of life, among whom they would naturally look for husbands, becomes repulsive to them; while at the same time their own training and acquirements scarcely qualify them to engage on fair terms with those above them'.[44] As for female intellectuals, they were a shameful breed comparable only to those other unmentionables, the male devotees of the 'love that dare not speak its name':[45]

There are women who are really almost epicene; whose brains are so analogous to those of men that they run nearly in the same channels, are capable of nearly the same toil, and reach nearly to

---

* Though this was the last thing on Greg's mind, those who did emigrate found themselves far freer to choose an active way of life. Charlotte Brontë's friend Rose Taylor, who emigrated to New Zealand, did so because (as Charlotte wrote to her sister Emily) 'she has made up her mind she cannot and will not be a governess, a teacher, a milliner, a bonnet-maker, nor a housekeeper.' She kept a store in Wellington, New Zealand, and wrote a series of articles for the *Victorian Magazine* in which she asserted that the first duty of women is 'the duty of earning money'.

the same heights ... women who live in and by their intelligence alone ... They are objects of admiration, but never of tenderness, to the other sex. Such are ... abnormal and not perfect natures.[46]

Greg took refuge in the well-worn argument of men's and women's complementary natures: 'The brain and frame of woman are formed with admirable suitability to their appropriate work, for which subtlety and sensitiveness, not strength and tenacity of fibre, are required. The cerebral organisation of the female is far more delicate than that of the man; the continuity and severity of application needed to acquire real *mastery* in any profession, or over any science, are denied to women.'[47]

Sixty years earlier, when these arguments had first evolved, an insecure society had clutched at patriotic reaction as a weapon to ward off revolution, Napoleon, shortages and discontent. Now, however, things were very different. Religion itself – the basis of Greg's social universe, in which female inferiority was an expression of divine will – was under attack from science; after the publication of Darwin's *Origin of Species* in 1859, it could no longer be unanimously conflated with literal biological truth. Nevertheless, neither Darwin nor reasoned argument would ever move such as Greg. As John Stuart Mill observed, writing *On the Subjection of Women* in 1869,

> So long as an opinion is strongly rooted in feelings it gains rather than loses in stability by having a mass of argument against it. For if it were accepted as a result of argument the refutation of that argument might shake the solidity of the conviction; but when it rests solely on feeling, the worse it fares in argumentative contest the more persuaded its adherents are that their feeling must have some deeper ground which the arguments do not reach; and while the feeling remains, it is always throwing up fresh entrenchments of argument to repair any breach in the old.[48]

By 1862, the 'Reform Firm' was riven by tensions. Political campaigns such as theirs can be very seductive: solidarity binds the beleaguered activists into an all-absorbing round of endless activity and ever-increasing demands – and suddenly the boundary lines no longer exist and there is no life beyond the campaign. In the hothouse atmosphere at the *EWJ*, emotions overflowed and resentments flourished. Barbara, whose marriage had somewhat detached her from this turmoil, lived in terror lest the *EWJ*'s sworn foe – Mrs Lynn Linton's reactionary *Saturday Review*, which in 1860 had published an article dropping heavy hints about suspicious sexual tendencies in Langham Place, should unearth a genuine scandal.

Her fears were realized in 1864 with the notorious Codrington versus Codrington divorce hearing, a case whose gleeful reporting affords a rare glimpse into the carnal realities of respectable Victorian life. Admiral Codrington, a bullying and authoritarian man, had married a flighty girl twenty years his junior. His wife's habitually flirtatious and probably adulterous behaviour drove her husband almost insane with jealousy. He would neither let her leave the house without his permission, nor escort her in public, nor would he give her any authority over their children. He also refused to have sex with her, on one occasion throwing her out of his room. And thus denied all male company, Helen Codrington found consolation in the willing arms of Emily Faithfull, proprietor of the feminist Victoria Press.

Miss Faithfull moved into the Codrington house in Eccleston Square in 1854 and stayed until 1857, keeping Mrs Codrington company during her husband's frequent absences. 'From time to time,' reported *The Times*, 'Mrs Codrington had proposed that she should sleep with Miss Faithfull, stating that she was subject to asthma, and in the spring of 1857, she positively and absolutely declined ever again to enter the same bed with the admiral, and she insisted on having a separate bed and sleeping with Miss Faithfull.'[49] Mrs Codrington claimed that one night in October 1856, her husband had come into the room where she and Emily were in bed on the pretext of stoking the fire; his own fire being well stoked by what he saw, he had tried to rape Miss Faithfull. Called to the witness box, however, Emily refused to confirm this, claiming that she had been asleep throughout and remembered nothing.

Robert Browning, in a letter to his poetess friend Isa Blagden, attributed this sudden change of allegiance to a sealed letter containing scandalous allegations, which the admiral had threatened to open should the case go against him. One of the counsel in the case had told a friend of Browning that the letter contained a charge I shall be excused from even hinting to you – fear of the explosion of which, caused the shift of Miss E. from one side to the other. As is invariably the case, people's mouths are opened, and tell you 'what they knew long ago' though it seems that did not matter a bit so long as nobody else knew; Mrs Procter, for instance, told me of a lie she (E) had invented to interest Adelaide, about as pretty a specimen as I ever heard, tho' familiar with such sportings of fancy.[50]

Mrs Codrington affirmed the rape, the admiral denied it, and Emily failed to return to court, though Mr Parkes, who took an avid interest in the case, told Bessie that at the time she had been reported still in London, dressed in male attire.[51]

Whether the *EWJ* was or was not, as its detractors insisted, a hotbed of unnatural practices, it is hard to know. The Victorian style tended to hyperbole while at the same time leaving much unsaid; much of the correspondence between those involved concerned situations and allegiances with which both parties were familiar, and which therefore needed no describing. But Adelaide Procter, who was at the centre of much of this activity, was certainly lesbian, as were 'Max' Hays and Emily Faithfull; and as partnerships changed, jealousies raged. Thus, in 1862, Bessie, feeling tired, wanted to retire from the editorship of the *Journal*, and suggested that Isa Craig might take over. Adelaide, however, was appalled: 'anything which throws the English Woman's Journal into E. Faithfull's power, which giving it to Isa does, is a positively wrong and wicked thing.'[52] The truth was that Emily had just deserted Adelaide for Isa and was now anathema. Adelaide, who wrote poetry, recognized the moral obligation to use the Victoria Press for her publications, while grumbling that 'I cannot afford so expensive a printer – and one who is so terribly slow besides ... delay – mistakes – confusion.' However, the letter's last sentence – 'The break with E.F. is made and is a final one' – confirmed that the disaffection was fundamentally emotional.[53] There were also tensions between 'Max' Hays and Adelaide. They, too, had been sentimentally entangled, but now Max had set up house with another member of the 'firm', Lady Monson. '[Max] is exceedingly subdued,' Bessie reported. 'I would do anything on earth to plant her away from the *English Woman's Journal* ... She mustn't be exposed to danger,' she added ominously and mysteriously.[54] (In the event Emily Davies took over the editorship.)

The problems were not confined to romantic spats. Some were religious: Maria Rye appeared to be discriminating against both Catholics and Unitarians when it came to providing emigration assistance or legal copying work. Some were matters of sheer incompatibility: Emily Davies, though single-minded and effective, was tactless and difficult to work with, always insisting on the overriding importance of opening university examinations to women, a topic with which Bessie, for one, had little sympathy.

By 1864, Bessie felt increasingly trapped. And that year, various events would finally force her away from what, for the past seventeen years, had been her life.

The first blow was Adelaide's death. For years her health had been doubtful and she had finally been diagnosed with tuberculosis – in those days, an almost certain death sentence. She had been an especially dear friend. There were old family connections: Adelaide's grandfather, Basil Montagu, then a circuit judge, had been an early supporter of Bessie's father Joseph Parkes when Parkes was still a solicitor in Warwick. And there was also a strong religious and emotional tie. Both Adelaide and Bessie had fallen under the charm of Dr (later Cardinal) Manning, a high-profile convert from Anglicanism to Catholicism who had become a famous society proselytizer. Adelaide, attracted by the ceremonial, and perhaps by the possibility of the all-female society of the convent, had entered the Church in 1851. 'I want you to come and go with me to receive the Palms,' she told Bessie in 1855, explaining why it would be impossible for her – and, she hoped, Bessie – to visit Anna Jameson on Palm Sunday.[55] By the time she died she had become Sister Mary Frances of the Irish Sisters of Mercy. Barbara, along with her sadness – 'Adelaide's death has come to me like an earthquake'[56] – felt a terrible apprehension that Bessie, too, was slipping away from her into Catholicism. How could any liberal impulse survive conversion to this most authoritarian and misogynistic of churches? Up to a point Adelaide had held the two in balance, but she had not been an activist in the same way as Bessie. 'I cannot tell you how wrong your views seem to me to be, and what a bar to anything you ought to wish for, & which we both love to do,' Barbara appealed in desperation. 'God forbid you should go over, & God forbid that the Catholic Church should ever take you in. It is no place for women.'[57]

What Barbara feared was true: Bessie was becoming a different person. The political activity that had hitherto so wholly absorbed her no longer provided the emotional fulfilment she craved and which Catholicism offered. Unitarians, she felt, were 'great in schools & baths & washhouses, & equal laws, & all the elements of moral sanitariness',[58] but that was no longer enough. How, without the certainty that Adelaide had not really died, merely moved on to join her maker – without the memory of Adelaide's own joy as this prospect drew near – could she possibly have borne this death? 'I feel as if with our dear Adelaide a great chapter of my life were read at last,' Bessie told Barbara. 'It has made me feel as if I were beginning quite another part of my life.'[59]

This sense of a break was reinforced when the following month, March, she caught scarlet fever and nearly died.

> This fever has dropped a dense veil between me and all my young women, or middle-aged women. And oh! how sick I am of them! I really laugh to myself as I sit reading Ivanhoe, and think that good little Miss Lewin can't get at me to torture me by hugging me! And that worthy Emily Davies can't write me letters about those awful University Examinations, which I certainly couldn't pass – not one paper. And that nobody can worry me about matrons, schools, workhouses, the Poles, the Italians, the epileptic idiots, the Danes, governesses, social sciences, temperance, Sunday leagues, cruelty to animals. Ugh![60]

Bessie's illness had been severe, and in 1865 there was yet another blow when her father died, leaving her alone with a mother whose views had never really coincided with her own. (To give a trivial but perhaps not insignificant example, Mrs Parkes had always felt indignant at Bessie's refusal to wear stays: an interesting (whale)bone of contention, given stays' literal and metaphorical role in the constriction of women.) She was at the end of her tether: until she should become stronger, she would keep away from feminist work. On the face of it, this was a wholly reasonable decision. But her friends realized that it was as much emotional as medical, and saw it as a betrayal.

Bessie had always felt a great affinity with France – the language, the culture, the practical way in which Frenchwomen got on with life, the way they participated in commercial activity and were valued as social equals. In the spring of 1867 she and Barbara took a holiday there, Barbara enjoying one of her regular absences from Algiers and the husband who remained admirable but who interested her less and less. Towards its end they rented, for six weeks, a small house in La Celle St Cloud, just outside Paris.

The house belonged to a Madame Belloc, who lived in a larger house near by and who was renting out this summer chalet because most of her income had recently vanished on the death of her artist husband. While Barbara spent her time painting, Bessie got to know and love Louise Belloc and the dear friend, Mademoiselle de Montgolfier, who lived with her. She also met Louis Belloc, Madame Belloc's youngest child, who was then thirty-seven – Bessie's own age – and who lived a semi-invalid life, never having fully recovered from a 'brain-fever' suffered thirteen years earlier.

Although Louis was often present when Barbara and Bessie came to visit, he rarely joined in the conversation. One afternoon, however, when Barbara was receiving company, and Madame Belloc and Mademoiselle de Montgolfier were away in Paris, Bessie and Louis went for a long walk together. It was their only time alone with each other during the whole six weeks, yet the day that Bessie and Barbara returned to Paris, Bessie announced to her horrified friend that she had made up her mind to marry Louis Belloc.[61] His mother knew nothing of her feelings; Louis had said not a word. Nevertheless Bessie had no doubt on the matter; and within a week Louis had written to her, to ask for her hand.

Barbara did everything she could to block the marriage. It was now ten years since her own marriage to Eugène Bodichon, and as the years passed she found it increasingly frustrating to spend so much of her life away from what still most engaged her – family, friends, political preoccupations. She could not bear the thought of Bessie suffering a similar disappointment. The wedding was to take place in September; on 26 August, Barbara wrote to Louis's mother, copying the letter to Bessie:

Dear Madame Belloc, —
  Although you are not aware of it, for after all you do not really know

her, Bessie is far too nervous and too delicate to undertake married life under what would be, as I am sure you must agree, unusual difficulties.

She *is unaware of it, but* I *know that in time she will feel intensely the abandonment of all she has gained by her noble life of work for others in England. She has built up, though she may not be conscious of it, a position of great distinction. All this she now proposes to give up, apparently without a thought. And I fear she has not consulted any man who would give her honest and impartial advice.*

As for me, her oldest, closest, and most devoted friend, I feel compelled to tell you that I entirely disapprove of this hasty marriage, and I beg you earnestly to ask her to pause, and to think, even now, well over what she is about to do.

I was amazed when I heard the news. Indeed it was a fearful shock. I also feel the terrible responsibility of being the only person who knows both Bessie and Monsieur Belloc.

Should the marriage take place, I implore you, Madame, to try and feel – not as a mother-in-law feels, but as a real mother feels.

Still, as Bessie knows, I feel that I am her sister, and, as I am constant in my relations, if she marries Monsieur Belloc, then I shall consider him exactly as I should do were he in truth my brother-in-law. And I am not going to tell anyone but Bessie and you what I think.

I hope you will not think it strange of me to say that I shall feel free, if you all wish it, after having told you my opinion, to continue my lifelong relation to Bessie. But I was bound to write this letter, on no other terms could I have done so.[62]

We do not know what Bessie thought of this extraordinary letter. Perhaps she realized that what it expressed most clearly was the lack of satisfaction Barbara had found in her own, childless marriage. Bessie's case, however, was very different from Barbara's. One reason her political work no longer absorbed her was that she craved the emotional fulfilments of family life and saw, in the close, warm, French and Catholic Bellocs – so very different from the cool Parkeses, the family of her dreams. The marriage went ahead and Bessie had two children in short order, Marie and Hilaire, plunging into a joyful domestic round that entirely absorbed her. Louis would survive for only five years after the wedding; but Bessie told her daughter, in the last year of her long life, that those five years, and the nine summers that followed them, spent at La Celle St Cloud with her beloved mother-in-law, represented her true vision of Arcadia.

When Emily Davies first moved to London and the *EWJ* in 1862, she and Bessie lobbied hard for the admission of ladies to the examinations of London University, knowing that, as with the establishment of women doctors, success would have repercussions far beyond the small numbers of people actually involved. In this first attempt they failed. But Emily persisted, and by sheer doggedness and canny politicking succeeded in breaking down one barrier after another. First she got women admitted to the Local Examinations of Cambridge University; then got the university to accept the idea of a women's college that might be associated with it; then, in 1869, she found a house in Hitchin where the first incarnation of this college might be established; finally, in 1873, she achieved her own buildings at Girton, three miles outside the Cambridge city limits, where the college remains to this day.

Even though Barbara is always cited as Girton's co-founder, neither she nor Bessie truly grasped the importance of its existence. Bessie did not much like Emily, and soon grew impatient with her examination obsession, while Barbara was really more interested in female suffrage and tried to persuade Emily to devote her energies to that. It was in vain. Emily kept a pad of paper on her desk at home where she noted anything that occurred to her as necessary but still lacking, and on reading her notes over one day realized that they all boiled down to one thing: university education *on the same terms as men*. Only that would destroy the pernicious and convenient notion that women were physiologically and mentally incapable of equality. And only then could women truly take on the world of men.

The men's desperate efforts not to concede the possibility of equal terms showed that they, too, recognized the importance of this point. In 1874, a year after Girton had opened its new buildings, Dr Henry Maudsley, in the *Fortnightly Review*, basing his argument on medical science, insisted that women could never hope to equal men because 'for one quarter of each month during the best years of life [they were] more or less sick and unfit for hard work'. This was merely the first of six articles he had prepared on the subject. Emily, terrified that parents of prospective students would be put off, persuaded her friend Dr

Elizabeth Garrett Anderson to reply in the next issue, which she did to such effect that Maudsley's succeeding articles were abandoned. But the attacks continued on more purely academic fronts. Why must Miss Davies insist on the inconvenient and expensive business of importing Cambridge university lecturers to tutor her girls, first in Hitchin, later in Girton? Would it not be better in every way if her young ladies were to take specially designed exams of their own – exams that would be better suited to their capacities and the inferior preparation they had inevitably received? Would not that save everyone a good deal of money, effort and disappointment? Sometimes the proposals were insidiously attractive: the Cambridge examination system was antiquated and outmoded and about to be replaced – why should not Miss Davies' students plunge straight into a more modern syllabus, letting the men catch up with them in good time? Others were obviously patronizing. Another young ladies' establishment (that would eventually become Newnham College) had been set up in Cambridge; *they* were basing their studies on a course of special ladies' lectures whose popularity had already been proved among governesses; why would not Miss Davies agree to join forces? 'I am sure it is generous consistency and not cruel mockery that makes you say you are willing to help us when your scheme is the serpent that is gnawing at our vitals,' Emily sternly replied to Professor Henry Sidgwick, these lectures' chief proponent. 'It glides in everywhere ... We meet this hindrance at every step and lately it has seemed to me that it bids fair to crush us. However we are not going to give in yet.'[63]

When Emily Davies first mooted her college in 1862, Bessie Parkes predicted that its first students would probably be 'ladies intending to be governesses'.[64] But this only showed how fundamentally she failed to see the point of what Emily was attempting. Barbara and Bessie had realized that women must act for themselves and not wait for men to help them. That had been their great break with the previous generation. Emily Davies went a step further. She saw that the reason men could not be trusted to help women was that their interests were antithetical – and that the governess, and all she implied, represented men's interests, not women's. Ill-educated, worse-paid than the male tutor doing exactly the same work, without influence or prospects, she not only perpetuated her own powerlessness but focused upon her person the nineteenth century's dislike of independent women, as well as its determination to neutralize the threat they might pose. Girton graduates, far from intending to be governesses, would be the living antithesis of this downtrodden figure. The essential thing about them was that by stepping outside the realm of designated women's occupations to compete with men on their own terms, they would at last fulfil the dreams of all those ladies who had signed up on the Langham Place register of positions vacant, hoping *not* to be governesses. However, if Girtonians' qualifications differed one iota from those of their male compeers, all would be lost. That difference would instantly be seized upon, and used to nudge women back to the margins of supposed congenital inferiority.

Philosophically, then, the establishment of Girton College may be seen as the beginning of the end of the governess. Other, material factors also hastened her decline. As career choices increased, and servants became harder to find, the middle classes were forced to abandon the expansive way of life, with large houses and armies of retainers, of which governesses had been part. As late as 1929 a feminist writer still complained that 'too many women become governesses because they can think of no other way of earning a living'.[65] Yet by then most girls went to school and governesses, as in Agnes Porter's day, were once again confined to the aristocracy.

However, although the objective situation had changed, a century's conditioning was harder to undo. In 1928, in the speech to female undergraduates that eventually became the essay *A Room of One's Own*, Virginia Woolf pointed out that, although 'there must be at this moment some 2,000 women capable of earning over £500 a year in one way or another',[66] they were not doing so. Even into the 1960s, a century after Girton's foundation, female professors, doctors and lawyers remained a rarity.

Some of this had to do with male obduracy: in the late 1950s and early 1960s at least one female barrister (and future judge) found it necessary to sign off court documents using only her initial – J. Bracewell – because if her gender were discovered, future supplies of work would dry up.[67] But obduracy can be overcome by determination. More insidious, and far harder to destroy, was women's internalizing of the notion that they were somehow inferior to men, a complementary species designed (in W.R. Greg's words) to 'complet[e], sweeten, and embellish the existence of others'.[68] They still chose to become nurses rather than doctors, secretaries rather than bosses: to be ill-paid facilitators for people no more talented nor, in many cases, better educated than themselves, but who simply happened to be men. The notion that they might be their bosses' equals penetrated only very slowly; the possibility that they might even be their superiors, though accepted in theory, has perhaps still not wholly sunk in.

Nevertheless, young women today grow up in the world that Mary Wollstonecraft dreamed of. And perhaps the final moment of change can be pinned down in Girton's own history: to the day in 1979 when it was agreed that all-women's colleges were no longer necessary, and the very first women's college of all admitted men.

Notes

1: 'There is nobody in the house with whom I can be on equal terms'

1 Miss Weeton, *Journal of a Governess 1811–25*, ed. Edward Hall, vol. 2, 1939, pp. 68–9.
2 Jane Austen, *Emma*, 1816, vol. 2, Chapter 17.
3 *Ladies' Journal* (1841).
4 George Stephen, *Guide to Service: The Governess*, 1844, p. 361.
5 *Hints to Governesses, by One of Themselves*, 1856, p. 8.
6 W.M. Thackeray, 'Book of snobs', 1848, Chapter 25.
7 Charlotte Brontë, *Shirley*, 1849, Chapter 21.
8 Lady Eastlake, '*Vanity Fair* – and *Jane Eyre*', *Quarterly Review*, 84 (December–March 1848-9), p. 177.
9 Anthony Trollope, *The Eustace Diamonds*, 1872, Chapter 29.
10 Louisa M. Alcott, *Little Women*, 1868, Chapter 12.
11 The social doyen in question was Ward McAllister, who told his story and set out his social principles in *Society as I Have Known It*, New York, 1890.
12 Eliza Bishop to Everina Wollstonecraft, February 1793, Abinger papers, Bodleian Library.
13 'The right spirit', *Work and Leisure* (1880), 259–60.
14 See for example W.R. Greg, 'Why are women redundant?', *National Review*, 14 (April 1862), pp. 434–60.
15 An average of £305 a week over and above board and lodging. Survey by gumtree.com, quoted in the *Guardian*, 15 May 2007.
16 Harriet Martineau, 'The governess', *Once a Week*, 3 (1860), pp. 267–72.
17 Charlotte Brontë to Ellen Nussey, 8 June 1839, *The Brontë Letters*, ed. Muriel Spark, London, 1954.
18 Elizabeth Gaskell, *The Life of Charlotte Brontë* (first published 1857, reprinted 1901), p. 154.
19 Anna Jameson, *Memoirs and Essays*, 1846, p. 277.
20 Eastlake, '*Vanity Fair* – and *Jane Eyre*', p. 176.
21 Greg, 'Why are women redundant?', p. 436.
22 Thackeray, 'Book of snobs', Chapter 25.
23 Martineau, 'The governess'.
24 *Hints to Governesses*, p. 4.
25 Weeton, *Journal of a Governess 1811–25*, vol. 2, pp. 68–9.

26 Ibid.
27 Charlotte Brontë to Ellen Nussey, 3 March 1841, *Brontë Letters*, ed. Muriel Spark, London, 1954.
28 Martineau, 'The governess'.
29 Weeton, vol. 2, p. 82.
30 Weeton, vol. 2, p. 67.
31 Weeton, vol. 2, p. 120.
32 'Going a-governessing', *English Woman's Journal*, 1, 1859, p. 397.
33 Greg, 'Why are women redundant?', p. 441.
34 J.A. Banks and Olive Banks, *Feminism and Family Planning in Victorian England*, 1965, p. 28.
35 Banks and Banks, *Feminism and Family Planning*, p. 30.
36 Wanda Neff, *Victorian Working Women*, 1929, p. 12.
37 *The Times*, 2 July 1861.
38 'Keeping up appearances', *The Cornhill Magazine*, vol. 4, 1861, pp. 305–18.
39 Anthony Trollope, *The Eustace Diamonds*, Chapter 30.
40 J.H. Walsh, quoted in Banks and Banks, *Feminism and Family Planning in Victorian England*, p. 75.
41 *Economy for the Single and Married*, 1845, quoted in J.A. Banks, *Prosperity and Parenthood: A Study of Family Planning among the Victorian Middle Classes*, 1954, pp. 74, 81.
42 Small advertisement in *The Times*, January 1845.
43 'How girls should be educated', *Ladies' Journal*, 1840.
44 *Hints to Governesses*, p. 27.
45 Martineau, 'The governess'.
46 'Society and the daily governess', Eliza Cook, *Eliza Cook's Journal*, 1853, p. 270.
47 *The Times*, 27 June 1845.
48 Charlotte Brontë to Ellen Nussey, 3 March 1841, *Brontë Letters*, ed. Muriel Spark, London, 1954.
49 *The Times*, 14 January 1895.
50 'The right spirit', *Work and Leisure* (December 1880), pp. 258–60.
51 Frances Power Cobbe, *Life of Frances Power Cobbe, By Herself*, 1894, pp. 69–70.
52 Stephen, *Guide to Service*, p. 353.
53 'The right spirit'.
54 *Hints to Governesses*, p. 27.
55 'The right spirit'.
56 Weeton, vol. 2, p. 379.
57 Advertisement in *The Times*, January 1845.
58 Report of the Governesses' Benevolent Institution, 1844, London Metropolitan Archives.
59 Martineau, 'The governess'.

2: 'In these days, there do not exist such people as Miss Porter'

1 C.R.M. Talbot to Charlotte Traherne, 22 March 1846. From a letter-book in Penrice Castle, with thanks to Joanna Martin.
2 Joanna Martin (ed.), *A Governess in the Age of Jane Austen: The Journals and Letters of Agnes Porter*, 1998 (hereafter referred to as *Journals and Letters of Agnes Porter*), journal entry, July 1791.
3 Charlotte Brontë to Ellen Nussey, 3 March 1841, *Brontë Letters*, ed. Muriel Spark, London, 1954.
4 Ibid.
5 Anne Brontë, *Agnes Grey*, 1847, Chapter 3.
6 John Tasker, whose nieces Eliza taught, had made his money with the East India Company, and had recently bought Upton Castle from the family whose ancestral home it had been.
7 We know that Lady Ilchester had not felt the same friendship for Miss Porter's predecessor, Jane Arden, who was 'let go' after two years, according to her employer because

she was 'untrustworthy'. Arden's story, as recounted years later by her daughter, was that she had left because Redlynch was too far from her family in Yorkshire. But whatever the ostensible reason, it is clear that the parties did not get on.

8 Charlotte Brontë to Ellen Nussey, 1839, *Brontë Letters*, ed. Muriel Spark, London, 1954.

9 Brontë, *Agnes Grey*, Chapter 3.

10 Figures from the Duke of Kingston's household: G.E. Mingay, *A Social History of the English Countryside*, 1990, p. 227.

11 *Journals and Letters of Agnes Porter*, journal entries for 29 April and 25 November 1791.

12 W.M. Thackeray, *Vanity Fair*, 1848, Chapter 6.

13 *Journals and Letters of Agnes Porter*, Agnes Porter to Lady Mary Strangways, 7 April 1792.

14 *Journals and Letters of Agnes Porter*, Agnes Porter to Lady Mary Talbot, 25 April 1812.

15 *Journals and Letters of Agnes Porter*, journal entry, 23 August 1803.

16 *Journals and Letters of Agnes Porter*, Agnes Porter to Lady Mary Talbot, 11 September 1794.

17 Ibid.

18 *Journals and Letters of Agnes Porter*, Agnes Porter to Lady Mary Talbot, 9 July 1797.

19 *Journals and Letters of Agnes Porter*, Agnes Porter to Lady Mary Talbot, 7 June 1798.

20 *Journals and Letters of Agnes Porter*, journal entry, February 1797.

21 *Journals and Letters of Agnes Porter*, journal entry, 28 March 1797.

22 *Journals and Letters of Agnes Porter*, Agnes Porter to Lady Mary Strangways, 7 April 1792.

23 Fanny Burney, *Camilla*, London 1796.

24 *Journals and Letters of Agnes Porter*, Agnes Porter to Lady Mary Talbot, 22 July 1794.

25 *Journals and Letters of Agnes Porter*, journal entry, 24 January 1791.

26 *Journals and Letters of Agnes Porter*, journal entries, 28 November 1790– 29 January 1791.

27 *Journals and Letters of Agnes Porter*, journal entry, 2 June 1791.

28 *Journals and Letters of Agnes Porter*, journal entry, 16 July 1791.

29 *Journals and Letters of Agnes Porter*, journal entry, 12 April 1805.

30 Stephen, *Guide to Service*, p. 361.

31 Joanna Martin, *Wives and Daughters: Women and Children in the Georgian Country House*, 2004, p. 230.

32 *Journals and Letters of Agnes Porter*, journal entry, June 1796.

33 *Journals and Letters of Agnes Porter*, journal entry, May 1797.

34 *Journals and Letters of Agnes Porter*, journal entry, May 1797.

35 *Journals and Letters of Agnes Porter*, journal entry, 24 March 1804.

36 *Journals and Letters of Agnes Porter*, journal entry, 21 October 1802.

37 *Journals and Letters of Agnes Porter*, 22 November 1806.

38 *Journals and Letters of Agnes Porter*, Agnes Porter to Lady Mary Talbot, 3 March 1807.

39 C.R.M. Talbot to Charlotte Traherne, 22 March 1846. From a letter-book in Penrice Castle, with thanks to Joanna Martin.

40 Anna Jameson, *On the Relative Social Position of Mothers and Governesses*, 1843, *Memoirs and Essays*.

3: Mary and her sisters: the problem of girls' education

1 Mary Wollstonecraft, *A Vindication of the Rights of Woman*, 1792,

Chapter 4, 'Observations on the State of Degradation to Which Woman is Reduced by Various Causes'.

2 Wollstonecraft, *A Vindication of the Rights of Woman*, Chapter 1.

3 Wollstonecraft, *A Vindication of the Rights of Woman*, Chapter 10.

4 Wollstonecraft, *A Vindication of the Rights of Woman*, Chapter 6.

5 Mary Wollstonecraft, *Correspondence*, ed. Janet Todd (hereafter referred to as *Wollstonecraft Correspondence*), 2003, Mary Wollstonecraft to Jane Arden, mid-1779.

6 *Wollstonecraft Correspondence*, Mary Wollstonecraft to Jane Arden, early 1780.

7 William Godwin, *Memoirs of Mary Wollstonecraft*, ed. J. Middleton Murry, 1928, p. 11.

8 Mary Wollstonecraft, *Mary: A Fiction*, 1788, Chapter 2.

9 *Wollstonecraft Correspondence*, Mary Wollstonecraft to Jane Arden, 1780.

10 Godwin, *Memoirs*, p. 27.

11 *Hints to Governesses*, p. 10.

12 *Wollstonecraft Correspondence*, Mary Wollstonecraft to Jane Arden, April 1781.

13 For an interesting discussion of this, see Amy Froide, *Never Married: Single Women in Early Modern England*, Oxford, 2005.

14 Mary Wollstonecraft, *Thoughts on the Education of Daughters*, 1786.

15 Mary Wollstonecraft, *Collected Works*, eds. Janet Todd and Marilyn Butler, 1989, vol. 4, p. 25.

16 Mary Wollstonecraft, *Maria, or, The Wrongs of Woman*, 1798, vol. 1, Chapter 8.

17 Eliza Bishop to Everina Wollstonecraft, April 1794. Eliza's letters to Everina are in the Abinger papers, Bodleian Library, dep. b. 210/7.

18 *Wollstonecraft Correspondence*, Mary Wollstonecraft to George Blood, July 1785.

19 *Wollstonecraft Correspondence*, Mary Wollstonecraft to Eliza Bishop, August 1781.

20 *Wollstonecraft Correspondence*, Mary Wollstonecraft to Everina Wollstonecraft, 10 February 1787.

21 *Wollstonecraft Correspondence*, Mary Wollstonecraft to Everina Wollstonecraft, 3 March 1787.

22 *Wollstonecraft Correspondence*, Mary Wollstonecraft to Eliza Bishop, late 1790.

23 Wollstonecraft, *Maria, or, The Wrongs of Woman*, Chapter 9.

24 *Wollstonecraft Correspondence*, Mary Wollstonecraft to Jane Arden, late 1782.

25 *Wollstonecraft Correspondence*, Mary Wollstonecraft to Everina Wollstonecraft.

26 *Wollstonecraft Correspondence*, Mary Wollstonecraft to Everina Wollstonecraft, 7 January 1784.

27 *Wollstonecraft Correspondence*, Mary Wollstonecraft to Everina Wollstonecraft, 12 or 19 January 1784.

28 *Wollstonecraft Correspondence*, Mary Wollstonecraft to Everina Wollstonecraft.

29 *Wollstonecraft Correspondence*, Mary Wollstonecraft to Everina Wollstonecraft.

30 Fanny Blood to Everina Wollstonecraft, Abinger papers, Bodleian Library, b. 210/9.

31 Wollstonecraft, *Thoughts on the Education of Daughters, Collected Works*, vol. 4, p. 25.

32 Wollstonecraft, *Thoughts on the Education of Daughters, Collected Works*, vol. 4, p. 22.

33 Erasmus Darwin, *Plan for the Conduct of Female Education in Boarding Schools*, 1797.

34 Elizabeth Firth Manuscripts, Special Collections, Sheffield University, 13 May, 1812.

35 Elizabeth Firth Manuscripts, 1 May 1812.

36 *Annual Register for 1759*.

37 Frances Edgeworth, *A Memoir of Maria Edgeworth*, 1867, p. 9.

38 E.P. Cooper to William Godwin, 1790s, Bodleian Library, Abinger papers, dep. b. 214/1(b).

39 Wollstonecraft, *Thoughts on the Education of Daughters*.

40 Godwin, *Memoirs of Mary Wollstonecraft*, pp. 34–5.

41 Mary Wollstonecraft, *Mary, A Fiction*, 1788, Chapter 8.

42 *Wollstonecraft Correspondence*, Mary Wollstonecraft to George Blood, 20 July 1785.

43 Godwin, *Memoirs*, p. 34.

44 *Wollstonecraft Correspondence*, Mary Wollstonecraft to George Blood, February 1786.

45 Godwin, *Memoirs*, p. 38.

46 Eliza Bishop to Everina Wollstonecraft, 17 August 1786, Abinger papers, Bodleian Library, b. 210/1.

47 *Wollstonecraft Correspondence*, Mary Wollstonecraft to Eliza Bishop, 23 September 1786.

48 *Wollstonecraft Correspondence*, Mary Wollstonecraft to George Blood, 6 July 1786.

49 Ibid.

50 *Wollstonecraft Correspondence*, Mary Wollstonecraft to George Blood, 25 August 1786.

51 *Wollstonecraft Correspondence*, Mary Wollstonecraft to Everina Wollstonecraft.

52 *Wollstonecraft Correspondence*, Mary Wollstonecraft to Everina

Wollstonecraft, 15 January 1787.

53 *Wollstonecraft Correspondence*, Mary Wollstonecraft to Everina Wollstonecraft, 30 October 1786.

54 Ibid.

55 Wollstonecraft, *Thoughts on the Education of Daughters*.

56 *Wollstonecraft Correspondence*, Mary Wollstonecraft to Everina Wollstonecraft, 9 October 1786.

57 Margaret King (Mrs Mason), letter to her daughters Laura and Nerina, Abinger MSS, quoted in E. McAleer, *The Sensitive Plant*, 1958, p. 5.

58 *Wollstonecraft Correspondence*, Mary Wollstonecraft to Everina Wollstonecraft, 30 October 1786.

59 *Wollstonecraft Correspondence*, Mary Wollstonecraft to Eliza Bishop, 5 November 1786.

60 *Wollstonecraft Correspondence*, Mary Wollstonecraft to Everina Wollstonecraft, 17 November 1786.

61 Margaret King (Mrs Mason) to William Godwin, 1803, Abinger MSS, quoted in McAleer, p. 66.

62 Margaret King (Mrs Mason), letter to her daughters Laura and Nerina, quoted in McAleer, p. 5.

63 *Wollstonecraft Correspondence*, Mary Wollstonecraft to Everina Wollstonecraft, 15 January 1787.

64 *Wollstonecraft Correspondence*, Mary Wollstonecraft to Joseph Johnson, 14 April 1787.

65 *Wollstonecraft Correspondence*, Mary Wollstonecraft to George Blood, 7 November 1786.

66 *Wollstonecraft Correspondence*, Mary Wollstonecraft to Eliza Bishop, 5 November 1786.

67 Godwin, *Memoirs*, p. 41.

68 *Wollstonecraft Correspondence*, Mary Wollstonecraft to Everina Wollstonecraft, 25 March 1787.

69 *Wollstonecraft Correspondence*, Mary

Wollstonecraft to Eliza Bishop, 5 November 1786.

70 *Wollstonecraft Correspondence,* Mary Wollstonecraft to George Blood, 7 November 1786.

71 *Wollstonecraft Correspondence,* Mary Wollstonecraft to Everina Wollstonecraft, 17 November 1786.

72 *Wollstonecraft Correspondence,* Mary Wollstonecraft to Eliza Bishop, 5 November 1786.

73 *Wollstonecraft Correspondence,* Mary Wollstonecraft to Eliza Bishop, 5 November 1786.

74 *Wollstonecraft Correspondence,* Mary Wollstonecraft to Everina Wollstonecraft, 30 October 1786.

75 Ibid.

76 *Wollstonecraft Correspondence,* Mary Wollstonecraft to Everina Wollstonecraft, 17 November 1786.

77 Ibid.

78 *Wollstonecraft Correspondence,* Mary Wollstonecraft to Eliza Bishop, 22 December 1786.

79 *Wollstonecraft Correspondence,* Mary Wollstonecraft to Everina Wollstonecraft, 3 March 1787.

80 *Wollstonecraft Correspondence,* Mary Wollstonecraft to Everina Wollstonecraft, February 1787.

81 *Wollstonecraft Correspondence,* Mary Wollstonecraft to Everina Wollstonecraft, 30 October, 1786.

82 *Wollstonecraft Correspondence,* Mary Wollstonecraft to Everina Wollstonecraft, 25 March 1787.

83 Ibid.

84 Ibid.

85 *Wollstonecraft Correspondence,* Mary Wollstonecraft to Everina Wollstonecraft, 11 May 1787.

86 Quoted in Ruth Brandon, *The New Women and the Old Men,* 1991, pp. 38–9.

87 *Wollstonecraft Correspondence,* Mary Wollstonecraft to Everina Wollstonecraft, November 1787.

88 Harriet Martineau, *Deerbrook,* 1839, vol. 3, p. 166.

89 Ibid.

90 *Wollstonecraft Correspondence,* Mary Wollstonecraft to Everina Wollstonecraft, November 1787.

91 Wollstonecraft, *Thoughts on the Education of Daughters,* p. 26.

92 *Wollstonecraft Correspondence,* Mary Wollstonecraft to Joseph Johnson, 1790.

93 *Wollstonecraft Correspondence,* Mary Wollstonecraft to Everina Wollstonecraft, November 1787.

94 *Wollstonecraft Correspondence,* Mary Wollstonecraft to Joseph Johnson, 1790.

95 *Wollstonecraft Correspondence,* Mary Wollstonecraft to Everina Wollstonecraft, November 1787.

96 *Wollstonecraft Correspondence,* Mary Wollstonecraft to George Blood, 16 May 1788.

97 Abinger papers, Bodleian Library, dep. f. 65.

98 Wollstonecraft, *Thoughts on the Education of Daughters,* p. 25.

99 Richard Price, *A Discourse on the Love of Our Country,* 1789.

100 Ibid.

101 Edmund Burke, *Reflections on the Revolution in France,* 1790.

102 Burke, *Reflections on the Revolution in France.*

103 Godwin, *Memoirs,* pp. 51–2.

104 Mary Wollstonecraft, *Vindication of the Rights of Men,* 1790, *Collected Works,* vol. 5, p. 18.

105 Mary Wollstonecraft, *A Vindication of the Rights of Men,* 1790.

106 Jean-Jacques Rousseau, *Emile,* Book 5, Pléiade Edition, p. 703.

107 Wollstonecraft, *A Vindication of the Rights of Woman,* Chapter 12.

108 Wollstonecraft, *A Vindication of the Rights of Woman,* Chapter 2.

109 Wollstonecraft, *A Vindication of the Rights of Woman*, Chapters 9 and 13.

110 Helen Braithwaite, *Romanticism, Publishing and Dissent: Joseph Johnson and the Cause of Liberty*, 2003, p. 206, n. 25.

111 *Wollstonecraft Correspondence*, Mary Wollstonecraft to Catherine Macaulay, December 1790.

112 Wollstonecraft, *A Vindication of the Rights of Woman*, Chapter 1.

113 Godwin, *Memoirs*, p. 57.

114 Wollstonecraft, *A Vindication of the Rights of Woman*, Author's Introduction.

115 Wollstonecraft, *A Vindication of the Rights of Woman*, Chapter 12.

116 Wollstonecraft, *A Vindication of the Rights of Woman*, Chapter 12.

117 Catherine Macaulay, *Letters on Education*, 1790.

118 Wollstonecraft, *A Vindication of the Rights of Woman*, Chapter 4.

119 *Wollstonecraft Correspondence*, Mary Wollstonecraft to George Blood, 6 October 1791.

120 *Wollstonecraft Correspondence*, Mary Wollstonecraft to Everina Wollstonecraft, 7 November 1787.

121 *Wollstonecraft Correspondence*, Mary Wollstonecraft to George Blood, 4 February 1791.

122 *Wollstonecraft Correspondence*, Mary Wollstonecraft to George Blood, 11 September 1787.

123 Eliza Bishop to Everina Wollstonecraft, May 1791.

124 Charlotte Brontë, *Jane Eyre*, 1847, Chapter 11.

125 Eliza Bishop to Everina Wollstonecraft, 4 October 1791.

126 Eliza Bishop to Everina Wollstonecraft, 4 November 1791.

127 Eliza Bishop to Everina Wollstonecraft, December 1791.

128 Eliza Bishop to Everina Wollstonecraft, December 1791.

129 Eliza Bishop to Everina Wollstonecraft, 8 December 1791.

130 Eliza Bishop to Everina Wollstonecraft, 4 November 1791.

131 Eliza Bishop to Everina Wollstonecraft, 8 December 1791.

132 William Godwin to J. Marshal, 1800, quoted in C. Kegan Paul, *William Godwin*, 1876, vol. 2, p. 369.

133 Eliza Bishop to Everina Wollstonecraft, December 1791.

134 Eliza Bishop to Everina Wollstonecraft, 3 July 1792.

135 *Wollstonecraft Correspondence*, Mary Wollstonecraft to Mary Hays, c. April–May 1796.

136 Eliza Bishop to Everina Wollstonecraft, February 1793.

137 *Wollstonecraft Correspondence*, Mary Wollstonecraft to Joseph Johnson, 26 December 1792.

138 *Wollstonecraft Correspondence*, Mary Wollstonecraft to Eliza Bishop, 20 January 1793.

139 Abinger papers, Bodleian Library, dep. b. 214.

140 Ibid.

141 Eliza Bishop to Everina Wollstonecraft, December 1792.

142 *Wollstonecraft Correspondence*, Mary Wollstonecraft to Eliza Bishop, 24 June 1793.

143 Virginia Woolf, 'Mary Wollstonecraft', in *The Common Reader*, second series, 1932, vol. 2.

144 *Wollstonecraft Correspondence*, Mary Wollstonecraft to Eliza Bishop, 13 June 1793.

145 *Wollstonecraft Correspondence*, Mary Wollstonecraft to Everina Wollstonecraft, 10 March 1794.

146 Eliza Bishop to Everina Wollstonecraft, 1794.

147 Eliza Bishop to Everina Wollstonecraft, 24 May 1794.

148 Eliza Bishop to Everina Wollstonecraft, 17 November 1794.

149 Eliza Bishop to Everina Wollstonecraft, 1 December 1794.

150 *Wollstonecraft Correspondence*, Mary Wollstonecraft to Eliza Bishop, 23 April 1795.

151 Godwin, *Memoirs*, p. 83.

152 Eliza Bishop to Everina Wollstonecraft, 29 April 1795.

153 Eliza Bishop to Everina Wollstonecraft, 10 May 1795.

154 Eliza Bishop to Everina Wollstonecraft, 28 March 1795.

155 *Wollstonecraft Correspondence*, Mary Wollstonecraft to William Godwin, 21 February 1797.

156 *Wollstonecraft Correspondence*, Mary Wollstonecraft to William Godwin, 6 March 1797.

157 William Godwin to Mary Wollstonecraft, 10 June 1797, quoted in Paul, vol. 1, p. 256.

158 Eliza Fenwick to Everina Wollstonecraft, 12 December 1797, quoted in Paul, vol. 1, p. 283.

159 Everina Wollstonecraft to Eliza Bishop, Abinger papers, Bodleian Library, dep. 210/5e.

160 Ibid.

161 Ibid.

162 Miss Mary Hutton to Edward Dowden (Shelley's biographer), E. Dowden, *Life of Shelley*, 1909, vol. 2, nn. 50–1.

163 Harriet Martineau, 'The governess', *Once a Week*, 3 (1860).

4: Claire Clairmont: after the fall

1 Claire Clairmont to Jane Williams, December 1826. All Claire Clairmont's letters are from *The Clairmont Correspondence: Letters of Claire Clairmont, Charles Clairmont and Fanny Imlay Godwin*, in 2 vols., ed. Marion Kingston Stocking, 1995 (hereafter referred to as Clairmont, *Letters*).

2 Lady Caroline Lamb, quoted in Elizabeth Jenkins, *Lady Caroline Lamb*, 1932, chapter 6.

3 Claire Clairmont to Lord Byron, 22 April 1816, Claire Clairmont, *Letters*, vol. 1.

4 All this information is from H. Crabb Robinson, *Henry Crabb Robinson on Books and their Writers*, 1938, vol. 1, p. 234.

5 In fact this was probably mythical, as it was not set down until 1878.

6 C. Kegan Paul, *William Godwin*, 1876, vol. 2, p. 190.

7 Aaron Burr, *The Private Journal of Aaron Burr*, ed. Wm. K. Bixby, 1903.

8 Claire Clairmont to Edward John Trelawney, in Claire Clairmont, *Letters*, vol. 2, p. 618.

9 Charles Lamb, *Letters*, vol. 1, p. 273.

10 Mary Shelley to Maria Gisborne, 16 October 1820, *Selected Letters of Mary Wollstonecraft Shelley*, ed. Betty T. Bennett.

11 Mary Godwin to Maria Gisborne, July 1820.

12 Claire Clairmont, *Letters*, vol. 2, p. 644.

13 Claire Clairmont to Edward John Trelawny, April 1871.

14 Burr, *Private Journal*, 2 December 1808.

15 Burr, *Private Journal*, 15 February 1812.

16 Claire Clairmont, *Journals*, ed. Marion Kingston Stocking, 1968, p. 432.

17 Edward Silsbee's notebooks, Peabody Essex Museum, Salem, Massachusetts, box 7, file 2.

18 Claire Clairmont, *Journals*, p. 424.

19 Percy Bysshe Shelley to T.J. Hogg, 4 October 1814, in P.B. Shelley, *Letters*, ed. F.L. Jones, 1964.

20 Burr, *Private Journal*, 24 February 1812.

21 Maria Gisborne, journal, 9 July 1820, quoted in Clairmont, *Letters*, p. 88.

22 Quoted in Paul, *William Godwin*, vol. 2, p. 214.

23 Claire Clairmont to E.J. Trelawny, April 1871, Clairmont, *Letters*, vol. 1.

24 Claire Clairmont's journal, quoted in Mary Shelley, *Journals*, ed. Paula R. Feldman and Diana Scott-Kilvert, 1987, vol. 1, p. 18.

25 Claire Clairmont, *Journals*, first journal, p. 31 (27 August 1814).

26 Claire Clairmont, *Journals*, first journal, p. 48 (7 October 1814).

27 Edward Silsbee's notebooks, Peabody Essex Museum, Salem, Massachusetts, box 7, file 3.

28 Mary Shelley, *Journals*, vol. 1, p. 69.

29 Ibid.

30 *The Times*, 17 March 1815, quoted in Claire Clairmont, *Letters*, vol. 1, p. 12.

31 Mary Shelley, *Journals*, vol. 1, p. 71.

32 Mary Shelley, *Journals*, vol. 1, p. 78.

33 Charlotte Brontë, *Jane Eyre*, Chapter 17.

34 Claire Clairmont, *Journals*, 2nd leaflet, 1828–30, p. 437.

35 Edward Silsbee's notebooks, Peabody Essex Museum, Salem, Massachusetts, box 7, file 3, quoted in Claire Clairmont, *Letters*, p. 25n.

36 Claire Clairmont, *Letters*, vol. 1, March or April 1816.

37 Claire Clairmont, *Letters*, vol. 1, March or April 1816.

38 Claire Clairmont, *Letters*, vol. 1, pp. 26–7n.

39 In R.B. Sheridan, *The Rivals*, 1775.

40 Lord Byron to Douglas Kinnaird, quoted in Leslie A. Marchand, *Byron: A Biography*, 1957, vol. 2, p. 681.

41 Marchand, *Byron*, vol. 2, p. 627.

42 Thomas Love Peacock, *Nightmare Abbey*, 1818.

43 Lord Byron to Augusta Leigh, 21 September.

44 Claire Clairmont, *Letters*, vol. 1, March or April 1816.

45 Claire Clairmont, *Letters*, vol. 1, April 1816.

46 Edward Silsbee's notebooks, Peabody Essex Museum, Salem, Massachusetts, box 7, file 3.

47 Also known as the Poverty Year, or Eighteen Hundred and Froze to Death.

48 Lord Byron to Augusta Leigh, 8 September 1816.

49 Lord Byron to Douglas Kinnaird, quoted in Marchand, *Byron*, vol. 2, p. 681.

50 Edward Silsbee's notebooks, Peabody Essex Museum, Salem, Massachusetts, box 7, file 2.

51 Claire Clairmont to E.J. Trelawney, 1870, quoted in Clairmont, *Letters*, vol. 2, p. 603.

52 Mary Shelley to P.B. Shelley, 5 December 1816, *Selected Letters of Mary Wollstonecraft Shelley*, 1817.

53 Robinson, *Henry Crabb Robinson on Books*, vol. 2, 15 December 1816.

54 Quoted in J. Buxton Forman, *The Elopement of Percy Bysshe Shelley and Mary Wollstonecraft Godwin as narrated by William Godwin*, 1911.

55 Claire Clairmont to Lord Byron, 12 January 1818, Claire Clairmont, *Letters*, vol. 1.

56 Leslie A. Marchand (ed.), *Byron's Letters and Journals*, vol. 6, 13 January 1818.

57 Mary Wollstonecraft Shelley, *Selected Letters of Mary Wollstonecraft Shelley*, 1817, vol. 1, pp. 48–9.

58 Claire Clairmont to Lord Byron, 12 January 1818, Claire Clairmont, *Letters*, vol. 1, pp. 48–9.

59 Lord Byron to P.B. Shelley, April 1818.

60 Claire Clairmont to Lord Byron, 27 April 1818, Claire Clairmont, *Letters*, vol. 1.

61 Lord Byron to Augusta Leigh, 3 August 1818.

62 Lord Byron to Augusta Leigh, 10 September 1819, Lord Byron, *Letters and Journals*, vol. 6, pp. 222–3.

63 Lord Byron to J.C. Hobhouse, 20 November 1819, Lord Byron, *Letters and Journals*, vol. 6, pp. 244–5.

64 Hubert Jerningham, *Reminiscences of an Attaché*, p. 106, quoted in Claire Clairmont, *Letters*, vol. 1, p. 130n.

65 Mrs Hoppner to Mary Shelley, 8 January 1819, Abinger papers, Bodleian Library.

66 Lord Byron to Augusta Leigh, 21 September 1818, Lord Byron, *Letters and Journals*, vol. 6.

67 Claire Clairmont to E.J. Trelawney, c. 1870, Claire Clairmont, *Letters*, vol. 2.

68 Claire Clairmont, *Letters*, vol. 1, p. 129n.

69 Mary Shelley to Maria Gisborne, 5 June 1819, Mary Wollstonecraft Shelley, *Selected Letters of Mary Wollstonecraft Shelley*.

70 Lord Byron to Mrs Hoppner, 22 April 1820, Lord Byron, *Letters and Journals*, vol. 7, p. 80.

71 Claire Clairmont to Antonia Clairmont, 16 August 1856, Claire Clairmont, *Letters*, vol. 2.

72 Mrs Mason to P. B. Shelley, Abinger papers, Bodleian Library, dep. c. 517.

73 For a discussion of this see Richard Holmes, *Shelley – The Pursuit*, 1974, pp. 465 ff.

74 Claire Clairmont to Lord Byron, 24 March 1821, Claire Clairmont, *Letters*, vol. 1.

75 Quoted in Iris Origo, *A Measure of Love*, 1957, p. 58.

76 Maria Gisborne's journal, 9 July and 28 August 1820.

77 Mrs Mason to Mary Shelley, 22 August 1824, Abinger papers, Bodleian Library, dep. c. 517.

78 Thomas Medwin, *Shelley*, 1847, pp. 169–70.

79 Ibid.

80 Claire Clairmont, *Journals*, 29 October 1820.

81 Claire Clairmont, *Journals*, 21 April 1821.

82 Origo, *A Measure of Love*, pp. 62–3.

83 Claire Clairmont to Lord Byron, 18 February 1822, Claire Clairmont, *Letters*, vol. 1.

84 P.B. Shelley, *Letters*, ed. F.L. Jones, 1964.

85 Silsbee notebooks, box 7, file 2.

86 P.B. Shelley, *Letters*, ed. F.L. Jones, 1964.

87 Mary Shelley to Claire Clairmont, quoted in Origo, pp. 69-70.

88 Claire Clairmont, *Letters*, vol. 1.

89 Claire Clairmont, *Letters*, vol. 1, p. 173n.

90 Lord Byron to Percy Bysshe Shelley, quoted in Origo, *A Measure of Love*, p. 75.

91 Holmes, *Shelley*, p. 713.

92 Origo, *A Measure of Love*, p. 75.

93 Origo, *A Measure of Love*, p. 76.

94 Holmes, *Shelley*, p. 715.

95 Mrs Mason to Percy Bysshe Shelley, Abinger papers, Bodleian Library, dep. c. 517.

96 Claire Clairmont, *Journals*, p. 436.

97 Percy Bysshe Shelley to John Gisborne, Claire Clairmont, *Letters*, vol. 1, p. 177n.

98 Claire Clairmont, *Letters*, vol. 1, p. 177n.

99 Claire Clairmont to Leigh Hunt, 19 July 1822, Claire Clairmont, *Letters*, vol. 1, p. 176.

100 Claire Clairmont to Mary Shelley, 28–30 March 1830, Claire Clairmont, *Letters*, vol. 1, p. 268.

101 Claire Clairmont to Mary Shelley, 11–12 September 1822, Claire Clairmont, *Letters*, vol. 1, p. 178.

102 Claire Clairmont, *Letters*, vol. 1, p. 171n.

103 Mary Shelley to Maria Gisborne, 27 August 1822, Mary Wollstonecraft Shelley, *Selected Letters of Mary Wollstonecraft Shelley*.

104 E.J. Trelawney to Claire Clairmont, 4 December 1822, quoted in J. Buxton Forman (ed.), *Letters of Edward John Trelawny*, 1910, p. 30.

105 E.J. Trelawney to Claire Clairmont, Claire Clairmont, *Letters*, vol. 1, p. 174n.

106 Claire Clairmont, *Journals*, 25 August–6 September 1825.

107 Mary Shelley to Claire Clairmont, 16 September 1822, Mary Wollstonecraft Shelley, *Selected Letters of Mary Wollstonecraft Shelley*.

108 Amelia Lyons, *At Home with the Gentry: A Victorian English Lady's Diary of Russian Country Life*, ed. John McNair, 1998, p. 3.

109 Vladimir Nabokov, *Speak Memory: A Memoir*, 1951.

110 Charles Clairmont to Mary Shelley and Claire Clairmont, 18 September 1822, in Claire Clairmont, *Letters*, vol. 1, p. 181.

111 Ibid.

112 Claire Clairmont to Jane Williams, 24 October 1822, Claire Clairmont, *Letters*, vol. 1.

113 Charles Clairmont to Mary Shelley, 22 February 1823, in Claire Clairmont, *Letters*, vol. 1, p. 208.

114 Claire Clairmont, *Letters*, vol. 1, p. 209n.

115 Charles Clairmont to Mary Shelley, 22 February 1823, Claire Clairmont, *Letters*, vol. 1.

116 Clairmont to Mary Shelley, 22 February 1823, Claire Clairmont, *Letters*, vol. 1.

117 J. Buxton Forman (ed.), *Letters of Edward John Trelawny*, 1910.

118 Charles Clairmont to Mary Shelley, 22 February 1823, Claire Clairmont, *Letters*, vol. 1.

119 Charles Clairmont to Mary Shelley, 22 February 1823, Claire Clairmont, *Letters*, vol. 1.

120 Claire Clairmont to Jane Williams, 22 January 1827, Clairmont, *Letters*, vol. 1.

121 Claire Clairmont, *Journals*, pp. 333–4, fifth journal, Islavsky, 1825.

122 Claire Clairmont to Jane Williams, 11 September 1824, Clairmont, *Letters*, vol. 1.

123 Claire Clairmont to Jane Williams, 27 October 1825, Clairmont, *Letters*, vol. 1.

124 Claire Clairmont, *Journals*, p. 315, fifth journal, Islavsky, 1825.

125 Claire Clairmont, *Journals*, p. 343, 13 August 1825, Islavsky.

126 Claire Clairmont, *Journals*, p. 338, 17 July 1825, Islavsky.

127 Claire Clairmont to Jane Williams, 27 October 1825, Claire Clairmont, *Letters*, vol. 1.

128 Claire Clairmont, *Letters*, vol. 1, p. 373, n. 15.

129 Claire Clairmont to Jane Williams, 20 June 1825, Claire Clairmont, *Letters*, vol. 1.

130 Ibid.

131 Claire Clairmont, *Journals*, p. 312, 19 May 1825, Islavsky.

132 Lyons, *At Home with the Gentry*, p. 4.

133 Claire Clairmont to Jane Williams, 20 June 1825, Claire Clairmont, *Letters*, vol. 1.

134 Lyons, *At Home with the Gentry*, p. 4.

135 A Lady, *The Englishwoman in Russia*, 1855, p. 27.

136 Claire Clairmont to Mary Shelley, 29 April 1825, Claire Clairmont, *Letters*, vol. 1.

137 Claire Clairmont, *Journals*, 3 June 1825.

138 Claire Clairmont to Mary Shelley, 29 April 1825, Claire Clairmont, *Letters*, vol. 1.

139 Claire Clairmont to Jane Williams, 20 June 1825, Claire Clairmont, *Letters*, vol. 1.

140 A Lady, *The Englishwoman in Russia*, pp. 143–4.

141 Claire Clairmont to Mary Shelley, 29 April 1825, Claire Clairmont, *Letters*, vol. 1.

142 Claire Clairmont, *Journals*, 6 January 1827.

143 Ibid.

144 Claire Clairmont to Jane Williams, 11 September 1824, Claire Clairmont, *Letters*, vol. 1.

145 Claire Clairmont to Mary Shelley, 14 May 1826, Claire Clairmont, *Letters*, vol. 1.

146 A Lady, *The Englishwoman in Russia*, p. 138.

147 Claire Clairmont to Mary Shelley, 2–14 May 1826, Claire Clairmont, *Letters*, vol. 1.

148 Claire Clairmont to Jane Williams, 20 June 1825, Claire Clairmont, *Letters*, vol. 1.

149 Abinger papers, Bodleian Library, dep. c. 517.

150 Claire Clairmont to Jane Williams, December 1826, Claire Clairmont, *Letters*, vol. 1.

151 Claire Clairmont to Jane Williams, December 1826, Claire Clairmont, *Letters*, vol. 1.

152 Claire Clairmont, *Journals*, p. 411.

153 Claire Clairmont, *Journals*, p. 422.

154 Claire Clairmont, *Letters*, vol. 1, p. 574.

155 E.J. Trelawny to Claire Clairmont, 19 November 1828, quoted in Forman (ed.), *Letters of Edward John Trelawny*, p. 114.

156 Claire Clairmont to Lord Byron, 12 September 1816, Claire Clairmont, *Letters*, vol. 1.

157 Claire Clairmont to Jane Williams, December 1826, Claire Clairmont, *Letters*, vol. 1.

158 Forman (ed.), *Letters of Edward John Trelawny*, p. 116.

159 E.J. Trelawny to M.W. Shelley, 11 March 1829, quoted in Forman (ed.), *Letters of Edward John Trelawny*, p. 114.

160 Claire Clairmont to Mary Shelley, March 1832, Claire Clairmont, *Letters*, vol. 1.

161 E.J. Trelawney to Mary Shelley, 29 June 1831, Forman (ed.), *Letters of Edward John Trelawny*, p. 114.

162 Claire Clairmont to Mary Shelley, 22 July 1828, Claire Clairmont, *Letters*, vol. 1.

163 Claire Clairmont to Mary Shelley, 30 October 1840, Claire Clairmont, *Letters*, vol. 2.

164 Claire Clairmont to Mary Shelley, 28 April 1844, Claire Clairmont, *Letters*, vol. 2.

165 Clairmont, *Letters*, vol. 2, p. 621 n.

166 Ibid.

167 Governesses' Benevolent Institution Report, 1843.

168 Nabokov, *Speak Memory*, Penguin edn, 1987, p. 85.

169 Henry James, *The Aspern Papers*, 1888, preface.

170 His notes of their conversations are to be found at the Peabody Essex Museum, Salem, Massachusetts.

171 Paul, *William Godwin*, vol. 1, p. 218.

172 Clairmont, *Letters*, vol. 2, p. 658.

5: Nelly Weeton: the cruelty of men

1 Miss Weeton, *Journal of a Governess 1811-1825*, ed. Edward Hall, 1939, vol. 2, p. 379.
2 Miss Weeton, *Journal of a Governess 1807-1811*, ed. Edward Hall, 1936, vol. 1, p. xiii.
3 Weeton, *Journal of a Governess*, vol. 1, p. 139.
4 Weeton, *Journal of a Governess*, vol. 2, p. 151.
5 John Ruskin, *Praeterita*, 1886, Chapter 8.
6 Weeton, *Journal of a Governess*, vol. 1, p. 13.
7 Ibid.
8 Weeton, *Journal of a Governess*, vol. 1, p. 14.
9 Weeton, *Journal of a Governess*, vol. 1, p. 58.
10 Weeton, *Journal of a Governess*, vol. 1, p. xv.
11 John Gregory, *A Father's Legacy to his Daughters*, 1774, p. 6.
12 Gregory, *A Father's Legacy to his Daughters*, p. 32.
13 William St Clair, *The Godwins and the Shelleys*, 1989.
14 Hannah More, *Strictures on the Modern System of Female Education*, 1799, 1, p. 31.
15 Weeton, *Journal of a Governess*, vol. 1, p. 197, 15 November 1809.
16 Weeton, *Journal of a Governess*, vol. 1, p. 259.
17 Jane Austen, *The Watsons*, 1871.
18 Weeton, *Journal of a Governess*, vol. 1, p. 64.
19 Weeton, *Journal of a Governess*, vol. 1, p. 26.
20 Weeton, *Journal of a Governess*, vol. 1, p. 36.
21 Ibid.
22 Weeton, *Journal of a Governess*, vol. 1, p. 187, August 1809.
23 Weeton, *Journal of a Governess*, vol. 2, p. 214.
24 Weeton, *Journal of a Governess*, vol. 1, p. 72.
25 Weeton, *Journal of a Governess*, vol. 1, p. 78.
26 Weeton, *Journal of a Governess*, vol. 1, p. 124.
27 Weeton, *Journal of a Governess*, vol. 1, p. 131.
28 Weeton, *Journal of a Governess*, vol. 1, p. 133, 4 December 1808.
29 Weeton, *Journal of a Governess*, vol. 1.
30 Weeton, *Journal of a Governess*, vol. 1, p. 258.
31 Weeton, *Journal of a Governess*, vol. 1, p. 202, December 1809.
32 Weeton, *Journal of a Governess*, vol. 1, p. 217.
33 Weeton, *Journal of a Governess*, vol. 1, p. 217.
34 Weeton, *Journal of a Governess*, vol. 1, p. 220.
35 Weeton, *Journal of a Governess*, vol. 1, p. 218.
36 Ibid.
37 Weeton, *Journal of a Governess*, vol. 1, p. 233.
38 Nelly Weeton to Tom Weeton, Weeton, *Journal of a Governess*, vol. 1, p. 237.
39 Weeton, *Journal of a Governess*, vol. 1, p. 238.
40 Ibid.
41 Ibid.
42 Weeton, *Journal of a Governess*, vol. 1, p. 260.
43 Weeton, *Journal of a Governess*, vol. 1, pp. 259–60, April 1810.
44 Weeton, *Journal of a Governess*, vol. 1, p. 360.
45 Weeton, *Journal of a Governess*, vol. 2, p. 10.
46 Weeton, *Journal of a Governess*, vol. 2, p. 57.

47 Weeton, *Journal of a Governess*, vol. 2, p. 72, January 1813.

48 Weeton, *Journal of a Governess*, vol. 2, p. 97.

49 Weeton, *Journal of a Governess*, vol. 2, p. 58, July 1812.

50 Weeton, *Journal of a Governess*, vol. 2, pp. 70–1, December 1812.

51 Weeton, *Journal of a Governess*, vol. 2, p. 110.

52 Weeton, *Journal of a Governess*, vol. 2, p. 132.

53 Weeton, *Journal of a Governess*, vol. 1, p. 317.

54 Weeton, *Journal of a Governess*, vol. 1, p. 178, July 1809.

55 Henry Fielding, *The Covent Garden Tragedy*, 1732.

56 Weeton, *Journal of a Governess*, vol. 2, p. 152, October 1816.

57 Weeton, *Journal of a Governess*, vol. 2, p. 162.

58 Weeton, *Journal of a Governess*, vol. 2, p. 169, January–February 1818.

59 Weeton, *Journal of a Governess*, vol. 2, pp. 145–6, June 1816.

60 Nelly Weeton to Tom Weeton, January 1818, in Weeton, *Journal of a Governess*, vol. 2, p. 162.

61 Weeton, *Journal of a Governess*, vol. 2, pp. 176–7.

62 Weeton, *Journal of a Governess*, vol. 2, p. 159, January 1818.

63 Nelly Weeton to Miss C. Armitage, July 1822, in Weeton, *Journal of a Governess*, vol. 2, p. 228.

64 Weeton, *Journal of a Governess*, vol. 2, p. 337, March 1825.

65 Weeton, *Journal of a Governess*, vol. 2, pp. 356–7, May 1825.

66 Weeton, *Journal of a Governess*, vol. 2, pp. 338–9.

67 Weeton, *Journal of a Governess*, vol. 2, p. 345.

68 Anne Brontë's 1845 diary paper, quoted by Stevie Davies in her introduction to the 1996 Penguin edn of *The Tenant of Wildfell Hall* (first published 1848). The Ashbys' marriage in *Agnes Grey* (first published 1847) is similarly disastrous.

69 Weeton, *Journal of a Governess*, vol. 2, p. 73.

70 Weeton, *Journal of a Governess*, vol. 2, p. 57.

71 Ibid.

72 Charlotte Brontë, *Jane Eyre*, 1847, Chapter 28.

73 For an interesting discussion of this, see Ruth Perry, *Novel Relations*, 2004.

74 Weeton, *Journal of a Governess*, vol. 1, p. 74.

75 Weeton, *Journal of a Governess*, vol. 2, p. 353.

76 Nelly Weeton to Mrs Price, June 1816, in Weeton, *Journal of a Governess*, vol. 2, p. 146.

77 Caroline Norton, quoted in Sheila R. Herstein, *A Mid-Victorian Feminist, Barbara Leigh Smith Bodichon*, 1985, p. 49.

78 Lady Eastlake, '*Vanity Fair* – and *Jane Eyre*', *Quarterly Review*, 84 (December–March 1848–9), p. 174.

79 Charlotte Brontë, *Shirley*, 1849, Chapter 37, 'The Winding-Up'.

6: Anna and the King: the unbreakable bonds of class

1 Robin Duke, introduction to the Folio Society edn of Anna Leonowens, *The English Governess at the Siamese Court*, first published 1870.

2 Margaret Landon, *Anna and the King of Siam*, Introduction.

3 Anna Leonowens, *Siamese Harem Life*, first published 1893, reprinted London, 1952, p. xi.

4 Anna Leonowens, *Siamese Harem Life*, p. 117.

5 *Time Magazine*, 17 August 1970.

6 W.S. Bristowe, *Louis and the King of Siam*, 1976, p. 33.

7 Anna Leonowens, *Siamese Harem Life*.

8 Bristowe, *Louis and the King of Siam*, p. 24.

9 Ibid.

10 Bristowe, *Louis and the King of Siam*, pp. 24–30.

11 Bristowe, *Louis and the King of Siam*, p. 30.

12 Amelia Lyons, *At Home with the Gentry: A Victorian English Lady's Diary of Russian Country Life*, ed. John McNair, 1998; and A Lady, *The Englishwoman in Russia*, 1855.

13 Anna Leonowens, *The English Governess at the Siamese Court*, 1980 edn., Preface.

14 Anna Leonowens, *The English Governess at the Siamese Court*, 1980 edn, pp. 24–5.

15 Anna Leonowens, *The English Governess at the Siamese Court*, 1980 edn, p. 26.

16 Bristowe, *Louis and the King of Siam*, p. 30.

17 Anna Leonowens, *The English Governess at the Siamese Court*, 1980 edn, p. 198.

18 Emmeline Lott, *The English Governess in Egypt and Turkey*, 1866, vol. 1, p. 256.

19 Bristowe, *Louis and the King of Siam*, pp. 30–1.

20 Lott, *The English Governess in Egypt and Turkey*, vol. 1, p. 130.

21 Lott, *The English Governess in Egypt and Turkey*, vol. 1, p. 132.

22 Eastlake, '*Vanity Fair* – and *Jane Eyre*', p. 177.

23 Quoted in Wanda Neff, *Victorian Working Women*, 1929, p. 167.

24 Neff, *Victorian Working Women*, p. 166.

25 Eastlake, '*Vanity Fair* – and *Jane Eyre*', p. 177.

26 Harriet Martineau, 'The governess', *Once a Week*, 3 (1860), 271.

27 Eastlake, '*Vanity Fair* – and *Jane Eyre*', p. 177.

28 *Governess Life; its trials, duties and encouragements. By the Author of 'Memorials of two Sisters'*, etc., London, 1849, pp. 14–15.

29 Ibid.

30 W.M. Thackeray, *Vanity Fair*, 1848, Chapter 1.

31 'The right spirit', *Work and Leisure* (December 1880).

32 Ruskin, *Praeterita*, p. 115.

33 Ruskin, *Praeterita*, p. 20.

34 Ruskin, *Praeterita*, p. 120.

35 Ibid.

36 See Hermia Oliver, *Flaubert and an English Governess: The Quest for Juliet Herbert*, 1980.

37 Anna Leonowens, *The English Governess at the Siamese Court*, 1980 edn, p. 181.

38 Anna Leonowens, *The English Governess at the Siamese Court*, 1980 edn, p. 149.

39 Anna Leonowens, *The English Governess at the Siamese Court*, 1980 edn, p. 90.

40 Anna Leonowens, *The English Governess at the Siamese Court*, 1980 edn, p. 180.

41 Anna Leonowens, *The English Governess at the Siamese Court*, 1980 edn, p. 70.

42 Anna Leonowens, *The English Governess at the Siamese Court*, 1980 edn, p. 75.

43 Anna Leonowens, *The English Governess at the Siamese Court*, 1980 edn, pp. 76–7.

44 Lott, *The English Governess in Egypt and Turkey*, vol. 1, pp. 157–8.

45 Anna Leonowens, *The English*

Governess at the Siamese Court, 1980 edn, p. 77.

46 Lott, *The English Governess in Egypt and Turkey*, vol. 1, pp. 157–8.

47 Lott, *The English Governess in Egypt and Turkey*, vol. 1, p. 254.

48 Eastlake, '*Vanity Fair* – and *Jane Eyre*', p. 178.

49 Bristowe, *Louis and the King of Siam*, p. 30.

50 Lott, *Harem Life*, vol. 1, pp. 139–40.

51 Margaret Landon, *Anna and the King*, 1952, p. 244.

7: Anna Jameson: the pursuit of independence

1 Anna Jameson, 'Woman's "Mission" and Woman's Position', *Memoirs and Essays*, 1846, pp. 215, 242–3.

2 Jameson, 'Woman's "Mission" and Woman's Position', pp. 213–14.

3 Charlotte Brontë, *Jane Eyre*, first published 1847, Penguin Popular Classics edn, 1994, p. 314.

4 Eastlake, '*Vanity Fair* – and *Jane Eyre*', pp. 172–3.

5 Ibid.

6 Emma Pitman, *My Governess Life*, 1833, p. 55.

7 Quoted in Daphne Bennett, *Emily Davies and the Liberation of Women*, 1990, p. 105.

8 Charlotte M. Yonge, response to Barbara Bodichon and Emily Davies, 1868, in M.C. Bradbrook, '*That Infidel Place': A Short History of Girton College*, 1969, pp. 24–5.

9 In the 1891 census.

10 Bessie Rayner Parkes, *Anna Jameson*, in *Vignettes: Twelve Biographical Sketches*, London, 1866.

11 Anna Jameson, 'On the Relative Social Position of Mothers and Governesses', *Essays and Memoirs*, p. 281.

12 Gerardine Macpherson, *Memoirs of*

the Life of Anna Jameson, 1878, p. 45.

13 Miss Emily Mason of Detroit, June 1837. See clarke.cmich.edu/detroit/jameson1837.ht

14 Quoted in Clara Thomas, *Love and Work Enough: The Life of Anna Jameson*, 1967, p. 216.

15 Anna Jameson, *A Commonplace Book of Thoughts, Memories and Fancies*, 1855, p. 123.

16 Macpherson, *Anna Jameson*, p. 152.

17 Jameson, *A Commonplace Book*, p. 118.

18 Anna Jameson to Ottilie von Goethe, November 1833, quoted in Mrs Steuart Erskine (ed.), *Anna Jameson: Letters and Friendships*, 1915, pp. 109–10.

19 Macpherson, *Anna Jameson*, p. 22.

20 Erskine (ed.), *Anna Jameson: Letters and Friendships*, p. 23.

21 Ibid.

22 Jameson, *Memoirs and Essays*, p. 273.

23 Anna Jameson, *Diary of an Ennuyée*, 1826, p. 31.

24 Jameson, *Diary of an Ennuyée*, p. 50.

25 Anna Jameson to Camilla Murphy, Easter 1822, quoted in Erskine (ed.), *Anna Jameson: Letters and Friendships*, p. 65.

26 Erskine (ed.), *Anna Jameson: Letters and Friendships*, p. 68.

27 Jameson, *Memoirs and Essays*, p. 285.

28 Jameson, *Memoirs and Essays*, p. 259.

29 Ibid.

30 Erskine (ed.), *Anna Jameson: Letters and Friendships*, pp. 69–70.

31 Macpherson, *Anna Jameson*, p. 47n.

32 Macpherson, *Anna Jameson*, p. 41.

33 Macpherson, *Anna Jameson*, p. 85.

34 Thomas, *Love and Work Enough*, p. 36.

35 Thomas Carlyle, *Letters to his Wife*, quoted in Thomas, *Love and Work Enough*, p. 44.

36 G.H. Needler (ed.), *Letters of Anna*

Jameson to Ottilie von Goethe, 1939, p. 6.

37 Needler (ed.), *Letters of Anna Jameson to Ottilie von Goethe*, 1939, p. 17.

38 Quoted in Thomas, *Love and Work Enough*, p. 153.

39 Macpherson, *Anna Jameson*, p. 145.

40 Robert Jameson to Anna Jameson, 30 October 1834, quoted in Macpherson, *Anna Jameson*, p. 100.

41 Macpherson, *Anna Jameson*, pp. 107–9.

42 Macpherson, *Anna Jameson*, p. 109.

43 Ibid.

44 Needler (ed.), *Letters of Anna Jameson to Ottilie von Goethe*, pp. 55–9.

45 Ibid.

46 Macpherson, *Anna Jameson*, pp. 116–17.

47 Macpherson, *Anna Jameson*, p. 119.

48 Macpherson, *Anna Jameson*, p. 125.

49 Macpherson, *Anna Jameson*, p. 108.

50 Bessie Rayner Parkes, 'Anna Jameson', *English Woman's Journal* (March 1861).

51 Macpherson, *Anna Jameson*, p. 129.

52 British and Foreign Review, 8 (1839), quoted in Thomas, *Love and Work Enough*, p. 140.

53 Jameson, 'Woman's "Mission" and Woman's Position', *Memoirs and Essays*, pp. 239–40.

54 'Isolation and combination', *Work and Leisure* (December 1880), 223.

55 Governesses' Benevolent Institution (GBI) archive, London Metropolitan Archives.

56 GBI archive.

57 Alice Renton, *Tyrant or Victim? A History of the British Governess*, 1991, p. 94.

58 Report of the GBI, 1844.

59 Reports of the GBI.

60 Jameson, 'Relative Social Position', *Memoirs and Essays*, p. 261.

61 Ibid.

62 'Experiences in Search of a Governess', *Work and Leisure* (December 1880).

63 For an interesting discussion of this, see Mary Poovey, *Uneven Developments: The Ideological Work of Gender in Mid-Victorian England*, 1989, p. 242.

64 Eliza Lynn Linton, 'The girl of the period', *Saturday Review* (1868).

65 Ibid.

66 W.R. Greg, 'Why are women redundant?', *National Review*, 14 (April 1862), 451.

8: The Reform Firm: what do women want?

1 Edward Trelawny to Anna Jameson, 2 July 1838, in H. Buxton Forman (ed.), *The Letters of Edward John Trelawny*.

2 William Thompson, *Appeal of One-Half of the Human Race, Women, against the Pretensions of the other Half, Men, to retain them in political and thence in Civil and Domestic Slavery*, 1825.

3 Harriet Martineau, *Autobiography*, 1877. Both these quotes, as well as this part of my argument, are taken from Barbara Caine, 'Victorian feminism and the ghost of Mary Wollstonecraft', *Women's Writing*, 4: 2 (1997), a most interesting and suggestive discussion of Wollstonecraft's reputation and influence at this time.

4 Martineau, *Autobiography*.

5 William Godwin, *Memoirs of Mary Wollstonecraft*, ed. J. Middleton Murry, 1928.

6 Godwin, *Memoirs of Mary Wollstonecraft*, p. 55.

7 Godwin, *Memoirs of Mary Wollstonecraft*, p. 132.

8 Pam Hirsch, *Barbara Leigh Smith Bodichon: Feminist, Artist and Rebel*, 1998, p. 19.

9 Bessie Rayner Parkes to Barbara Leigh Smith, 1848, Parkes papers, Girton College, Cambridge.

10 Barbara Leigh Smith to Bessie Rayner Parkes, 1847, Parkes papers, Girton College, Cambridge.

11 Sheila R. Herstein, *A Mid-Victorian Feminist: Barbara Leigh Smith Bodichon*, 1985, p. 10.

12 Dante Gabriel Rossetti to Christina Rossetti, 8 November 1855, quoted in Herstein, *A Mid-Victorian Feminist*, p. 17.

13 Marie Belloc Lowndes, *I Too Have Lived in Arcadia*, 1941, p. 3.

14 Bessie Rayner Parkes, biographical memoir, 1849, Parkes papers, Girton College, Cambridge.

15 Joseph Parkes to Bessie Rayner Parkes, 24 September 1858, Parkes papers, Girton College, Cambridge, II/64.

16 Bessie Rayner Parkes, diary fragment, 1849, Parkes papers, Girton College, Cambridge.

17 Barbara Leigh Smith to Bessie Rayner Parkes, quoted in Margaret Crompton, 'Prelude to Arcadia', Parkes papers, Girton College, Cambridge, A/70/30.

18 Bessie Rayner Parkes, diary, 24 November 1849, Parkes papers, Girton College, Cambridge.

19 Greg, 'Why are women redundant?', p. 455.

20 Emily Davies to Henry Tomkinson, April 1864, quoted in Bennett, *Emily Davies and the Liberation of Women*, p. 56.

21 Bessie Rayner Parkes to Barbara Leigh Smith, 12 February 1847, Parkes papers, Girton College, Cambridge.

22 Anna Jameson to Bessie Rayner Parkes, 1856, Parkes papers, Girton College, Cambridge.

23 From *Nachlass* of Ottilie von Goethe, 'Jameson, Anna, varia von ihrer Hand', quoted in Needler (ed.), *Letters of Anna Jameson and Ottilie von Goethe*, p. 234.

24 Anna Jameson to Bessie Rayner Parkes, 1858, Parkes papers, Girton College, Cambridge.

25 Anna Jameson to Bessie Rayner Parkes, 1859, Parkes papers, Girton College, Cambridge.

26 Bessie Rayner Parkes, *Remarks on the Education of Girls*, 1854.

27 Bessie Rayner Parkes, 'The changes of eighty years', *Essays on Women's Work* (1865), 61.

28 Bessie Rayner Parkes to Barbara Bodichon, 17 November 1859, Parkes papers, Girton College, Cambridge.

29 Barbara Bodichon, *Women and Work*, 1859.

30 Elizabeth Parkes to Bessie Rayner Parkes, 13 February 1857, Parkes papers, Girton College, Cambridge, II/28.

31 Elizabeth Blackwell, *Pioneer Work for Women*, 1895, quoted in Hirsch, *Barbara Leigh Smith Bodichon*, p. 53.

32 Paper read at the National Association for the Promotion of Social Science, August 1860, and reprinted in the *English Woman's Journal*, October 1860.

33 Cynthia Asquith, *Haply I May Remember*, 1950, p. 212.

34 Jessie Boucherett, 'Obstacles to the employment of women', *English Woman's Journal* (February 1860).

35 *The Autobiography of Benjamin Franklin*, Penguin Classics edn, 1986, p. 112.

36 Boucherett, 'Obstacles to the employment of women'.

37 Bessie Rayner Parkes, *Essays on Woman's Work*, 1865, p. 182.
38 Charlotte Brontë to W.S. Williams, at her publishers, Smith and Elder, 1853.
39 Jameson, 'Woman's "Mission" and Woman's Position', *Essays and Memoirs*, p. 245.
40 'Mr Brown's letters to a young man about town', *Punch* (7 July 1849).
41 W.M. Thackeray to Isabella Thackeray.
42 Alexander Walker, *Woman Physiologically Considered as to Mind, Morals, Marriage, Matrimonial Slavery, Fidelity and Divorce*, London, 1839.
43 Greg, 'Why are women redundant?', pp. 443–4.
44 Greg, 'Why are women redundant?', p. 450n.
45 Lord Alfred Douglas, 'Two Loves', 1896.
46 Greg, 'Why are women redundant?', p. 439.
47 Greg, 'Why are women redundant?', p. 456.
48 John Stuart Mill, *On the Subjection of Women*, 1869.
49 *The Times*, 30 July 1864.
50 Quoted in Martha Vicinus, 'Lesbian perversity and Victorian marriage: the 1864 Codrington divorce trial', *Journal of British Studies*, Chicago (January 1997).
51 Joseph Parkes to Bessie Rayner Parkes, 1864, Parkes papers, Girton College, Cambridge.
52 Adelaide Procter to Bessie Rayner Parkes, 1862, Parkes papers, Girton College, Cambridge.
53 Ibid.
54 Bessie Rayner Parkes to Barbara Bodichon, 1862, Parkes papers, Girton College, Cambridge.
55 Adelaide Procter to Bessie Rayner Parkes, 1855, Parkes papers, Girton College, Cambridge.
56 Quoted in Hirsch, *Barbara Leigh Smith Bodichon: Feminist, Artist and Rebel*, p. 209.
57 Quoted in Hirsch, *Barbara Leigh Smith Bodichon: Feminist, Artist and Rebel*, p. 207.
58 Bessie Rayner Parkes to Barbara Bodichon, November 1863, Parkes papers, Girton College, Cambridge.
59 Ibid.
60 Bessie Rayner Parkes to Barbara Bodichon, March 1864, Parkes papers, Girton College, Cambridge.
61 Lowndes, *I Too Have Lived in Arcadia*, p. 29.
62 Lowndes, *I Too Have Lived in Arcadia*, p. 66.
63 Quoted in Bennett, *Emily Davies and the Liberation of Women*, p. 137.
64 'The Means of Education', *English Woman's Journal*.
65 Neff, *Victorian Working Women*, p. 182.
66 Virginia Woolf, *A Room of One's Own*, 1929.
67 Dame Joyanne Bracewell, b. 1934, obituary in *Guardian*, 25 January 2007.
68 Greg, 'Why are women redundant?', p. 436.

Select Bibliography

The dates given are those of first publication.

Adburgham, Alison, *A Punch History of Manners and Modes, 1841–1940*, London, 1961.

Alcott, Louisa M., *Little Women*, New York, 1868.

Amies, Marion, 'The Victorian governess and colonial ideals of womanhood', *Victorian Studies*, 31 (Summer 1988).

Anon, *The Private Governess*, The Literary Souvenir, 1826.

Ariès, Philippe (trans. Robert Baldick), *Centuries of Childhood: A Social History of Family Life*, London, 1962.

Asquith, Cynthia, *Haply I May Remember*, London, 1950.

Austen, Jane, *Emma*, 1816.

——————, *The Watsons*, 1871.

Bage, Robert, *Hermsprong, or, man as he is not*, London, 1796.

Bailey, F.M., *Mission to Tashkent*, London, 1946.

Balfour, Mrs Clara Lucas, *A Sketch of Mrs Barbauld*, London, 1854.

Banks, J.A., *Prosperity and Parenthood: A Study of Family Planning among the Victorian Middle Classes*, London, 1954.

Banks, J. A., and Banks, Olive, *Feminism and Family Planning in Victorian England*, London, 1965.

Barbauld, Anne Laetitia, *Legacy for Young Ladies – miscellaneous pieces in Prose and Verse by the late Mrs Barbauld*, Boston, 1826.

Beatty, J.W., *The Story of the Governesses' Benevolent Institution*, privately printed, Southwick, Sussex, 1971.

Beloe, William, *The Sexagenarian*, London, 1817.

Bennett, Daphne, *Emily Davies and the Liberation of Women*, London, 1990.

Bennett, Judith, and Froide, Amy M. (eds.), *Single Women and the European Past 1250–1800*, Philadelphia, 1999.

Berington, Joseph, *An Essay on the Immateriality and Immortality of the Soul, and its instinctive sense of good and evil, in opposition to the opinion advanced in the essays introductory to Dr Priestley's abridgment of Dr Hartley's Observations on Man*, London, 1778.

Blake, Mrs Warrenne (ed.), *An Irish Beauty of the Regency – compiled from 'Mes Souvenirs', the journals of the hon. Mrs Calvert*, 1911.

Blessington, Marguerite, *The Governess*, 1839.

Bloch, Jean, *Rousseauism and Education in Eighteenth-Century France*, Oxford, 1995.

Bodichon, Barbara, *An American Diary 1857–8*, London, 1972.

———, *Women and Work*, London, 1857.

Bradbrook, M.C., *'That Infidel Place': A Short History of Girton College*, London, 1969.

Bradley, Ian, *The Call to Seriousness: The Evangelical Impact on the Victorians*, 1976.

Braithwaite, Helen, *Romanticism, Publishing and Dissent: Joseph Johnson and the Cause of Liberty*, London, 2003.

Bristowe, W.S., *Louis and the King of Siam*, London, 1976.

Brontë, Anne, *Agnes Grey*, 1847.

———, *The Tenant of Wildfell Hall*, 1848.

Brontë, Charlotte, *The Professor*, 1846.

———, *Jane Eyre*, 1847.

———, *Shirley*, 1849.

———, *Villette*, 1853.

Brown, Ford K., *The Life of William Godwin*, London and Toronto, 1926.

Brown, Peter, *The Chathamites*, London, 1967.

Browning, E. Barrett, *Aurora Leigh*, 1857.

Burke, Edmund, *Reflections on the Revolution in France*, London, 1790.

Burnett, John (ed.), *Destiny Obscure: Autobiographies of Childhood, Education and Family from the 1820s to the 1920s*, London, 1994.

Burney, Fanny, *Camilla*, 1796.

Burns, J.H., 'Clio as a governess', *History Today*, 36: 8 (August 1986), 10–15.

Burr, Aaron, *The Private Journal of Aaron Burr*, ed. Wm. K. Bixby, Rochester, 1903.

Burstyn, Joan N., *Victorian Education and the Ideal of Womanhood*, 1980.

Butler, Marilyn, *Maria Edgeworth*, London, 1971.

———, (ed.), *Burke, Paine, Godwin and the Revolutionary Controversy*, Cambridge, 1984.

Byron, George Gordon, Lord, *Letters and Journals*, vol. 6, ed. Leslie Marchand, London, 1976.

Cahen, L., *Condorcet et la Révolution française*, Paris, 1904.

Caine, Barbara, 'Victorian feminism and the ghost of Mary Wollstonecraft', *Women's Writing*, 4: 2 (1997).

Calhoun, Mrs Lucia Gilbert, *Modern Women and What is Said of Them*, New York, 1868.

Chandler, George, *William Roscoe of Liverpool*, London, 1953.

Charke, Charlotte, *A Narrative of the Life of Charlotte Charke, by herself*, London, 1755.

Clairmont, Claire, 'The Pole', *English Annual* (1836).

———, *Journals*, ed. Marion Kingston Stocking, Cambridge, Mass., 1968.

———, *The Clairmont Correspondence: Letters of Claire Clairmont, Charles Clairmont and Fanny Imlay Godwin*, in 2 vols, ed. Marion Kingston Stocking, Cambridge, Mass., 1995.

Clarke, Patricia, *The Governesses: Letters from the Colonies, 1862–1882*, 1985.

Cobbe, Frances Power, *Life of Frances Power Cobbe, By Herself*, London, 1894.

Collier, Jane, *The Art of Ingeniously Tormenting*, London, 1753.

Colquhoun, Patrick, *Treatise on the Police of the Metropolis*, London, 1797.

Condorcet, Marie Jean Antoine Nicolas Caritat, Marquis de, *Sur l' Instruction publique 1791–2, Collected Works*, vol. 7.

———, *On the Admission of Women to the Rights of Citizenship*, trans. Alice Drysdale Vickery, 1893.

Cook, Eliza, *Eliza Cook's Journal*, London (1849–54).

Craik, Diana Mulock, *Bread Upon the Waters: A Governess's Life*, (for the Governesses' Benevolent Institution), 1852.

Cunningham, Allan, *Lives of Painters*, London, 1829.

Cunnington, C. Willett, *Feminine Attitudes in the 19th Century*, London, 1935.

Darwin, Erasmus, *Plan for the Conduct of Female Education in Boarding Schools*, London, 1797.

Davidoff, Leonore, and Hall, Catherine, *Family Futures: Men and Women of the English Middle Class 1780–1850*, Chicago, 1987.

Dowden, Edward, *Life of Shelley*, London, 1909.

Eastlake, Lady, '*Vanity Fair* and *Jane Eyre*', *Quarterly Review*, 84 (December–March 1848–9).

Edgeworth, Frances, *A Memoir of Maria Edgeworth*, London, 1867.

Edgeworth, Maria, *The Good French Governess*, 1801.

———, 'Madame de Fleury', in *Tales of Fashionable Life*, 1812.

Edgeworth, M. and R. L., *Essays on Practical Education*, London 1811.

Edgeworth, Richard Lovell, *Memoirs*, London, 1844.

Ellis, Sarah Stickney, *Wives of England*, London, 1843.

———, *Daughters of England*, London, 1845.

Erskine, Mrs Steuart (ed.), *Anna Jameson: Letters and Friendships*, London, 1915.

Fane, Julian, *Morning*, London, 1956.

'Female labour', *Fraser's Magazine* (March 1860).

Fielding, Sarah, *The Governess*, London, 1749.

Fordyce, James, *Sermons to Young Women*, London, 1765.

Forman, H. Buxton, *The Elopement of Percy Bysshe Shelley and Mary Wollstonecraft Godwin as narrated by William Godwin*, London, 1911.

———, (ed.), *The Letters of Edward John Trelawny*, Oxford, 1910.

Froide, Amy, *Never Married: Singlewomen in Early Modern England*, Oxford, 2005.

Gardiner, Everilda Anne, *Recollections of a Beloved Mother*, London, 1842.

Gaskell, Elizabeth, *The Life of Charlotte Brontë*, first published 1857, reprinted London, 1901.

———, *Wives and Daughters*, London, 1865,

Gathorne-Hardy, Jonathan, *The Rise and Fall of the British Nanny*, Newton Abbot, 1973.

Genlis, Stephanie de, *Leçons d'une Gouvernante à ses élèves*, 1791.

———, *Memoirs*, London, 1825.

George, Margaret, *One Woman's 'Situation'*, Illinois, 1970.

———, *Women in the First Capitalist Society: Experiences in 17th-Century England*, Brighton, 1988.

Gisbourne, Thomas, *An Enquiry into the Duties of the Female Sex*, London, 1797.

Gittings, Robert, and Manton, Jo, *Claire Clairmont and the Shelleys 1798–1879*, Oxford, 1992.

Godwin, William, *Memoirs of Mary Wollstonecraft*, ed. J. Middleton Murry, London, 1928.

Governess Life; its trials, duties and encouragements. By the Author of 'Memorials of two Sisters', etc., London, 1849.

Graham, Maria, *Journal of a Residence in Chile*, London, 2003

Greg, W.R., 'Why are women redundant?', *National Review*, 14 (April 1862), 434–60.

Gregory, John, *A Father's Legacy to his Daughters*, London, 1774.

Grylls, R. Glynn, *Claire Clairmont*, London, 1939.

——, *Queen's College*, London, 1948.

Hall, Anna Maria, *Stories of the Governess* (for the Governesses' Benevolent Institution), 1852.

Hayley, William, *A Philosophical, Historical and Moral Essay on Old Maids. By a Friend to the Sisterhood*, London, 1785.

Hays, Mary, *Memoirs of Emma Courtney*, London, 1796.

——, 'Mary Wollstonecraft', in *Annual Necrology for 1797–8*.

Herstein, Sheila R., *A Mid-Victorian Feminist: Barbara Leigh Smith Bodichon*, New Haven and London, 1985.

Highsmith, Patricia, 'The Heroine' (short story), in *O. Henry Prize Stories*, 1946.

Hill, Bridget, *Women, Work and Sexual Politics in Eighteenth-Century England*, Oxford, 1989.

'Hints on the modern governess system', *Fraser's Magazine*, 30 (November 1844).

Hints to Governesses, by One of Themselves, London, 1856.

Hirsch, Pam, *Barbara Leigh Smith Bodichon: Feminist, Artist and Rebel*, London, 1998.

Hobsbawm, Eric, *The Age of Capital, 1848–1875*, London, 1975.

Holmes, Richard, *Shelley – the Pursuit*, London, 1974.

——, *Sidetracks*, London, 2000.

Howe, Bea, *A Galaxy of Governesses*, London, 1954.

Hufton, Owen, *The Prospect Before Her: A History of Women in Western Europe*, London, 1995.

Hughes, Kathryn, *The Victorian Governess*, London, 1993.

James, Henry, *The Turn of the Screw*, 1898.

——, *The Aspern Papers*, 1888.

Jameson, Anna, *Memoirs and Essays*, London, 1846.

——, *Diary of an Eunuyée*, London, 1826.

——, *A Commonplace Book of Thoughts, Memories and Fancies*, 1855.

Jones, Frederick (ed)., *Maria Gisborne and Edwin E. Williams: Shelley's Friends – Their Journals and Letters*, Norman, Oklahoma, 1951.

Jones, M. Gladys, *Life of Hannah More*, Cambridge, 1952.

Kamm, Josephine, *Hope Deferred: Girls' Education in English History*, London, 1965.

Kelly, Gary, *Women, Writing and Revolution 1790–1827*, Oxford, 1993.

Kemble, Fanny, *Records of a Girlhood*, 1895.

Laboucheix, R., *Richard Price*, London, 1971.

Lacey, Candida Ann (ed.), *Barbara Leigh-Smith Bodichon and the Langham Place Group*, London, 1987.

A Lady, *The Englishwoman in Russia*, London, 1855.

Lamb, Charles and Mary Anne, *Letters*, ed. Edwin W. Marrs Jr, Ithaca (NY) and London, 1975–8.

Lanser, Susan, 'Singular Politics – the Rise of the British Nation and the Production of the Old Maid', in Bennett and Froide (eds.), *Single Women and the European Past 1250–1800*, Philadelphia, 1999.

Le Breton, Anna Laetitia, *Memories of Mrs Barbauld*, London, 1874.

Le Fanu, Sheridan, *A Lost Name*, 1868.

———, *Uncle Silas*, 1864.

Leonowens, Anna, *The English Governess at the Siamese Court*, London, 1870, reprinted London, 1980.

———, *Siamese Harem Life*, 1893, reprinted London, 1952.

Lewis, Sarah, 'On the social position of governesses', *Fraser's Magazine*, 37 (April 1848).

Lott, Emmeline, *The English Governess in Egypt and Turkey*, 2 vols, London, 1866.

Lowndes, Marie Belloc, *I Too Have Lived in Arcadia*, London, 1941.

Lucas, Charles M.A., *The Infernal Quixote: A Tale of the Day*, London, 1801.

Lyons, Amelia, *At Home with the Gentry: A Victorian English Lady's Diary of Russian Country Life*, ed. John McNair, Nottingham, 1998.

McAleer, E., *The Sensitive Plant*, London, 1958.

McAllister, Ward, *Society as I Have Known It*, New York, 1890.

Macaulay, Catherine, *Letters on Education*, London, 1790.

Maclean, Fitzroy, *Eastern Approaches*, London, 1949.

Macpherson, Gerardine, *Memoirs of the Life of Anna Jameson*, London, 1878.

Mangnall, R.M., *Historical and Miscellaneous Questions*, London, 1800.

Marchand, Leslie A., *Byron: – A Biography*, 2 vols, London, 1957.

Martin, Joanna (ed.), *A Governess in the Age of Jane Austen: The Journals and Letters of Agnes Porter*, London, 1998.

———, *Wives and Daughters*, London, 2004.

Martineau, Harriet, *Deerbrook*, 3 vols, London, 1839.

———, 'Female industry', *Edinburgh Review*, 109 (April 1859).

———, 'The governess', *Once a Week*, 3 (1860), 271.

———, *Autobiography*, London, 1877.

Maurice, F.D., Charles Kingsley et al, *Introductory Lectures delivered at Queen's College, London*, London, 1849.

Milbank, Alison, *Daughters of the House: Modes of the Gothic in Victorian Fiction*, Basingstoke, 1992.

Mingay, G.E., *A Social History of the English Countryside*, London, 1990.

Mitford, Nancy (ed.), *The Stanleys of Alderley: Their Letters between the Years 1851–1865*, London, 1939.

More, Hannah, *Strictures on the Modern System of Female Education*, London, 1799.

Morgan, Lady Sydney, *O'Donnel, a National Tale*, 1814.

Murch, Jerome, *Mrs Barbauld and her contemporaries*, London, 1877.

Nabokov, Vladimir, *Speak Memory: A Memoir*, London, 1951.

Neale, Shirley, 'The Governesses' Benevolent Institution: care of aged governesses in Kentish Town and Kent', *Camden History Review*, 24 (2000).

Needler, G.H., (ed.), *Letters of Anna Jameson to Ottilie von Goethe*, London, 1939.

Neff, Wanda, *Victorian Working Women*, New York, 1929.

Nightingale, Florence, *Letters to Dr Pincoff*, London, 1857.

'The non-existence of women', *North British Review*, 22 (August 1855).

Oliphant, Margaret, 'The condition of women', *Blackwood's Magazine*, 83 (February 1858).

Oliver, Hermia, Flaubert and an English Governess: The Quest for Juliet Herbert, Oxford, 1980.

Origo, Iris, *A Measure of Love*, London, 1957.

Papendiek, Charlotte, *Court and Private Life in the time of Queen Charlotte*, London, 1887.

Parkes, Bessie Rayner, *Remarks on the Education of Girls*, London, 1854.

————, *A Year's Experience in Women's Work*, Transactions of the National Association for the Promotion of Social Science, London, 1860.

————, *Essays on Woman's Work*, London, 1865.

————, *Vignettes*, London, 1866.

Paul, C. Kegan, *William Godwin*, 2 vols, London, 1876.

Perry, Ruth, *Novel Relations*, Cambridge, 2004.

Peterson, M. Jeanne, *Family, Love and Work in the Lives of Victorian Gentlewomen*, Bloomington, 1989.

Pilkington, Laetitia, *Memoirs*, London, 1784.

Pitcher, Harvey, *When Miss Emmie was in Russia: English Governesses before, during and after the October Revolution*, London, 1977.

Pitman, Emma, *My Governess life*, London, 1883.

Pollock, Linda, 'Teach her to live under obedience', *Continuity and Change*, 4: 2 (1989).

Poovey, Mary, *Uneven Developments: The Ideological Work of Gender in Mid-Victorian England*, London, 1989.

Priestley, Joseph, *Observations on Education*, London, 1779.

————, *Autobiography*, ed. Jack Lindsay, Bath, 1970.

Py, Gilbert, *Rousseau et les educateurs*, Oxford, 1997.

'Queen bees or working bees?', review of a paper read by Miss Bessie Parkes to the Social Science Congress, *Saturday Review* (12 November 1859).

Reader, W.J., *Professional Men: The Rise of the Professional Classes in 19th Century England*, 1966.

Rendall Jane, 'Friendship and Politics: Barbara Leigh Smith Bodichon (1827–91) and Bessie Rayner Parkes (1829–1925)', in *Sexuality and Subordination*, Susan Medus and Jane Rendall (eds.), London, 1989.

Renton, Alice, *Tyrant or Victim? A History of the British Governess*, London, 1991.

'The right spirit', *Work and Leisure* (December 1880).

Ritchie, Anne Thackeray, *Chapters from some Memoirs*, London, 1894.

————, *Journals and Letters*, ed. Abigail Burnham Bloom and John Maynard, Columbus, Ohio, 1994.

————, 'Toilers and spinsters', *Cornhill*, 3: 15 (1861).

Robinet, J.F.E., *Condorcet*, Paris, 1893.

Robinson, H. Crabb, *Henry Crabb Robinson on Books and their Writers*, 2 vols, London, 1938.

Ross, Miss, *The Governess; or Politics in Private Life*, 1836.

Rousseau, Jean-Jacques, *La nouvelle Héloïse*, 1761.

————, *Emile*, 1762.

————, *Confessions 1770*, first published 1782.

Rudolf, Anthony, *Byron's Darkness and Nuclear Winter*, London, 1984.

Ruskin, John, *Sesame and Lilies*, 1864.

————, *Praeterita*, London, 1886.

Rye, M.S., 'On female emigration', *Transactions of the National Association for the Promotion of Social Science* (1862).

St Clair, William, *The Godwins and the Shelleys*, London, 1989.

Sanders, Valerie, *The Private Lives of Victorian Women*, Hemel Hempstead, 1989.

Scargill, William, *Blue Stocking Hall*, London, 1827.

Schimmelpenninck, Mary Anne, *Life*, London, 1895.

Sewell, Miss E.M., *Principles of Education, drawn from Nature and Revelation, and applied to female education in the upper classes. By the author of 'Amy Herbert', etc.*, London, 1865.

Shelley, Mary, *Journals*, in 2 vols, ed. Paula R. Feldman and Diana Scott-Kilvert, Oxford, 1987.

————, *Selected Letters* ed. Betty T. Bennett, Baltimore and London, 1995.

————, *Frankenstein*, 1818.

Shelley, P.B., *Letters*, ed. Frederick L. Jones, vols 1 and 2, Oxford, 1964.

Sherwood, Mary Martha, *Caroline Mordaunt, or, The Governess*, London, 1853.

Shirreff, Emily, *Intellectual Education and its Influence on the Character and Happiness of Women*, London, 1858.

Shorter, Clement, *The Brontës and their Circle*, London, 1908.

Showalter, Elaine, *A Literature of their Own: British Women Novelists from Brontë to Lessing*, Princeton, 1977.

Sibbald, Susan, *Memoirs*, ed. F.P. Hett, London, 1926.

'Sisters of misery', *Punch*, 7: 15 (July–December 1848), 24–5.

Smith, Mary, *The Autobiography of Mary Smith: Schoolmistress and Nonconformist*, London, 1892.

Spark, Muriel, ed., *The Brontë Letters*, London, 1954.

Stephen, George, *Guide to Service: The Governess*, London, 1844.

Stickney Ellis, Sarah, *The Daughters of England*, London, 1864.

Stone, Lawrence, *Family, Sex and Marriage in England*, London, 1977.

Stourton, Margaret, *M.S. or, A year of governess life*, London, 1863.

Thackeray, W.M., *Vanity Fair*, London, 1848.

————, 'The Book of Snobs', London, 1848.

The Governess; or, Politics in Private Life, London, 1836.

Thomas, Clara, *Love and Work Enough: The Life of Anna Jameson*, Toronto, University of Toronto Press, 1967.

Thompson, William, *Appeal of One-Half of the Human Race, Women, against the Pretensions of the other Half, Men, to retain them in political, and thence in Civil and Domestic Slavery*, London, 1825, reproduced with an introduction by Michael Foot and Marie Mulvey Roberts, Bristol, 1994.

Thomson, Patricia, *The Victorian Heroine: A Changing Ideal, 1837–1873*, London, 1956.

Thornley, Margaret, *The True End of Education and the Means Adapted to It*, Edinburgh, 1846.

Trelawny, Edward John: *Letters*, ed. H. Buxton Forman, Oxford, 1910.

Trollope, Frances, *Domestic Manners of the Americans*, London, 1830.

Uglow, Jenny, *The Lunar Men*, London, 2002.

Vicinus, Martha, 'Lesbian perversity and Victorian marriage: the 1864 Codrington divorce trial', *Journal of British Studies*, Chicago (January 1997).

Walkowitz, Judith: *Prostitution and Victorian Society: Women, Class and the State*, Cambridge, 1980.

Weeks, Jeffrey, *Sex, Politics and Society: The Regulation of Sexuality since 1800*, London, 1981.

Weeton, Miss, *Journal of a Governess 1807–1811*, ed. Edward Hall, vol. 1, Oxford, 1936.

———, *Journal of a Governess 1811–1825*, ed. Edward Hall, vol. 2, Oxford, 1939.

West, Katherine, *A Chapter of Governesses: A Study of the Governess in English Fiction 1800–1949*, London, 1949.

Wilmot, Catherine, *An Irish Peer on the Continent*, 1801–3.

Wollstonecraft, Mary, *Thoughts on the Education of Daughters*, London, 1786.

———, *Mary: A Fiction*, 1788.

———, *A Vindication of the Rights of Men*, London, 1790.

———, *A Vindication of the Rights of Woman*, London, 1792.

———, *Collected Works*, ed. Janet Todd and Marilyn Butler, London, 1989.

———, *Correspondence*, ed. Janet Todd, London, 2003.

Wood, Mrs Henry, *East Lynne*, 1860–1.

Woolf, Virginia, 'Mary Wollstonecraft', in *The Common Reader*, second series, London, 1932.

Wright-Henderson, P.A. (ed.), *Letters hitherto unpublished, written by members of Sir Walter Scott's family to their old governess*, London, 1905.

Yonge, Charlotte M., *Hopes and Fears, or, Scenes from the Life of a Spinster*, London, 1861.

———, *Womankind*, London, 1878.

———, *The Daisy Chain*, London, 1856.

Zimmern, Alice, *The Renaissance of Girls' Education in England*, London, 1898.

Manuscript collections

Bodleian Library, Correspondence of Lady Mountcashel, and of Eliza Bishop and Everina Wollstonecraft, Abinger collection.

Chatsworth Archives, The letters of Selina Trimmer.

London Metropolitan Archives, Minutes and Yearbooks of the Governesses' Benevolent Institution.

Parkes Papers, Girton College.

Peabody Essex Museum, Salem, Mass. Edward Silsbee's notebooks: MS 74, boxes 4, 7, 8.

Pforzheimer Collection, New York Public Library, Cini papers.

Sheffield University Library, Special Collections, Elizabeth Firth's diary, 1812–13.

The Women's Library, Autograph Letter collection.

The Women's Library, Records of the Committee for Promoting the Higher Education of Women.

Index